More Finishes
and Finishing Techniques

More Finishes
and Finishing Techniques

The Best Of Fine WoodWorking

The Taunton Press

Cover photo by Vincent Laurence

BOOKS & VIDEOS

for fellow enthusiasts

First printing: 1997
Printed in the United States of America

A FINE WOODWORKING Book

FINE WOODWORKING® is a trademark of The Taunton Press, Inc.,
registered in the U.S. Patent and Trademark Office.

The Taunton Press, Inc.
63 South Main Street
P.O. Box 5506
Newtown, Connecticut 06470-5506

Library of Congress Cataloging-in-Publication Data

More finishes and finishing techniques : the best of Fine woodworking.
    p. cm.
    "A Fine woodworking book."
    Includes index.
    ISBN 1-56158-190-9
    1. Wood finishing.   I. Fine woodworking.
TT325.M67   1997
684'.084—dc20
                                   96-35218
                                     CIP

Contents

Introduction

An article in an early issue of *Fine Woodworking* sang the praises of a simple wood finish you could mix up in a Mason jar and slop on with a rag. It consisted of turpentine, varnish and boiled linseed oil, ingredients available at most any hardware store. As the author pointed out, this home brew is easy to mix, easy to apply, and gives wood a pleasing, burnished glow. It is a finish that's almost impossible to screw up, and that alone helped make it my first and only choice for a long time.

Eventually I realized I was missing a lot by not learning how to use different kinds of finish. Varnish, shellac, lacquer, and paint all have their own strengths and their advocates. Of course the trick is in choosing the right finish and applying it correctly to a surface that has been properly prepared. That's what this collection of articles from *Fine Woodworking* will help you do.

In more than two dozen articles, authors explore the many finish choices that woodworkers can learn to enjoy. In addition to explaining how different finishes are applied, these experts explain finish removal and repair, how to mix and use stains and other wood colorants, and how to rub out a finish to glassy perfection. Whatever your usual finish of choice,these articles will give you the confidence to broaden your finishing repertoire.

—Scott Gibson, editor

The "Best of *Fine Woodworking*" series spans more than 12 years of *Fine Woodworking* magazine. There is no duplication between these books and the popular "*Fine Woodworking* on..." series. A footnote with each article gives the date of first publication; product availability, suppliers' addresses, and prices may have changed since then.

Brush a complicated surface in several stages, working from the deepest surfaces, like the bevel on this raised panel door, to details, like the molding the author is brushing here with a sash brush. Apply finish to the panel field and door frame last.

Brushing on a Finish

Good preparation and flowing strokes yield smooth results

by Chris A. Minick

If you learned to use a brush by painting your house, the clear finish you brushed on your latest woodworking project probably doesn't look too good. Why? Because paint and varnish are very different materials. Paint needs to be vigorously brushed back and forth to get it to lay out thin because it's *thixotropic*, meaning that it's thicker when at rest, thinner when energy is applied to it. But varnish applies most evenly when it's gently flowed onto a surface.

My flow-and-go method for brushing a clear finish on woodwork was taught to me by my grandfather who was a professional finisher. I've found his combination of finish preparation and brush handling to give my projects a final appearance that rivals the smoothness of spraying. The method works for most common wood finishes like oil-based varnish, brushing lacquer, water-based finish and shellac. But before dipping the brush in the can, we must choose and prepare the finishing material.

Picking and preparing the finish

Fast-drying finishes are harder to apply by brush than slower drying finishes. Oil-based varnishes dry slowly enough to allow ample time for leveling, allowing you to work at a leisurely pace. For that reason, oil-based polyurethane varnish is my favorite brush-on finish. At the other end of the spectrum, shellac is probably the most difficult common finish to apply, especially to large areas—it just dries too quickly. I limit my shellac brushing to small projects

that I can completely coat in about 10 minutes. Likewise, most water-based finishes brush well but require a quick hand. Solvent-based lacquers are easier to brush, and retarders can be added to them to slow down drying.

Most finishes are too thick to brush right out of the can. Thinning with the appropriate solvent is usually necessary. Brushing a too-thick finish will show brush marks and streaks while an over-thinned finish tends to run, sag and drip. To get the ideal mix, start by transferring the finish to a clean coffee can, so you can thin only the amount you want to use. Now measure the finish's thickness with a viscosity drip cup and a stopwatch. A viscosity drip cup holds a predetermined amount and has a precisely sized hole in the bottom; you fill it up with finish, then time how long it takes all the finish to drip out through the hole (see the photo at right). Cups are available in paint stores and, unfortunately, come in many sizes (in other words, there's no simple standard). I usually work with about a pint of finish, thinning it a little at a time and checking its viscosity as I go. If I over thin it, I add a little finish from its original container. I find a reading of 13-14 seconds with a Zahn #3 cup, 48-50 seconds with a Zahn #2 cup or approximately 20-22 seconds with a Wagner cup seems about right.

Begin brushing

Before dipping into the finish, wet your brush with the thinning solvent to condition the bristles and to prevent the buildup of

From *Fine Woodworking* (January 1993) 98:54-56

dried finish at the base of the brush. This minimizes the likelihood that any dried finish will flake off the brush and contaminate the freshly varnished surface, and it makes cleaning the brush easier. Strike off the excess solvent by dragging the bristles across the edge of the container.

Fill the brush with finish by dipping it so no more than half the bristle length is submerged. Capillary action will automatically fill the brush's reservoir (near the ferrule) with the proper amount of finish. Now tap the bristles on the inside of the can to remove the excess finish and to prevent dripping. Don't drag the brush over the edge of the can—this might cause bubbles to form.

Using the basic brushstroke described in the box at right, I always finish the unseen areas of my project first. This gives me a chance to judge the flowing and leveling properties of the finish before I've committed myself to the show side of the piece. If the viscosity doesn't seem right, I add more finish to increase the thickness or more solvent to decrease it.

If you're brushing a complicated surface, such as a carving or a raised panel door, it's best to brush the areas farthest away first, working outward from the center. I apply a coat to both sides of a door in one session by setting it on a nail board (a piece of thin plywood the size of the door with one nail in each corner).

Normally, I scuff-sand between each coat with 220-grit sandpaper to remove nibs or dust specks. Three or four coats is about right for most projects. After the final coat has dried for a few days, I rub out the finish and apply a coat of paste furniture wax.

Dealing with defects

Drips, runs and sags are a normal part of any finishing operation. Fresh runs and sags can be removed from the surface by back brushing the affected area with an unloaded brush; capillary action draws off the excess finish. Hairs, brush bristles or other goobers should be picked out immediately. A quick tipping off (see the box at right) blends and removes your fingerprints.

Sanding out a dried drip or run flush with the surrounding finish can create a halo around the defect. It's better to slice the drip off with a sharp chisel to remove the drip quickly and cleanly, only a little touch sanding is needed with 400-grit paper. ☐

Chris Minick is a chemist and woodworker in Stillwater, Minn.

The basic brushstroke

A smooth finish depends on smooth brush handling. My basic method begins with a back stroke 3 in. to 4 in. from the leading edge of the panel (right). Pull the brush smoothly, and lift it just before it goes over the edge. This back stroke virtually eliminates runs along the edge. I finish the stroke by starting just behind the back stroke's wet edge and pulling the brush in one slow and continuous motion across the panel (left). Pull the brush along slowly enough to allow an even sheet of finish to flow out of the brush, but fast enough to prevent pooling. My 2-in. brush holds enough finish for a single stroke about 20 in. long, which takes between five and seven seconds.

I hold the brush loosely by the ferrule with the handle cradled between thumb and index finger. I start with the brush at about a 45° angle and gradually increase the angle to almost 90° by the end of the stroke. As the bristle angle increases, more varnish flows out. When my brush approaches the trailing edge of the panel, I decrease the pressure slightly so the bristles don't run over the edge. Each successive stroke just barely overlaps the previous one. After the whole panel is coated, I tip off the finish by lightly dragging the bristle tips through the wet finish. Tipping off with an unloaded brush levels any uneven areas and removes bubbles. Any small bubbles left can usually be dispersed by lightly blowing on them from close range. —*C.M.*

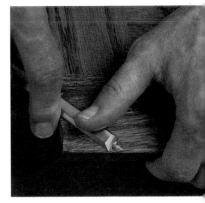

Checking the viscosity of a finish is the best way to know how much thinner you need to add to get the best finish flow. A stopwatch clocks the time it takes for a viscosity drip cup filled with finish to empty. Add more thinner until the time is optimal (see the section "Picking and preparing the finish" on the facing page).
Remove the excess from a loaded brush by tapping the bristles lightly on the sides of the can, side to side. This prevents the brush from dripping and doesn't create air bubbles, which can end up on the finished surface.
Slicing off a dried drip with a sharp chisel is probably the cleanest way to remove the defect.

Choose the right brush for the job, and keep it clean

Practically any brush you can buy at a paint or hardware store is capable of applying a finish to woodwork. But if you want to brush on a smooth finish with an even, streakless appearance, you must choose the right brush for the job (see the photo at right). The best brush has the correct type and style of bristles for applying the particular finish you choose. Generally, heavy-bodied finishes should be applied with a stiffer bristle brush while softer bristle brushes are better for applying thin finishes. Natural bristle brushes work best for applying solvent-based finishes.

A good-quality **China bristle** (hogs hair) brush has the proper stiffness and flexibility for applying oil-based varnishes, such as alkyd varnish and polyurethane. **Ox-hair** brushes, which are slightly stiffer than China bristle, hold their shape better when used for extended periods of time. Their stiffness also makes ox hair an excellent choice for smaller brushes of one inch or less. Softer **fitch** (skunk hair) brushes work best for applying thin finishes but **camel-hair** (actually, pony hair) brushes can be used.

Synthetic bristle brushes are best for waterborne finishes because natural bristles quickly splay in water and become unusable. The softness and flexibility of these brushes is determined by the polymers used for their bristles. **Nylon bristles** are the softest and are good for general-purpose finishing. If you can afford only one brush, it should be nylon. **Nylon/polyester bristle blends** are slightly stiffer, and like ox hair, make excellent small-sized brushes. Pure **polyester bristles** are very stiff, generally too stiff for applying thin furniture finishes and should only be used for applying heavy-bodied paints.

In addition to bristle material, brushes come with one of three tip styles: **blunt cut**, **flagged** and **tapered**. Some tip styles are better for certain finishing jobs than others (see the box below).

Most finishing projects require using more than one brush. I use a 1-in. sash brush for coating small or intricate areas like moldings, spindles or tight inside corners. A 2-in. brush is my favorite for large flat areas. Brushes wider than 2 in. are inappropriate for furniture finishing. They're just too hard to control.

Cleaning brushes

Proper care and storage of any brush ensures optimum performance and longevity. Each brush needs to be thoroughly cleaned and wrapped for hanging storage between uses. First, remove excess finish by scraping the brush's bristles across the lip of the finish container followed by wiping off the residue with a paper towel. Wash the bristles in the same solvent used to thin the finish. Periodically, check your cleaning progress by bending the bristles with one hand and feeling along their base with the thumb of your other hand (see the photo at right). A slimy feel indicates more cleaning is needed. Once all the finish has been removed, wash the brush in soap and water (I use dishwashing liquid, but any soap will do). After a clean water rinse to remove soap residue, wrap the brush tightly in brown paper to dry. Storing the wrapped brush by hanging it vertically on your shop wall prevents the bristles from taking a set and prolongs brush life. —C.M.

Woodworkers can choose from many brush types and styles including from left to right: nylon tapered bristle, nylon sash, ox hair, China bristle, nylon/polyester flagged bristle and nylon/polyester sash.

Keep a brush clean and properly stored *and it will last for years. After thorough solvent cleaning, bend the bristles and feel for remaining finish. Wrap the washed brush in brown paper and hang it up.*

Blunt cut
Also called straight cut, these bristles are usually only found on cheap, low-quality brushes that are better used for dusting than varnishing furniture.

Flagged bristles
With each filament broken into several small fiberals, flagged bristle tips have a fuzzy feel and appearance. Flagged nylon/polyester brushes are excellent varnish brushes.

Tapered bristles
These bristles taper from base to tip and end in a sharp point closely resembling natural bristles. Good for all varnishing, especially with water-based finishes.

Drawing: staff

Choosing a Finish

Appearance is just one consideration

by Chris A. Minick

Ask ten woodworkers what they like best about wood-working. I'll bet a truck-load of walnut that finishing isn't at the top of the list. Most woodworkers hate finishing—and with good reason. Finishing requires you to work with stinky chemicals rather than shaping wood. Because finishing is the last step in a long process, a mistake could ruin the whole project. Or the error could mean spending hours stripping off the finish with more smelly chemicals. Furthermore, there are so many types and brands of finish to choose from (see the photo below). It's no wonder why many woodworkers get accustomed to applying only one kind of finish to every project. While that approach may be efficient, it could lead to a visual sameness to your work. More importantly, your old standby finish may not be the most suitable treatment for your project's intended use.

I consider three things when choosing a finish: the application equipment I have, the appearance I want and the protection I need for a project (such as film hardness and moisture resistance).

To sort out the most common finishing-product options, it helps to know about their properties. I use the comparison chart on pp. 12-13 to weigh the strengths and weaknesses of each finish.

Penetration and application

The most important factor affecting how a finish performs is whether it penetrates the surface. Based on where the finish resides, woodworking finishes can be divided into three general classes: "in the wood," "in and on the wood" and "on the wood."

In-the-wood finishes—Penetrating finishes like tung, linseed and Danish oils are easy to use. Just wipe them on, and wipe off the excess. Because easy reparability is their biggest advantage, I often use oil finishes on projects that take abuse. A periodic reapplication of oil hides any scratches. The lack of a surface film allows oil finishes to be re-coated anytime without fear of adhesion loss.

Oil finishes darken wood but leave it natural-looking. That

Picking finishes and applicators—*Along with the most common wood finishes, author Chris Minick displays the applicators he prefers for each. From left: paste wax, linseed oil, Danish oil and mineral oil—all applied with a rag; semi-gloss interior paint—* *applied with a polyester brush; shellacs—applied with an ox-hair brush; polyurethane varnish—applied with a foam applicator; water-based acrylic—applied with a nylon/polyester brush; and nitrocellulose lacquer—applied with a spray gun.*

chocolate-brown color of the walnut box on the left in the photo below was achieved with three coats of linseed oil. I like the appearance of an oil finish on dark woods, but I find the yellow color of tung oil objectionable on light-colored woods like birch. In addition, tung oil tends to obscure subtle figure.

Not all so-called oil finishes are purely oil. Danish oils, for example, which add a rich, satin luster to certain hardwoods (see the photo on the facing page), are usually dilute varnish solutions to which oils have been added for increased penetration.

In-and-on-the-wood finishes—Oil-based varnishes and lacquers have the unique ability both to penetrate the wood and to form a protective coating on the surface. This class of finish produces that wonderful illusion of depth associated with fine furniture. Some woodworkers steer away from polyurethane varnishes, fearing they will give projects a plastic-coated look, but I've found an easy way to avoid the plastic look. Because I don't have a good touch at spraying on an oil-based varnish, I usually brush on three or four coats of thinned varnish to a piece. Then I burnish the final coat (after it has dried) with a soft cloth to kill the plastic look. The key to getting a nice finish with oil-based varnish is to apply thin coats and then rub out the last. The walnut box on the right in the photo below has a brushed-on varnish finish.

Nitrocellulose lacquer is an in-and-on-the-wood finish that exhibits marvelous depth, high luster and is quick-drying. These attributes make it the preferred finish of professional furniture-makers. Brush-on formulations of nitrocellulose lacquer are available, but I've found them difficult to apply. Spraying is the most practical way to apply nitrocellulose lacquers. Unfortunately, I don't have a spray booth or the other explosion-proof equipment needed to safely apply highly flammable finishes. As a consequence, I only use solvent-based lacquers on small projects.

On-the-wood finishes—As the name implies, on-the-wood finishes lay on the surface and do little to accentuate the grain or color of wood. The shellac finish on the center walnut box (see the photo below left) has the typical satiny look of this class of finish. Wax is an obvious on-the-wood finish, too. And aside from its easy repairability, one of the best things about wax is its nontoxic nature (see the story on p. 14).

It may surprise you to learn that the new water-based finishes also lay on the surface of the wood. The chemical composition of a typical water-based finish prevents the resin from penetrating the wood. This accounts for the no-depth look that these finishes impart to bare wood. However, I've found water-based finishes look great when applied over sealed surfaces (see the photo at right on p. 15) rather than directly to the wood. A fair amount of practice is needed to acquaint oneself with the idiosyncrasies of applying water-based finishes. But because water-based finishes are non-flammable, have little odor and are easy to clean up, I find the benefits are worth the application effort.

Surface preparation—Of course the final finish you achieve is only as good as the surface you prepared. In some instances, sanding to 600-grit is all you need. In other cases, you may want a scraped surface. If you do sand, it's best to work your way up through the grades of grit, as described in *FWW* #99, p. 40. I often use my random-orbit sander to smooth a surface (see the photo on the facing page) because I can sand cross-grain without scratches or swirls. Smoothing between coats and after the topcoat will further improve the look and feel of your finish.

Appearance: color and luster

Clear finishes are far from colorless. While the color of a finish is not usually my primary consideration when selecting a finish, color can have a profound effect on the final appearance of the project. The samples shown in the photos above the chart are all cherry with three coats of finish. Paints were not included in the chart because of their wide variety.

Solvent-based acrylic lacquers (commonly found in auto supply stores) are clear and make good coatings for light-colored wood or as a clear coat over whitewashed, stained or painted pieces. Wa-

Same wood, different lusters—*These three boxes were made from a single piece of walnut (a strip is shown at bottom), but finished differently: The left box was coated with linseed oil to give a dull look; the center box was wiped with shellac and waxed to a satin sheen; the right box (with the reveal on the lid) was brushed with polyurethane varnish and burnished to a low gloss. The finishes also bring out variations in color and grain contrast.*

Comparison of translucent finishes

Finish type	Tung, linseed oils	Danish oil
Finish description		
Surface penetration	In	In
Stain resistance	Poor	Poor
Moisture resistance	Poor	Poor
Relative color ◆	Dark amber	Amber
Relative luster	Dull	Satin
Best applicator ✖	Wipe on	Wipe on
Repairability	Excellent	Excellent
Dry time (hours)	18-24	6-12

Notes: ◆ 3 coats of finish were used to achieve these colors on cherry.

ter-based acrylic finishes are just as colorless as their solvent-based kin, but they look hazy over dark stains. Oil finishes are on the other end of the color spectrum. These deep-colored finishes drastically alter the hues of wood. But because oils don't form a surface film, the dark yellow tint is only noticeable on light-colored wood. Standard alkyd varnishes, polyurethane varnishes and nitrocellulose lacquers impart an amber glow, often called "warmth," as displayed by the lacquered Queen-Anne highboy in the top photo on p. 14. By contrast, the bluish tint of a water-based polyurethane coating gives stained wood a cold cast, an effect that is even more pronounced on walnut. I prefer warmer finishes, so I rarely use water-based polyurethane in my shop.

Aside from color, there's another quality of finishes that affects appearance—luster. A finish's formulation, thickness and method of application cause a surface to be either dull, satin or glossy. It's usually the style of a furniture piece that dictates which looks best. For instance, we're accustomed to seeing a hand-rubbed finish on an 18th-century, French period piece. Yet we prefer a more rustic look on a Shaker-style bench. A hard and glossy polyurethane varnish looks out of place on either piece.

Layering different finishes on the same piece—Finishes can also be layered for special effects. The spruce guitar soundboard in the photo at right on p. 15 has a double-layer finish along the top. First I brushed on fresh, super-blond shellac to enhance the grain and chatoyance of the stock and to add an amber color to the finish. Next I applied the vertical bands of water-based finish, so I could compare each against the look of acrylic and nitrocellulose lacquers. When undercoated with shellac, the color and depth of the water-based finishes closely matched the lacquers.

My favorite finish for black walnut is a three-layer finish. I apply linseed oil to deepen the brown color; two coats of shellac seal in the oil and enhance the wood's highlights. Finally I apply a top coat of water-based lacquer to add depth. Layered finishes can produce unusual effects, so always test a layered finish on scrapwood before committing it to your project. Keep in mind, too, that

Good surface preparation and Danish oil do wonders for this piece of macacauba (a relative of rosewood). The rich colors of the dense tropical wood also come alive when the surface is sanded to 600-grit and waxed, as the back part of the board shows.

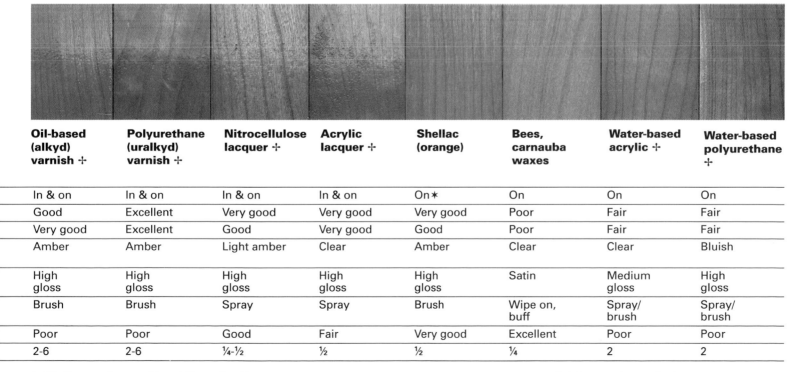

Oil-based (alkyd) varnish ÷	Polyurethane (uralkyd) varnish ÷	Nitrocellulose lacquer ÷	Acrylic lacquer ÷	Shellac (orange)	Bees, carnauba waxes	Water-based acrylic ÷	Water-based polyurethane ÷
In & on	In & on	In & on	In & on	On✷	On	On	On
Good	Excellent	Very good	Very good	Very good	Poor	Fair	Fair
Very good	Excellent	Good	Very good	Good	Poor	Fair	Fair
Amber	Amber	Light amber	Clear	Amber	Clear	Clear	Bluish
High gloss	High gloss	High gloss	High gloss	High gloss	Satin	Medium gloss	High gloss
Brush	Brush	Spray	Spray	Brush	Wipe on, buff	Spray/ brush	Spray/ brush
Poor	Poor	Good	Fair	Very good	Excellent	Poor	Poor
2-6	2-6	¼-½	½	½	¼	2	2

✷ Shellac can be considered "in and on" for dilute solutions.

÷ Most manufacturers add flatting agents to create a "satin" option.

✶ Many finishes can be applied (less effectively) by other methods.

Highboy gets a high-end finish. Andrew Davis of Santa Fe, N.M., hand-rubbed layers of lacquer to finish this mahogany Queen Anne highboy. Aniline dye and japan colors were used to add tint.

not all finish combinations are compatible. Generally, I've had good luck layering water-based finishes over solvent-based ones if I seal in between them with shellac.

Protection

Durability is an important consideration when I'm choosing a finish. Along with film hardness and adhesion, a finish often has to resist abrasion, distortion, heat and solvents. Generally, the higher the molecular weight of a finish, the more protection it offers. Oil finishes, although easy to repair, offer little protection from water or food stains. The varnish component of Danish oil increases the protection level of the finish only marginally. Likewise, paste wax performs rather poorly at resisting stains or moisture. By contrast, the superior protection of polyurethane varnish makes it my first choice for kitchen tabletops and other pieces that must stand hard use. Oil-based varnish, shellac and both acrylic and nitrocellulose lacquers protect wood against stains and water, but not quite as well as polyurethane. Water-based finishes are slightly less protective than a nitrocellulose lacquer.

So while certain finishes provide excellent stain and water protection without repairability, others repair easily but don't provide much protection (see the chart). Do you settle for protection or repairability? You may not have to make that choice. Combining different finishes on the same project provides a way to take advantage of the strong points of each.

Applying separate finishes on the same piece—I often use different finishes on the same project. Vertical and horizontal surfaces in a piece will wear differently, so you may want to finish them differently. And because of the effects of dust and gravity, you may want to apply the finishes differently as well. The top of my dining room table is finished with a polyurethane varnish, which is practically bulletproof—protecting against food stains, water and abrasion. Because the table's legs are subject to chair bangs and kicking feet (three teenagers live in my house), I oiled the legs with linseed. By occasionally re-coating them, I hide the scratches. The stool in the photo at left on the facing page was al-

Nontoxic finishes

Safe to apply—To add a nontoxic finish to his maple cheese board, the author rubs on mineral oil (above), also known as paraffin oil, which is prescribed as a laxative.

While browsing through my hardware store, I picked up a can of interior oil-based varnish. Plainly printed on the label was "nontoxic when dry." This statement surprised me because I knew the finish must contain metallic driers to function properly. Although lead compounds are no longer used as driers in varnish, manganese, zirconium and cobalt are used, and their low-level toxicity effects have not been fully explored. So why risk putting heavy metals on your salad bowl or breadboard?

Current research about food-preparation surfaces indicates that wooden cutting boards are better than synthetic ones (see *FWW* #101, p. 104). And the study suggests that if you finish the wood, you may actually impede some of the wood's beneficial effects (the tannins may deter bacteria). However, if you decide to finish the wood, there are several superior nontoxic finishes.

Mineral and linseed oil: My first choice for finishing wooden kitchen items is mineral oil, which is a petroleum-derived hydrocarbon. Sold as a laxative in my pharmacy, the bottle of mineral oil I use recommends "one to three tablespoons at bedtime." I feel pretty safe using this finish on a cheese board (see the photo at left). A few coats of mineral oil help protect against food stains and dishwater, and an occasional re-coating keeps the board looking new. Another laxative, raw linseed oil (not the boiled kind which may contain metal driers), imparts a yellow color to wood and also makes a fine nontoxic finish.

A layered finish adds depth. *This spruce soundboard stock (above) shows what effect an under layer of super-blond shellac (the top horizontal band) has. From the left, the vertical finish strips are nitrocellulose lacquer, acrylic lacquer, water-based acrylic and water-based polyurethane.*

Separate treatments—*Minick chose five finishes for this stool (left). The seat was coated with water-based acrylic; the legs were shellacked, painted and waxed; and the rungs were Danish oiled. Similarly, a guitar's body and neck may be finished differently.*

so treated with a combination of finishes. With a multi-finish approach, I like to finish the components separately. Before finishing, I mask off the surfaces that will be glued. Once the finish is dry, I assemble and glue up the components.

One last test of a finish comes when I stand back to admire a project. The finish should enhance the wood. If all I see is the finish, then I chose the wrong one. A close friend summed it up best, "You never see a perfect finish, you only see the bad ones." □

Chris Minick is a finishing chemist and a woodworker in Stillwater, Minn. He is a regular contributor to Fine Woodworking.

Further reading

To learn more about:

Brushing on a finish, see p. 8 and *FWW* #95, p. 46.

Finish durability, see *FWW* #82, p. 62.

Finishing hazards, see *FWW* #92, p. 80 and *FWW* #80, p. 58.

Spraying a finish, see *FWW* #82, p. 56.

Water-based finishes, see p. 24 and *The Woodfinishing Book,* by Michael Dresdner, The Taunton Press, 1992.

Tung and walnut oils: Pure tung and pure walnut oil dry without metallic driers. As long as their container says "pure," both walnut and tung oil are considered nontoxic. Products labeled tung-oil finish or tung-oil varnish may contain resins or metallic driers. One source for drier-free oils is Wood Finishing Enterprises (1729 N. 68th St., Wauwatosa, Wis. 53213; 414-774-1724).

Waxes and shellac: Carnauba wax (made from Brazilian palm trees) or paste furniture waxes that contain beeswax (secreted by honey bees) give a nice shine to a smooth piece of hardwood. Both waxes are approved by the Food and Drug Administration (FDA) as nontoxic food additives. I apply paste furniture wax to cutting boards fairly often because its protection against water is low.

Shellac, a nontoxic resin made from insect secretions, is also recognized by the FDA as a food additive. Used as a candy glaze (hence the name confectioners' glaze) and as a timed-release coating on oral medications, shellac makes an excellent choice for baby cribs and other pieces requiring a film-forming finish. Shellac has a short shelf life once dissolved in alcohol. So it's best to prepare your own solutions from fresh, dry shellac flakes. I've found the pre-mixed variety is often too old to dry properly.

Watch paints and water-based finishes: Most children's toys look best when painted. Don't use common house paint—oil-based or latex! These paints often contain pigments, biocides and

fungicides that may be harmful if ingested. Instead, use one of the specially developed nontoxic paints, which are available at most arts and crafts stores. Look for the seal of The Arts and Crafts Materials Institute or the words "conforms to ASTM D-4236" on the label. Either designation indicates the product meets government and industry standards for a nontoxic paint.

Similarly, don't assume water-based finishes are nontoxic just because they contain water. A clear, water-based finish can contain up to 15 separate additives, some of which are harmful if ingested. Also, be careful if you apply a clear finish over stain. It's best to read the can and call the manufacturer if you're unsure.

Material Safety Data Sheets: No discussion of finish toxicity is complete without mentioning Material Safety Data Sheets (MSDS). These sheets include information for the safe handling and disposal of a product, and they list most of the hazardous ingredients it contains. But except for special cases (carcinogenic and certain highly toxic materials), hazardous ingredients at concentrations of less than 1% of the formulation do not have to be listed on the MSDS. Just because a material doesn't appear on the MSDS does not mean it isn't in the finish. Metallic driers, for instance, typically fall below the 1% rule and do not have to be listed. If you have concerns about a particular finish, call the manufacturer. You'll be provided with the product's MSDS and other safety information. —*C.M.*

A Hand-Rubbed Oil Finish

Proper surface preparation underlies its beauty

by Tom Wisshack

T homas Sheraton, the 18th-century English furniture designer, recommended making a paste of linseed oil and ground brick dust and rubbing it into mahogany with a piece of cork. The result, enhanced by innumerable polishings with beeswax over the years, is the beautiful patina we see on many treasured antiques.

Oil finishes still have much to offer today's craftsman. An oil finish will accentuate the grain, color and figure of the wood rather than obscure it, as many coats of a surface finish (such as varnish, shellac or lacquer) are prone to do. Additionally, an oil finish will never chip, peel, develop fisheye or orange peel. And dust contamination is not an issue with oil finishes, making them a good choice for the craftsman without a separate finishing space. If dust lands before the piece is dry, simply wiping it down with a soft, clean cloth takes care of the problem. Finally, and perhaps most importantly, because an oil finish penetrates and bonds with the wood, rather than forming a film atop the wood, renewing the finish is as simple as rubbing in some fresh oil.

As simple and beautiful as oil finishes are, however, it would be a mistake to view oil finishing as a quick, easy solution or a cover-up for bad workmanship. On the contrary, there is quite a lot of work involved in preparing a surface for an oil finish, and an oil finish will magnify any imperfections in the wood. Also, an oil finish is only moderately resistant to water and alcohol, so it may not be the best choice for a dining room or kitchen table, but for a piece of furniture subject to less spillage and daily wear, it may be ideal. For many craftsmen, the beautiful, rich patina that an oil finish develops over time far outweighs the care needed to maintain it. In this article, I'll discuss preparing for and finishing new furniture as well as rejuvenating previously oil-finished pieces.

Surface preparation

Someone once said that you could put used motor oil on a perfectly prepared wood surface and it would look good. As shocking as that may sound, the statement points out a funda-

mental truth: An oil finish is only as good as the surface to which it's applied. You may be able to get by with a less than perfectly prepared wood surface if you plan to varnish or lacquer because these finishes form a relatively thick coating. But with an oil finish, any flaws in the unfinished surface will only become more evident when oiled, so you need to take extra care preparing the surface.

Some craftsmen prefer a handplaned or scraped surface to one that has been sanded a great deal. A surface finished by a cutting tool rather than sandpaper possesses a different tactile quality and will respond quite well to an oil finish. Most of us, however, find it necessary to sand at least a bit; how fine a grit you stop at is largely a matter of personal taste. A surface that has been sanded to 1,000-grit will respond as well to an oil finish as one that has been handplaned only, but the characters of their surfaces will differ.

After planing or scraping to remove any mill marks or other imperfections from the wood's surface, you should raise the grain with a sponge or rag soaked in hot water. This will make any unseen flaws in the surface evident, so you can scrape or sand them out. It will also make your project easier to repair if it comes into

Photos: Vincent Laurence

Achieving an open-pored look is as simple as eliminating all the intermediary sanding and jumping straight from plane or scraper to 600- or 1,000-grit sandpaper. More open-pored woods, such as the wenge in this tabletop, lend themselves better to this treatment than do cherry or maple.

contact with water after it's finished.

I usually begin sanding with 220-grit wet/dry sandpaper on an orbital sander or hand-held sanding block. I follow up with 320-, 400- and 600-grit paper, always sanding in long, straight strokes with the grain. A pine block faced with sheet cork (available from art-supply stores) will keep you from creating valleys as you would if you held the sandpaper in your hand; this is more important with the coarser grits because of their greater cutting effect. By the time you finish with the 400-grit, you'll start to see the wood grain and color come into focus. With the 600-grit, you're actually burnishing the surface. You may wish to use intermediate grits, or follow the 600-grit with finer automotive sandpapers, but I find the above routine generally sufficient.

After attending to all flat surfaces, I take a piece of worn 600-grit paper and gently round any sharp edges and corners. This will prevent finishing rags from catching and will also give the piece of furniture a slightly used or worn look. If you wish to retain a more open-pored look, or would like handplaning marks to be evident in the finished piece, skip straight from plane to 600- or 1,000-grit paper to polish the surface quite beautifully without filling all the pores (see the photo above).

It's important either to vacuum or to clean the surface thoroughly with compressed air after each successive grade of sandpaper to avoid scratching the surface with particles left over from the previous, coarser grit. I also check the surface with a strong light between each sanding and again when I think I'm done. This will often reveal minor flaws I might otherwise have missed. The wood's surface, ready for oil, should have a sheen and be glass-smooth even before any finish is applied.

I like to let a piece of furniture sit for several weeks after preparing its surface and before I apply any oil. This time allows the surface to oxidize somewhat, giving it a head start on the rich color it will acquire with age. Cherry, for example, will look rather greasy and anemic and may have an unpleasant orangey tone if finished with oil right away. By letting the wood mature prior to finishing—even for just a couple of weeks—a richer tone results and the patina will build up more quickly. Not all woods respond to this waiting period, and not all craftsmen can afford to wait or are willing to do so. For me, the results are well worth it, and because I normally have several projects going at once, time isn't a problem.

Repairs and rejuvenation

An oil finish needs to be maintained. I'll refurbish one of my own pieces every couple of years, or sooner if it's damaged. To rejuvenate a surface that is intact (no scratches, water marks or abrasions), I simply rub my homemade oil finish into the surface for a couple of minutes and then remove all traces of oil with a dry rag. Finally, I rub the surface with another dry, clean rag until the surface has a satiny sheen.

If the surface is scratched or otherwise blemished, it's usually possible to remove the blemish by rubbing it out with a pad of 0000 steel wool soaked in the oil finish. Sprinkling a little rottenstone (a gray, abrasive powder much finer than pumice) onto the wood surface while rubbing will restore its original sheen. If you're removing a blemish from one area, in order to keep the same color and sheen over the whole piece, it's important that you not forget to rub the whole piece out. With each rubdown, the wood gets more beautiful and begins to form a patina. A table I made about ten years ago has had its top rubbed down about six times and is quite striking in appearance.

If a blemish doesn't respond to rubbing out with the steel wool, you may need to use wet/dry sandpaper with the oil solution. Although it depends on how deep the scratch is, as a rule, I don't use anything coarser than 320-grit for repairs. I use a sanding block (to prevent my fingers from digging into the wood) and follow the grain of the wood. Once I've removed the blemish, I work my way through the various grades of sandpaper until I have a perfect surface again, and I finish up with 0000 steel wool and rottenstone. I'm very careful not to sand too deeply because this would expose the underlying (nonoxidized) wood color, necessitating a much more extensive repair. Using the finest grade of sandpaper you can get by with will generally keep you out of trouble.

If you need to repair a piece of furniture but don't want to darken it, rub the piece down with mineral oil instead of a finishing oil. I have a walnut writing table that the sun had started to fade. I liked its color and wanted to retain it, but the tabletop needed some attention. Using the mineral oil just as I've used the homemade finish on other pieces (with a pad of fine steel wool and some rottenstone), I was able to repair the table without changing its color.

Choosing and applying oil

As I've tried to stress already, the kind of oil you use isn't nearly as important as the preparation prior to the actual finishing. I generally use a homemade oil finish (see the sidebar on the facing page), but there are also a host of commercially available oil finishes. Danish oil finishes are among the most popular because they're simple to apply and the results are predictably successful.

Second in popularity to Danish oil finishes are tung oil finishes. The working properties of these finishes are similar to the Danish oil finishes, although tung oil generally cures faster and offers a bit more protection than most of the Danish oil products. (Keep in mind, however, that there is tremendous variability in formulation, drying time and working properties from one manufacturer to another. I've used tung oil finishes that have gone on like Mazola and stayed that way and others that started to tack up almost immediately upon application.) I find tung oil finishes too shiny, and in some cases, streaky for my tastes, especially with more than two coats, but a final rubdown with fine steel wool will generally both even out the finish and tone the gloss down to a satiny sheen.

My application procedure is similar for Danish oil and tung oil finishes. I brush on a first coat—liberally—and allow it to soak into the wood—about 10-15 minutes for Danish oil finishes but only 2-3 minutes for the tung oil finishes. Then I wipe up all oil remaining on the surface with a clean rag. I let this first coat dry for a few days (for either finish), and then I apply subsequent coats with a rag, wiping in a circular motion. Again, I eliminate all traces of oil remaining on the surface, using a clean, dry rag. Although there's no definite rule on how many coats you should apply, I usually give my pieces three to five coats. It's important to wait as long as possible between coats to avoid the greasy, hurried look that is characteristic of so many oil finishes.

Something to keep in mind, particularly with the more heavy-bodied oil finishes such as the tung oil finishes (although it's true to some degree with all oil finishes), is that the more coats you apply the more you lose the open-pored look. To retain this look on some of my contemporary pieces, I've applied only one coat of oil, and then followed that up a couple of weeks later with a coat of quality paste wax.

In instances where I want to finish a piece with oil, but a greater level of protection is required, I use Formby's Low Gloss Tung Oil Finish. The combination of tung oil and alkyd resins provides considerably more protection than most oil finishes, and the Formby's finish dries quickly and reliably. ☐

The hue of sun-bleached walnut suited the author, but the tabletop needed work. Using mineral oil and rottenstone, he rubbed out numerous minor scratches and scuffs, as well as gave the surface a new shimmer, without changing the color of the wood.

Tom Wisshack makes and restores fine furniture and is a woodfinishing consultant in Galesburg, Ill.

Homemade linseed-oil mixture rubs in best

Although there are a host of commercially available premixed oil finishes, I prefer to make my own. Call it part nostalgia, but it's the best oil finish I've used. I use this finish only on new furniture. If you're asked to restore an antique, you should seek the advice and expertise of a conservator before proceeding. Although eminently repairable, an oil finish is not removable save by sanding to bare wood.

I mix three parts boiled linseed oil (it must be boiled) to one part turpentine or high-quality mineral spirits and add a few drops of japan drier (generally available through commercial paint supply stores)—about two percent by volume. For the first coat, I warm the mixture in a double boiler or electric glue pot, being *extremely* careful to avoid spilling any. I work a liberal amount onto one surface at a time using a natural bristle brush. Then I let the oil sit and soak into the wood for about 30 minutes. Next, I sprinkle the wood surface with a small amount of rottenstone and rub with burlap until a paste develops. I continue rubbing into the wood's surface for several minutes (see the photos at right). Then I wipe all traces of oil and rottenstone off of the piece, using clean, dry rags. Remember that rags saturated with linseed oil are extremely flammable: submerge them in water immediately after use, or spread them flat outdoors to dry, and then be sure to put them in a closed garbage can outdoors at the end of the day.

I try to let the first coat dry in a well-ventilated, relatively warm area for about two weeks. If any oil beads appear on the surface during this time (they'll usually show up in the first couple of days), I wipe them off with a clean piece of terry-cloth towel. I apply the second coat more sparingly with a soft cotton cloth. After letting the oil soak in for about 15 minutes, I wipe off any oil remaining. I wipe until the rags come off the surface clean and dry and then give all surfaces a brisk rub. Two weeks later, I apply the third coat in the same fashion. If I'm going to apply a fourth or fifth coat, I'll wait another couple of weeks.

The drying time of this finish will vary tremendously depending on atmospheric conditions. The longer you can wait the better. It's possible to add more japan drier to the mixture to ensure drying, but the actual curing of an oil finish takes months and cannot be hastened chemically. Applying too many coats of oil in a short amount of time results in a greasy, slightly transparent tone. It's best to wait until the finish has begun to cure and form the beginnings of a patina before passing the piece on to a customer or gallery. —T.W.

Burlap, rottenstone and the author's homemade linseed-oil mixture combine for a finish that's second to none. Although the paste formed by the rottenstone and oil mixture looks as though it would darken the wood, as long as there are no cracks, the paste will all come off.

Making a Case for Varnish

The most beautiful and durable finish for fine furniture is applied with a brush

by Frank Pollaro

I'd just finished the most complex piece I had ever attempted, the reproduction of a desk by Emile-Jacques Ruhlmann, the greatest of the Art Deco furniture designers. The curvaceous desk, veneered in amboyna burl and shagreen, or sting-ray skin, had taken me more than 300 hours to complete. The original had been French polished, but I wanted to provide my reproduction with more protection than shellac affords while giving it the same clarity and brilliance.

I asked Frank Klausz, a friend and fellow woodworker, what he recommended, and he suggested that I use varnish. I experimented on scrap boards until I was satisfied with the results. And then I varnished the desk. It was the perfect finish with all the depth, clarity and brilliance I had hoped for.

Now varnish is the standard finish for all my fine work (see the photo above). I've experimented with a number of varnishes and brushes and refined my technique. Now I can brush on a finish that looks as though it has been sprayed.

Understanding varnish

A properly applied varnish finish is glass smooth, hard and resistant to most household chemicals, foods and drinks. It also has a warm, amber glow. That makes it best suited for darker woods, unless you want to add warmth to a light wood, such as maple or ash. Regardless of the choice of wood, a well-polished varnish surface will turn heads.

Varnish must be rubbed out—About the only downside to using varnish is that you

Always use a good brush. Look for a thick, firm brush with fine bristles, like this badger brush.

have to rub out and polish the finish if you want a blemish-free surface. Varnish is oil based, so it takes far longer to dry than lacquer or shellac. Lacquer thinner and denatured alcohol evaporate in minutes, leaving a hard, dry finish behind. Varnish can stay tacky for hours, vulnerable to anything in the air, whether that's dust or a wandering fly. So it's important to apply varnish in as clean an atmosphere as possible.

Depending on the style and function of the piece of furniture I'm finishing, as well as the client's tastes, I may polish it only to a satiny gloss, or I may take it all the way to a high gloss. Either way, though, it's not nearly as time-consuming as a lot of woodworkers think it is. Even a very large dining table won't take more than an afternoon to rub out and polish.

You must sand between coats—The other major difference between varnish and lacquer is that you cannot reactivate dried varnish with a fresh coat or with a solvent. With lacquer, every time you apply a new coat of lacquer, you effectively melt it into previous coats, creating what amounts to a single, thick coat. With varnish, you're building up a finish one layer at a time. Each new coat should bond mechanically to the one below it by gripping the scratches in the surface. For this reason, it's absolutely essential to sand between coats until there are no shiny, low spots.

One final detail about the varnish itself. Always use a high-quality product. It will brush on and flow out much better than cheaper stuff. I've settled on Behlen's Rockhard Tabletop varnish (distributed through Garrett Wade; 800-221-2942 and Woodworker's Supply; 800-645-9292). It's the best varnish I've found, and it dries the hardest, so it rubs out better than any other.

A good brush is the key

The single most important thing you can do to achieve a great varnish finish is to start with a good brush. They aren't cheap—expect to spend between $30 and $60 for a 3-in. brush. My first varnish brush was a badger brush from Behlen's (see the photo above), which I still use. It's a good value at $30 or so. But I discovered another brush last year that I like even better. It's made in Germany from the inner ear hair of oxen and is imported by Kremer Pigments (228 Elizabeth St., New York, N.Y. 10012; 212-219-2394). The brush, listed simply as the Pi72, costs nearly $60. But it has very fine bristles, which leave virtually no brush marks in the finish surface.

Whichever brush you decide to use should be thick, firm and made with fine, natural bristles. This will allow the brush to hold a good amount of varnish and distribute it evenly on the surface. A thin, skimpy brush won't hold enough varnish. A limp brush won't move the varnish around, and coarse bristles can leave marks in the finish. If you're going to use varnish, do yourself a favor and buy a good brush.

Brushing it on

The best place to varnish a piece of furniture is in a small, dust-free room with the windows closed. Few of us have that luxury, though. To reduce the number of little dust specks settling on the wet varnish, I often spray a mist of water in the air, on the ceiling and on the floor just before getting started. Try not to get any water on the piece you're about to finish. Don't get too worked up about dust, though, because any small bumps will be sanded off after each coat has dried.

I cut the first coat of varnish 50% with thinner and add a few drops of Behlen's Fish Eye Flo-Out. This is essentially just silicone, but it enhances the flow of the varnish, eliminates the likelihood of fisheyes and improves the scratch resistance and glossiness of the finish.

Brush technique is important with varnish. The object is to apply a thin, even coat. If you put on too much varnish, it will skin over and the varnish under the skin will never dry. If you use too little varnish, you'll have a hard time moving it around, and it will not flow out. With a little practice, though, the whole process will become second nature.

I find it helpful to let the brush soak in the varnish for a minute or two, so it can absorb some of the finish. Then I apply the first coat, brushing all the way across the table in long, smooth strokes (see the photo at left on p. 22). After covering the table with varnish, I quickly brush over the varnish I've just applied, but at 90° to the original direction and with a much lighter touch (see the top right photo on p. 22). Each coat is applied in the same way. On a piece of furniture with a predominant grain direc-

Brush on the varnish in long, smooth strokes (left). On a surface with a single or a predominant grain direction (unlike this sunburst veneer pattern), start by applying the finish across the grain. The first coat of varnish should be a 50/50 solution of varnish and solvent.

Brush out the varnish at 90° to the direction you laid it on (above), usually with the grain. Use a light touch. Just skim across the surface without exerting any downward pressure.

tion, I apply the varnish first across the grain and then brush it with the grain. You have to move quickly because even though the varnish will stay tacky for hours, it will start to set up after just a few minutes. You'll probably see brush marks, or striations, in the surface at first, but after 15 minutes or so, they'll level out.

I let this first coat dry for at least 24 hours and then sand it out with a random-orbit sander and a 220-grit disc. This gives the surface some tooth for the next coat to bind to. After sanding, I wipe down the surface with a tack cloth before applying the next coat.

I brush on the second coat, cut with 25% thinner and then wait another 24 hours for the coat to dry before sanding it. For a tabletop like this one, I'll apply four or five coats, allowing 24 hours between each coat and 72 hours after the last coat before starting to rub out the finish. The third and subsequent coats are full-strength varnish. Four coats are usually enough, but I've applied as many as eight. If you want the surface to be completely smooth and non-porous, keep applying coats until there are no pores showing after you've sanded with the 220-grit paper. Then just one final coat should do it.

Rub out and polish the finish

When you're happy with the last coat and have given it at least 72 hours to dry (a week

would be better), it's time to rub out the finish. For a satin finish, I just sand with 600-grit paper and polish with 0000 steel wool lubricated with Behlen's Wool-Lube. Then I rub down the surface with a clean cloth, and I'm done.

For a high-gloss finish, I used to wet-sand from 600-grit to 1,000-, 1,200- and, finally, 1,500-grit paper. Now I start and end my sanding with 1,200-grit paper (available at most auto-body supply shops). The advantage of working your way through the grits is that the rubbing out takes less time and the result is likely to be slightly flatter because you're starting with a more aggressive abrasive. The reason I stopped doing it is that I always found myself trying to eliminate a scratch or two from one of the coarser grits that only became apparent after I'd gotten to the 1,500-grit. I'd have to go through the whole routine again, losing any time I had saved.

To take down all the nubs or bumps in the surface of the finish caused by dust or other debris, I wrap the sandpaper around a wooden block (see the center photo at right). I've used naphtha, mineral spirits and water as wetting agents. For this table, I used water with a little Behlen's Wool-Lube in it to make things more slippery. A little rubber squeegee helps to clear away the slurry, so you can check to see if a bump is gone or if you have more sanding to do (see the photo at right). The auto-

Rub out nubs or bumps with 1,200-grit paper wrapped around a wooden block (above). Water, naphtha or mineral spirits may be used to lubricate the surface.

Use a rubber squeegee to clear slurry. The 1,200-grit paper works slowly, so keep rubbing and clearing the slurry until all the high spots are gone.

Polish the finish with a power buffer and automotive glaze. *Once you've sanded out all the nubs and bumps and gotten the surface flat, 10 minutes of power buffing will take the finish to a high-gloss shine.*

For porous woods, fill the grain

On very open-grained woods, such as burls, I collect all of the sawdust from my final dry-sanding (220-grit) in a jar. I mix this sawdust with full-strength varnish (see the top two photos below). I hone a square edge on a 2-in. putty knife and use it to apply this paste to the raw wood in place of the 50% dilution I normally use for the first coat.

I lay this paste down in one direction and spread it perpendicularly. I fill the voids, imperfections and pores (see the bottom photo), being careful not to scratch the surface. After 24 hours, I sand with 220-grit to reveal a glass-smooth surface. Two more full-strength coats of varnish and I'm ready to rub out and polish the finish —F.P.

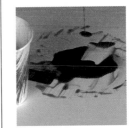

Mix full-strength varnish *and 220-grit sanding dust until it has the consistency of molasses.*

body supply dealer I do business with gives me these squeegees.

After I've sanded out all of the nubs and bumps, I swap the wooden block for a cork block and give the whole table an even sanding, trying to get it as flat as possible. It's important to take down any high spots after each coat. If you let these spots build up, you could sand through one coat into another. This shows up as a visible ring between the two coats, and the only way to fix it is to sand off the whole topcoat and apply it again.

Pay special attention to the edges, where the varnish can build up a little ridge. You can judge how flat the finish is by looking at the reflection of a light on the table. If it looks like it's reflecting off the surface of a wind-swept pond, then you have some more sanding to do. If it's relatively undis-

torted, you're in good shape.

To complete the gloss finish, I apply Meguiar's Mirror Glaze #1 (an automotive rubbing compound), buff it out and wipe it off. (For the closest dealer, call Meguiar's at 800-854-8073.) It's important to get the surface completely clean because any residue from the #1 compound will scratch the surface when you go to the next finer compound. I follow the Meguiar's #1 with the #3 compound, using a different buffing wheel—again, so the residue from the coarser compound doesn't undo what I'm trying to accomplish (see the photo above). After buffing with the #3 compound, I wipe off the table with a clean rag. The surface will shine like a mirror. □

Frank Pollaro designs and builds custom furniture in East Orange N.J.

Work mixture into the grain. *Apply it in one direction, and then work it into pores crosswise. Try to create a smooth surface.*

Water-Base Finishes

Tips and techniques for choosing and using these new materials

by Chris A. Minick

I f you've visited your local hardware or paint store lately, you've probably noticed some new cans on the shelves. Many longtime wood-finish manufacturers have recently introduced new lines of water-base wood-finishing products that promise to be environmentally safe and easy to clean up. Although these products are available in the form of familiar finishes, such as lacquer, varnish and polyurethane, they lack most of their traditional counterparts' harmful solvents and can be cleaned up with plain, clear water.

While water-base finishes, which are non-flammable and essentially non-toxic, hold the promise of healthier and safer application, as well as a cleaner environment, there is a price to pay. These new finishes have properties that make them *very* different from their traditional, solvent-base equivalents: Mixing and thinning them is different, applying them is different and troubleshooting their problems is different. They even *look* different straight out of the can. Even if you are an experienced finisher, all this means that you'll have to invest some time to relearn old habits before you'll get a good finish using water-base products. This article will give you an overview of the water-base finishing process, including how to prepare the wood, and some techniques I've learned for successfully applying these new materials. I'll also tell you how water-base and solvent-base finishes differ, how to avoid incompatibility and how to troubleshoot some common water-base dilemmas. But first, let's examine the legal impetus behind this latest finishing revolution.

Water-base products and the law—Why is there a sudden flurry of new water-base finishes? Many of these new products have come about largely in response to recent governmental regulations restricting the amount of solvent or "volatile organic compound" (VOC) in finishing materials, such as clear finishes, sealers, fillers, stains and paints. VOC legislation was first passed in California as a means to reduce air pollution, and several states in the East, notably New York, New Jersey and North Carolina, have adopted California-inspired VOC regulations. Many other states, as well as civic municipalities, are considering adopting similar standards. Industry experts anticipate that VOC regulations will be nationwide by the mid-1990s, at which time water-base and other VOC-compliant finishes will be the standard, rather than the exception to solvent-base finishes as they are currently.

But before you get rid of every can of solvent-base finish on your shelves, read on. Most current regulations state that those hobbyists and small-shop woodworkers who use *less than one gallon of finish per day* are exempt. However, there's a catch: VOC regulations are compelling finish manufacturers to concentrate on developing and producing mostly materials that meet VOC standards; so you can expect that many solvent-base products will be less available in the future. There are several types of wood finishes that won't be dramatically altered to comply with VOC regulations. Most oil finishes, such as 100% tung oil and boiled or raw linseed oil, will remain unchanged. Some oil-varnish mixtures, like Watco Danish oil, may be slightly reformulated to reduce VOCs, but the change should be hardly noticeable to the end user. Commercially prepared shellac will be available in not less than a 3-lb. cut, but you'll still be able to make your own shellac finish in any

With an increasing number of states and municipalities adopting regulations restricting the amount of volatile organic compounds (VOCs) allowed in paint and other coatings, many finish manufacturers have introduced new lines of non-toxic water-base stains and clear finishes.

From *Fine Woodworking* (July 1991) 89:52-55

strength you desire by mixing dry shellac flakes or buttons with alcohol. High-solids varnishes, such as McCloskey's Clean Air Formulation spar varnish, are in another class of low-VOC finishes. These are made compliant with VOC regulations by altering the resins to allow lower solvent levels, and they don't have a water base. I won't discuss these types of finishes here, but in general, they take longer to dry, may be more difficult to apply and have slightly lower protection qualities than their conventional counterparts.

Solvent base vs. water base – Most of the finishes you've used in your shop are probably solvent base, including traditional lacquers, varnishes, polyurethanes and shellac. Typically, solvent-base finishes are a mixture of resin (which forms the actual finish film), driers (to accelerate drying the resins) and solvent (which acts as a carrier for the resin and allows application). Water-base finishes come with the same general resin types, such as polyurethane and acrylic, as solvent-base finishes, but their formulations are considerably more complicated. In addition to resins and solvents, water-base finishes commonly contain surfactants, defoamers, thickeners, flow-out additives, mar reducers and other additives necessary to make the resin compatible with water. And, of course, water-base finishes contain lots of water, which is primarily what makes them low in VOCs.

Besides reducing VOCs and decreasing air pollution in the lower atmosphere, water-base finishes offer woodworkers several other important advantages. They are non-flammable, easy to clean up, practically non-toxic, and have very little odor. If you are a professional woodworker, there is an added bonus: since these finishes aren't flammable, you won't need an expensive explosion-proof spray booth; plus, you may lower your insurance rates. However, water-base materials also have a few disadvantages. Water-base products may develop poor film properties when dried in a humid environment, and they must be stored carefully to avoid freezing. Many are tricky to apply, and the first coat usually raises the grain of the wood substantially. Also, water-base materials may not be compatible with traditional (usually oil-base) stains, sealers and fillers. Finally, most water-base finishes appear milky white in the can and when they are first applied (see the photo above), which may make you apprehensive about using them. But don't worry; they dry quite clear.

Which type and brand of water-base finish should you use? Unfortunately, I don't think any one product is ideal for all wood-finishing situations. There are dozens of water-base finishes now available in hardware and paint stores and home centers, including many nationally distributed products made by major finish manufacturers, such as McCloskey, Fabulon, Star Bronze (ZipGuard), Flecto, Benjamin Moore and Carver Tripp (see the photo on the facing page). Though few cans clearly state that the product is water base, terms and phrases like "low in VOCs," "cleans up with water" or "environmentally safe" will usually tip you off to a water-base product. Before selecting a particular finish, I recommend you buy several different types and brands, make up some samples and conduct your own in-shop tests for stain resistance, hardness and adhesion, as each product has slightly different application characteristics and final-film properties. (For more on this, see "Evaluating Wood Finishes," *FWW* #82.) Regardless of the finish you select, you'll have to get used to its individual application characteristics. But despite the variations among different water-base products, many of the same basic procedures apply for using them, starting with the way the wood's surface should be prepared prior to finishing.

Surface preparation – Many problems with water-base finishes can be avoided by properly preparing the wood surface before appli-

Because most water-base finishes first appear milky white, applying them can be a little disconcerting. But fear not; they dry crystal clear. To avoid brush marks, hold the brush at about a 30° angle to the work and pull it across the workpiece in long, even strokes, allowing the finish to "flow" onto the wood.

cation. As mentioned earlier, the high water content of these finishes tends to raise the wood's grain, resulting in a fuzzy surface after the first coat. To avoid this, deliberately raise the grain by wetting the wood with clean water after sanding, and then sand it smooth again before finishing. Allow the wood to dry overnight, and then knock the grain down with fine grit sandpaper (no coarser than 180-grit). But be careful: The *type* of sandpaper you use can cause problems with water-base products. Non-loading sandpapers, like Norton's No-fil or 3M's Tri-M-ite, are coated with a wax-like substance (usually stearates), which prevents clogging and extends useful life, but can contaminate a surface and create fisheyes or brush streaks. Thoroughly cleaning a contaminated surface with a tack rag can alleviate the problem, but even the rag can cause problems. Most commercial tack cloths are saturated with a sticky, non-drying oil that can leave fisheye-causing residues behind after wiping. A better (and cheaper) alternative is to use a clean, water-dampened cloth, which works well as a water-base tack cloth. Also, *do not* use steel wool to smooth the wood or to rub out between coats of finish; small shards of steel can embed themselves and rust when a water-base finish is applied. Alternatively, use a plastic, non-woven sanding pad, such as a Scotch-Brite brand finishing pad.

Compatibility – Perhaps the biggest drawback to water-base materials is their limited compatibility with other standard finishing materials. Stains, fillers and sealers used under water-base finishes must be chosen carefully to ensure compatibility and adequate adhesion of subsequent coats. I've had water-base topcoats applied over an oil-base stain peel off in sheets (see the left photo on the following page). To avoid a catastrophe, experiment by staining and topcoating a sample before coating the workpiece. You can use a water-base stain like Smooth and Simple Wood Stain (available from Clearwater Color Co., 217 S. 5th St., Perkasie, Pa. 18944; 215-453-8663). Further, many stains, fillers and sealers are specifically designed for use with water-base finishes. Aniline wood dyes, either water or alcohol soluble, and NGR (non-grain-raising) stains, like

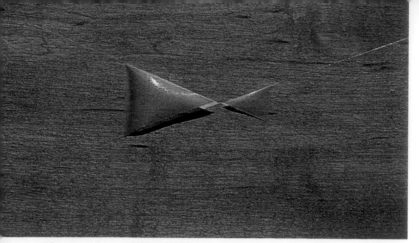

The incompatibility of many water-base finishes with other finishing materials can be a problem. The sample shown here was topcoated with a water-base polyurethane applied over an oil-base stain; after being scored with a razor knife (for demonstration purposes), the water-base finish peeled up easily.

Their tendency to foam during application, especially when brushed on, is a common problem with water-base finishes. The right half of the sample shows a clear water-base finish brushed on straight from the can (note the bubbles); the same clear finish was brushed on the left half after a defoaming agent was added.

Behlen's Solar Lux (available from Garrett Wade, 161 Ave. of the Americas, New York, N.Y. 10013; 800-221-2942, 212-807-1757), are completely compatible. In addition, a wash coat of shellac is a good sealer beneath water-base topcoats. In my trials, this wash coat didn't raise the wood grain objectionably, but rather imparted a slight yellow tint, adding a richness to the finish that I find lacking in many clear water-base materials. It's also possible to concoct a shopmade sealer by diluting a water-base material by 50% with distilled water. Only distilled water should be used, as "hard" (mineral-laden) tap water can cause sand-like specks (called gel specks) in the film, ruining the finish. However, some water-base finishes won't tolerate dilution; consult the label or manufacturer first.

Troubleshooting—Even if you've licked incompatibility dilemmas and have applied the finish properly (see the sidebar below),

problems may still arise. The key to good results with a water-base product is detecting and solving problems before they ruin your project. One of the most common and annoying problems that occurs while applying water-base finishes is foaming and bubbling, especially if you use a brush (see the above photo at right). The foaming is caused by soap-like materials (surfactants and leveling agents) that keep the resin in emulsion and help the finish flow out. I've found that I can eliminate the problem most of the time by adding a "defoamer" in the form of about 1 oz. of mineral spirits to a gallon of finish. Mineral spirits seems to decrease the final finish's gloss a bit, but this is barely detectable. Chicago, Ill., woodworker John Kriegshauser discovered that he could use 1 oz. of half-and-half (cream and milk) to a gallon of finish as a defoamer. Although this may seem a little unconventional, the chemical structure of milk fat is very similar to some commercially made de-

Applying a water-base finish

Water-base finishes don't look or handle much like their traditional solvent-base counterparts; so it shouldn't come as much of a shock that they'll probably require some getting used to. Water-base finishes can be applied directly from the can via a brush, a standard compressed-air spraying system or HVLP (high-volume low-pressure) spray equipment. But application techniques, such as brushing methods and spray-equipment setups, are somewhat different for water-base than for solvent-base materials. Before delving into the techniques, a few words about safety: While water-base finishes are low in toxicity, *they are not completely non-toxic.* Hence, the same safety precautions for solvent-base finishes also apply to water base: Avoid skin contact, provide adequate ventilation and use an approved mist-and-organic-vapor-rated mask for spray application.

Water-base finishes have a narrower "application window" than most solvent-

base finishes. In other words, they are less tolerant to low temperatures and high humidity. Ideal application conditions are between 60°F and 80°F and less than 80% relative humidity. If the temperature of the finishing room is too low or the humidity is too high, water-base finishes will not form an optimum film. Minimum temperatures are different for each product; so check the label. Many finishes have additives that ensure adequate film formation at high humidity levels, but it's better to avoid working on humid days if possible.

Brushing: Water-base materials are more difficult to brush on than solvent-base products for two reasons. First, they have a tendency to foam; so selecting the proper brush is crucial. The cheap, 59-cent variety won't work here, but neither will an expensive, natural-bristle brush; the bristles absorb water quickly, swell and splay, increasing the likelihood of brush marks. I've

found the best choice to be a nylon-bristle brush with tapered tips; mine cost about $8. Tapered bristles have fewer tip ends, generating fewer bubbles. Avoid brushes with flagged bristles—ones that look like they have been shredded—because they encourage bubble formation, particularly when the finish is brushed on too heavily. Some finishers have had good luck with "paint pads," which are inexpensive applicators with plastic handles and short, non-flagged bristles.

Brushing technique is especially important to attain a flat, smooth finish. First, wet the brush with distilled water. This keeps the finish that has soaked into the brush from drying and ruining the bristles or from peppering the finish with flecks of dried finish. Next, dip the brush in the finish and tap off the excess. Hold the brush at about a 30° angle to the work surface and pull it across the workpiece in long, even strokes (see the photo on p. 25). The

foamers. I've tried half-and-half and it worked amazingly well and didn't change the finish's final gloss.

Fisheyes—those little crater-like pockmarks in a finish—can occur with both solvent-base and water-base finishes; they're due to localized differences in the finish film's surface tension. The cause is frequently due to some kind of surface contamination, such as stearates left from sanding, traces of oil from compressed air or dirty handprints; almost any waxy or oily dirt can cause fisheyes. To combat the problem, don't make the mistake of adding "fisheye eliminator" to your mixture. Most of these additives, even some designed for use in water-base systems, contain silicone oil. Silicone is one of the banes of the finishing world because it contaminates everything it contacts—your brushes, spray equipment and the wood—and it actually *increases* the chances of fisheyes on your next finishing job. The way to eliminate fisheyes is to correct the problem at the source. Keep the workpiece as clean as possible, and wipe its surface with a clean cloth before finishing. If fisheyes persist, add a flow-out agent specifically designed for water-base materials. (I use one made by Amity; call 800-334-4259 or 608-837-8484 to find your local Amity dealer.) This additive can eliminate fisheyes by lowering the film's surface tension. If all else fails, try lightly resanding, wiping down the surface and then recoating.

As with traditional nitrocellulose lacquers, most water-base finishes dry rapidly: A thin coat will dry dust free in about 10 minutes or so, and it will be ready for recoating in about 80 minutes. This is a real plus when you need to complete a project in a hurry. But this rapid drying can be detrimental in some instances, such as when brushing finish on a large tabletop in a low-humidity environment. In this case, the finish brushed on one area dries before the adjacent area is covered, causing lap marks. To avoid this problem and maintain a "wet edge" when brushing, try adding a small amount of propylene glycol. (I use Hydrocote Glaze Extender

from Hood Products, PO Box 160, Tennet, N.J. 07763; 800-229-4937.) This retards the evaporation of the water in the finish slightly, prolonging the finish's "open time." About 1 oz. per gallon works in most situations, although a little more won't hurt.

Witness lines, faint lines that sometimes show up in a multiple-coat finish when it's sanded or rubbed out, may indicate poor adhesion between coats. Since the problem is caused by too little "coalescent solvent" in the mixture, the remedy is to add more of it. In most cases, small amounts (1 oz. per gallon) of standard lacquer thinner will serve this function because it increases the "bite" of each new coat to the previous one and allows the individual layers to meld together into a solid film.

If your final finish comes out looking good, but scratches or stains too easily, you can make the film more durable by adding a "cross-linker additive" to the finish before application. Carver Tripp makes one called Safe & Simple Super Strength Hardener (available in hardware and paint stores). It's designed for use with the company's own water-base products, but I've found it also works with many other water-base finishes.

One final consideration for water-base finishes: Since these products were created to be easier on the environment, you must dispose of old or unused finish properly. Many people think that because the finishes contain water, they can be dumped down the kitchen drain. *Don't do it!* Besides being illegal in many areas, it's also unwise. "Hard" water will turn the discarded liquid into a mass of sticky glop that's capable of thoroughly plugging your drain. A better alternative is to pour or brush heavy coats of the unwanted material onto some cardboard scraps and let it dry. Once the finish is dry, it is harmless and can be disposed of with your regular trash. □

Chris Minick is a product development chemist and an amateur woodworker in Stillwater, Minn.

finish should "flow" out of the brush and onto the surface with very few bubbles. This technique (traditionally used for applying shellac) works well on both horizontal and vertical surfaces; but thinner coats should be applied to vertical surfaces to avoid sags and runs. Also, avoid the temptation to brush out any bubbles that form; most will break before the film dries.

Spraying: If you spray water-base materials, first make sure your compressor's air filter and water trap are clean; any stray oil will contaminate the finish. Next, your spray gun setup may need changing. For best results with a conventional siphon-feed gun, install a tip with a slightly smaller orifice (and matching needle) than one you would use for nitrocellulose lacquer. Finishing consultant Michael Dresdner recommends using a fluid tip with an orifice between 0.040 in. and 0.055 in. in combination with a low-volume air cap (5 cu. ft./min. at 30 psi). Fluid apertures of HVLP spray guns should be similarly reduced for water-base finishes; a 0.9mm (0.036 in.) tip works well.

Spraying horizontal surfaces is fairly straightforward, but vertical surfaces can present problems. Too light of a coat can produce orange peel; too heavy a coat may run or sag. I like to mist on several light coats in close succession, applying just enough material to completely wet the surface each time. This method requires some practice, and you'll have to adapt it for the material you're using. Every brand of water-base finish I've tried has its own characteristic fluidity. Some are thin enough to be sprayed directly from the can, while others require thinning before use. How much to thin depends a lot on your spraying technique. If you do need to thin the water-base finish to achieve a good spray pattern, be sure to use only distilled water or a special water-base reducer.

Once you're done spraying, clean your gun and cup immediately with warm, soapy water followed by a clean-water rinse. Any dried finish left in the gun can usually be removed with lacquer thinner. To avoid rusting problems, most water-base finish manufacturers recommend using a gun that has stainless-steel fluid

passages. However, my gun has regular steel fluid passages; so after cleaning, I run some denatured ethyl alcohol (available at hardware stores) through the gun to remove the last traces of water.

Rubbing out: After the topcoats dry, you can rub out a water-base finish using automotive rubbing compounds or conventional techniques and materials (see "Rubbing Out a Finish," FWW #72). I've had good luck using either water or mineral oil as a lubricant along with pumice and followed by rottenstone compounds. One caution: don't let the rapid drying time of the water-base finishes fool you. Ultimate film properties won't fully develop for four to five *weeks* and the longer you wait, the less likely you are to experience water or oil damage during the rubbing process. (If you don't rub it out, the film is hard enough after about three days to put your project into service.) Waxing the finish right away somewhat delays the development of the film's hardness. Waiting about two weeks before waxing is usually sufficient, but the longer you can wait, the better. —C.M.

Padding on Shellac

A durable finish that's quick to apply, easy to repair

by Jeff Jewitt

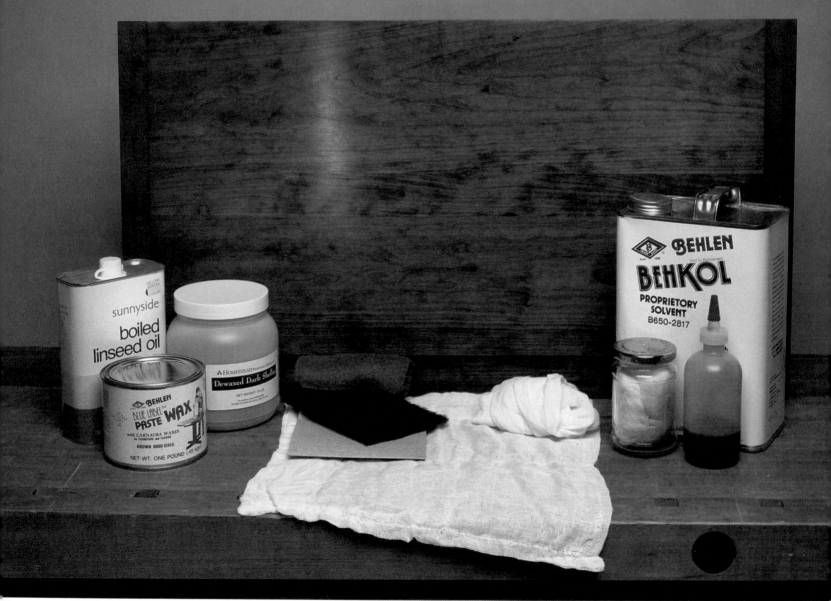

Padding on shellac doesn't require lots of fancy equipment. *You can get a beautiful finish with a minimum of materials: shel-* *lac flakes, solvent, boiled linseed oil and wax. The author finished the tabletop in the background by padding on shellac.*

P adding shellac is a low-tech process that is perfectly suited to the professional and amateur finisher. The advantages of shellac are numerous. It is a nontoxic, Food and Drug Administration-approved natural resin. The carrier for shellac, ethanol, is relatively nontoxic (ethanol is the same kind of alcohol that's found in liquor), and the fumes are not unpleasant. Shellac dries quickly, so dust does not pose a great problem, and finishes can be done in two to three days.

Applying shellac by padding it on is an easy technique to master. I rub on a freshly dissolved shellac solution over a sealer coat of oil, which increases the finish depth. I let each coat dry overnight and continue rubbing on shellac until I've achieved the desired depth and gloss I'm after. Shellac is a good-looking, durable finish that can easily be repaired if damaged. But because shellac can be dissolved by alcohol, this finish is not a good choice for a bar top.

The materials for padding shellac are inexpensive and easy to obtain through most finishing companies (see the sources of supply box on p. 30). They consist of shellac, denatured alcohol, padding cloth, a drying oil such as boiled linseed oil or tung oil, sandpaper and synthetic steel wool.

The materials

I prefer to make my own shellac solution of 2 lbs. of dry shellac flakes dissolved in a gallon of alcohol (a 2-lb. cut; for more on this,

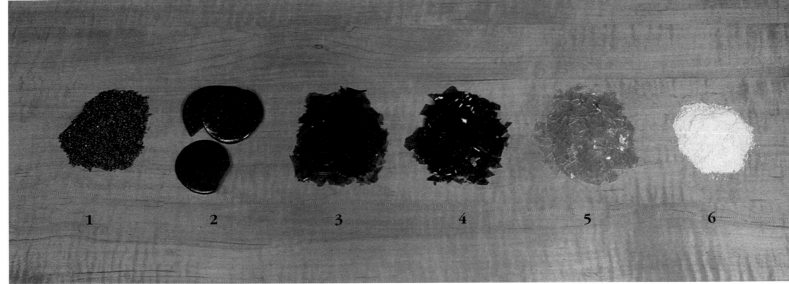

Shellac in dry form is available in a variety of grades. Seedlac (1) and buttonlac (2) are among the least refined forms of shellac. The most common shellac is #1 orange (3). The next two are more highly refined dewaxed shellacs, available in dark-golden brown (4) and pale amber (5). Bleached white shellac (6) yields a colorless solution.

see the story at right). Using fresh shellac will help you avoid one of the classic complaints against shellac as a finish—it won't dry. Shellac is made up of organic acids that react with alcohol in a process called esterification. This gradual reaction produces esters, gummy substances that inhibit drying in old shellac.

Although it's possible to use premixed shellac, any liquid shellac older than six months should be tested for drying problems (Wm. Zinsser Co. makes shellac with a longer shelf life). To test shellac, place a drop or two on a piece of glass. If it's not dry to the touch in five minutes, don't use it. Premixed shellac is available only in orange or white (chemically bleached) varieties; there are more choices if you buy it in dry form (see the photo above). And if you mix your own shellac, you are guaranteed a fresh solution.

There are four alcohol solvents for shellac—methanol, ethanol, butanol and propanol. Methanol is an excellent solvent, but it's extremely poisonous. The fumes will pass through organic vapor respirators, so I avoid using methanol in my shop. Ethanol is far better because of its low toxicity. Butanol has an odor I find disagreeable, so I don't use it as the main solvent. I do add it occasionally to ethanol-reduced shellac as a retarder because butanol's higher molecular weight makes it evaporate slightly more slowly than ethanol. Propanol, the alcohol in rubbing alcohol, can be hard to get in chemically pure form. Don't use rubbing alcohol to dissolve shellac; it is 30% water and will cause problems in the shellac film.

An excellent product made specifically for reducing shellac is a Behlen product called Behkol (see the sources box on p. 30), which is 95% anhydrous ethanol and 5% isobutanol. The isobutanol slows down the drying time slightly.

The best cloth for applying shellac is manufactured from bleached, 100% cotton and is sold as padding, trace or French polishing cloth. Whatever cloth you use, it should be clean, not dyed, lint-free and absorbent. Avoid old T-shirts or cheesecloth because of the lint. My favorite cloth comes in 12-in. squares and has a rumpled texture similar to surgical gauze, as shown in the photo on the facing page.

Use either boiled linseed oil or tung oil to seal the wood and to give greater depth to the finish (only a small amount is needed). I have not been able to discern a difference between the two under the shellac finish. Make sure the linseed oil is boiled, though, because raw linseed oil contains no driers and never really hardens.

What's shellac, and how is it used?

Shellac is derived from a natural resin secreted by a tiny insect called *Lucceifor laccu*. This insect alights on certain trees indigenous to India and Thailand and feeds off sap in the twigs. The insects secrete a cocoon-type shell, which is harvested by workers shaking the tree branches. In this form, the resin is called sticklac and contains bits of twig, insect and other contaminants. The sticklac is then washed to remove impurities. At this point, it may be refined either by hand or machine. The next step up is buttonlac, which is processed in India. It is reddish-brown and is sold in 1-in.- to 2-in.-wide buttons.

Seedlac is another impure form of shellac and is processed further in India for better-quality lacs or exported to other countries for further refining. White shellac is made in the United States by Wm. Zinsser Co. from imported seedlac that's dewaxed and bleached by bubbling chlorine gas through it.

Shellac grading is complex because it is a product with wide commercial applications. But the most important characteristics for woodworkers are those based on color and wax content. The best grades of shellac for finishing have less than 1% wax and are light-amber in color. Wax in shellac decreases its moisture resistance and makes it less transparent.

The most common shellac is industry-graded as #1 orange, which usually is 4% wax and is a brownish-orange color. Dewaxed shellacs can range in color from a dark-golden brown to a pale amber, as shown in the photo above. Fresh shellac is always better, so I mix my own, making just enough for the job at hand. For padding, I prefer a 2-lb. cut, which means 2 lbs. of shellac flakes dissolved in a gallon of alcohol. For most projects, a pint (¼ lb. of flakes in 1 pint of alcohol) is sufficient.

I mix shellac in a clean glass jar. Avoid metal cans because they will discolor the solution. Periodically shaking the jar prevents a jelly-like mass from forming at the bottom. Most shellacs take about a day to dissolve, so plan ahead. If it takes longer, the shellac may be bad. After dissolving in alcohol, lower-grade shellacs like buttonlac and seedlac always should be strained through a medium-mesh or fine-mesh filter to remove impurities. —*J.J.*

After the oil dries for a few minutes, charge the pad with a squeeze bottle to get just the right amount of shellac. The pad should be a lint-free cloth folded so that there are no wrinkles or seams on the bottom of the pad.

First apply a primer coat of oil for a deep finish. The author rubs in a light coat of oil, either boiled linseed or tung oil, to seal the wood. Shellac can be padded on after the oil has dried for several minutes.

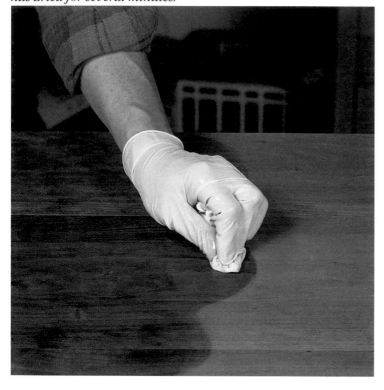

Preparation

No finish can hide sloppy surface preparation. On new wood, I plane, scrape and sand to 220-grit on highly visible surfaces. I also do as much surface preparation as I can on the project before it's glued up. For new work, I'll even apply the oil and the first coat of shellac before assembling a project. Applying at least the first coat of shellac before the piece has been glued up makes it much easier to get an even finish, even in hard to reach places.

I generally tape off tenons and other joints so that oiling doesn't contaminate the wood. If the wood is to be colored, I use water-soluble dyes before the oil sealer coat. These dyes raise the grain, so I knock down the raised fibers with maroon synthetic steel wool (equivalent to 00 steel wool or 320-grit sandpaper) after the dye dries. I prefer synthetic steel wool because it's not as likely to cut through the dye on the edges. After the wood is smoothed down, you're ready for the first finishing step.

Oiling

Oil seals the wood and gives it greater depth. On refinished pieces, you can omit this step. Oils will accentuate the figure and deepen the color of wood, particularly curly maple and cherry. I have used a variety of oils, but I like linseed and tung oil the best. Apply just enough oil to make the surface of the wood look wet (about a thimbleful per square foot), as shown in the photo at left. Do not flood the surface with oil. Apply the oil with a clean, soft cloth, and rub the surface briskly. It will penetrate quickly. After several minutes, begin applying the shellac.

Padding shellac

Fold the padding cloth into a rolled ball, as shown in the top photo. There should be no creases or seams on the pad bottom. Pour about 1 oz. of alcohol into the pad and work it in. Then pour about ¼ oz. to ½ oz. of a 2-lb. cut shellac into the bottom of the pad. I keep my shellac in round squeeze bottles to simplify dispensing into the pad. Use just a little; you shouldn't be able to squeeze shellac from the pad.

To apply the shellac, start at the top, right-hand edge of the board, and work across the board with the grain. Bring the pad down lightly, drag it across the board and right off the opposite

edge, as shown in the drawing. Reverse directions, working back from left to right. Continue down the board, applying the shellac in alternating stripes. When you've reached the bottom, start again at the top; the board will be dry enough to repeat the process.

When the pad dries out, recharge it with more shellac. The amount of shellac you'll use depends on the size of the piece. A 24-sq.-in. piece should take about 10 or 15 minutes and will use three or four charges of shellac. On tops, do the edges first, and then continue the same sequence as above. If there is a complex molded edge, make the pad conform to the shape of the molding. The other parts of the piece (aprons, legs and sides) get the same padding coat of shellac. When the board is tacky and the pad starts to stick, stop. Store the pad in a jar with a screw-type lid.

The first application of shellac should be dry enough to scuff-sand in approximately 1 hour. Using 320-grit, stearated sandpaper (aluminum oxide mixed with zinc stearate as a lubricant), lightly scuff-sand the surface. Scuff-sanding is applying just enough pressure to barely scratch the surface. After this, smooth out the surface with maroon synthetic steel wool. Then apply shellac to the other sides of all surfaces, such as the undersides of tops and the insides of carcases in the same way you did on the top.

When this coat of shellac is dry, after about an hour, scuff-sand and rub these surfaces with synthetic steel wool. After the first coat of finish has been applied, it's time to glue the project together. Be careful to avoid excess glue, and make sure that clamps are properly padded. If any glue squeezes out, you can pull it off like scotch tape after 30 minutes to an hour. Don't let the glue dry completely, it may pull off the finish when you try to remove it.

The next day, once the piece is glued up, the finishing sequence is repeated. The pad should glide easily over the surface, and you should have an even coat of shellac on the surface. As the pad starts to dry out, you can switch from polishing in a stripe pattern to a circular pattern or a series of figure eights to get even coverage on the board. Stop when the finish is tacky and the pad sticks. At this point, the surface should have an even shine, indicating a surface build of shellac. Put the pad back in the jar, and let the finish dry overnight.

The next day, examine the finish. You should have an even coating of finish on the surface. If you are working with open-pored woods like walnut or mahogany, you'll see crisp outlines to the open pores. This level of finish is appealing to some. If so, you can stop applying shellac; simply go on to the rubbing-out stage, which I'll explain in a minute, and you're done.

For surfaces that will receive a lot of wear and tear, you may want to apply several more coats for maximum protection. If so, repeat the procedure until you've built up the finish to the film thickness that you want, allowing each coat to dry overnight. You don't gain any added protection after four or five applications, but there is an aesthetic difference. After the final padding application, let the project dry for several days before rubbing it out.

Rubbing out

Rubbing out the shellac finish results in a smoother, better-looking surface. The beauty of the padding application is that there are no brush marks or other surface irregularities to level, so this step usually goes quickly. The first step is to level the surface of the finish with 400-grit, wet-or-dry silicon carbide finishing paper. Then switch to 0000 steel wool, squirting mineral spirits onto the pad and dipping it into a can of paste wax.

I prefer steel wool for rubbing out because it has a better bite and leaves a better-looking finish. My favorite wax is Behlen's Blue Label paste wax, available in brown for darker finishes and natural for lighter finishes. Working with the grain, I bear down fairly hard with the steel wool and rub the wax on the surface. I wait until it begins to haze, wipe off the excess and buff to a satiny sheen. If a higher gloss is desired, rub the surface with rottenstone mixed with mineral spirits before waxing.

Maintenance

If the piece is not subjected to a lot of wear and tear, a yearly re-waxing keeps it looking great. For tables, chairs and other high-wear items, you can rejuvenate the finish by removing the wax with mineral spirits and rubbing with maroon synthetic steel wool. Then apply a light coat of shellac, let dry and re-wax. □

Jeff Jewitt runs J.B. Jewitt Co., Inc., specializing in restoration and conservation of period furniture. He owns Homestead Finishing Products in North Royalton, Ohio.

Waterborne Finishes: Friendlier Than Ever

Simple shop tests help rate a new generation of clearcoatings

by Chris A. Minick

Finishes that use water as a carrier— *Waterborne finishes go by many names, such as lacquer, acrylic, urethane and conversion-varnish. But they all use water as a delivery medium. The waterborne finishes compared in this article (with their test panels below left) include both hardware-store and commercial-grade varieties.*

A cigarette advertising campaign gained fame, if not fortune, by telling women, "You've come a long way, baby." The ads are in bad taste. But that corny slogan would be perfect for describing products I'm sure advertising copywriters didn't have in mind—waterborne wood finishes.

Almost universally, the latest wave of clear, waterborne finishes (see the photo above) shows a dramatic improvement over those of just five years ago. Gone are the poor-performing, hard-to-use coatings that looked more like plastic wrap than furniture finish. They've been replaced by friendlier finishes, some of which out-perform nitrocellulose lacquer.

Waterborne finishes are not toxic to the environment. They meet the most recent limits for volatile organic compounds (VOCs) in finishes. The newest waterborne finishes adhere better and raise the grain less than the old formulations did. They are easy to use, dry fast, clean up with water and, generally, level out well. If you have good ventilation, you can set up a simple finishing area to spray waterborne finishes. You don't need an explosion-proof booth. If you're brushing, keep in mind that the coats dry quicker than solvent-based varnish (see the story on p. 36).

To see how the new field of waterborne finishes has changed, I chose 15 popular brands—eight over-the-counter finishes found at hardware stores and seven professional-grade finishes found at woodworking supply stores.

I picked gloss finishes because they're the most difficult to get right. I couldn't

From *Fine Woodworking* (November 1995) 115:48-53

Photos: Alec Waters

Six finish testing methods

There is no magic to testing finishes. For the test panels, I used ½-in. medium-density fiberboard (MDF) veneered with birch. I stained half of each panel with Glidden's walnut, oil-based stain and let the panels dry for a week.

To apply the finish uniformly, I used a draw-down bar (a rod wrapped with #40 wire). I applied a swath of finish on one end of the panel and used the wire-wrapped bar to drag the finish across the panel. (You could make your own bar by spiral-wrapping 20-gauge wire around a length of pipe.) I applied three consistent coats of finish, 3 mils thick, allowing each coat to dry four hours. I cured the panels in the shop for 10 days. —*C.M.*

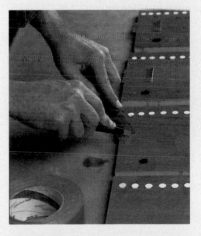

Adhesion

Slice an X on the finish with a razor or sharp knife guided by a straightedge (on the stained side of the panel). Apply a piece of duct tape over the cut area, and rub down well.

After a few minutes, yank off the tape. The finishes that pass will show no delamination. Finishes with marginal adhesion will have ragged edges along the cut. And failed finishes will have chunks missing.

(continued on p. 35)

evaluate every transparent waterborne finish on the market, but if the brand you're using isn't on the chart on pp. 34-35, some simple shop tests will tell you how good your finish is (see the box at right).

Choosing a finish depends on many factors (see the article on pp. 11-15). Because different waterborne finishes excel at different things, you can use the results summarized in the chart (or your own test results) to select the right finish. First, though, a brief discussion of the chemistry of waterborne finishes is in order.

Waterborne finishes have complex formulations

By definition, a lacquer always is soluble in its own solvent. That's why even dried nitrocellulose lacquer can be cleaned from a brush with lacquer thinner. It might surprise you that most waterborne finishes are lacquers. They're sold under every finish name under the sun, including acrylic and urethane.

But don't expect to clean up any of these dried waterborne finishes with water. Water is merely a convenient, nonhazardous carrier liquid that transports the resin from the can to the work. Special resin-soluble/water-soluble solvents, usually glycol ether (similar to lacquer retarder), are added to waterborne finishes. These solvents are critical to film formation. They also dissolve the dry film.

Besides solvent, water and resin, a myriad of other chemicals are needed to complete a waterborne finish formulation. Among the most important are surfactants, compounds which are added for stability, proper flow and leveling.

Defoamers minimize bubbles during application, and thickeners maintain proper viscosity. Flatting agents control finish sheen, and mar-aids protect the film from damage while curing. The formulation is a delicate balance of all these parts, plus some other minor ones. Over-thinning a waterborne finish will destroy this balance, resulting in finishing defects.

How waterborne finishes work

Waterborne finishes contain about 30% resin—much more than nitrocellulose lacquer, which has about 12% resin. That's why it's easy to apply too heavy a coat the first time you spray a waterborne finish. It's common to get sags and runs until you get used to spraying these finishes.

Waterborne finishes differ from solvent-based finishes not only in composition but also in the way a film is formed. If you could look into a can of waterborne finish with a powerful microscope, you'd see billions of tiny spheres of resin dispersed in water. Each resin ball contains solvent, which makes the ball sticky, and is surrounded by a protective layer of surfactant. The surfactant layer keeps the sticky balls from becoming one giant agglomeration in the can.

As the finish begins to dry, water evaporates from the emulsion. At the same time, the viscosity of the finish increases, and the resin balls start to bunch together, much like golf balls packed in a bucket. When enough water has evaporated, capillary action within the film deforms the balls into stacked, overlapping discs, called platelets. Residual solvents, called tail solvents, weld the discs together to form a continuous film.

The tail solvents also allow successive coats to burn into one another. The solvents gradually evaporate to complete the curing. One exception is Kemvar W made by Sherwin Williams. Because it is a conversion varnish, it's possible to get "witness lines" between coats if the directions aren't followed. Witness lines result when successive layers of finish don't melt into

each other and are rubbed out unevenly.

The whole film-forming process is known as coalescence. The makers of waterborne finishes often have "polymerized" written on the can because it's a sexy chemical term that attracts consumers. Some cans of waterborne finish also have "catalyzed" on the label, which means that a chemical (catalyst) is added to trigger the polymerization process. Finish polymerization, in theory, means that billions of tiny molecules link into one big one.

Testing the finishes and interpreting the results

I'm a sucker for new finishes. But experience has taught me that the worst way to select a new finish is by reading manufacturer's advertisements or what's listed on the label. Most of the product literature reads something like "Our finish is great on everything." The only way to tell whether those assertions are true is to test the finish. That's how this article was born. Half the waterborne finishes I tested are

Comparing waterborne finishes

Manufacturer	Product	Adhesion over oil stain	Stain Resistance (22 max.)	Heat resistance (200°F)	
Amity (800) 733-1776	Gloss	Fail	22	OK	
Behlen (518) 843-1380	Water-based urethane	Pass	17	Slight print	
Behr (714) 545-7101	#630 polyurethane	Fail	22	OK	
Carver Tripp (508) 679-5938	Safe & Simple	Fail	22	OK	
Crystalac (615) 727-6425	CL90	Marginal	14	Slight print	
Deft (714) 474-0400	Safe & Easy	Marginal	20	Slight print	
Fabulon (716) 873-6000	Crystal	Marginal	16	OK	
Eclectic Products (800) 288-4667	Famowood Super Lac	Pass	19	OK	
General Finishes (800) 783-6050	EF poly-acrylic blend	Pass	16	OK	
Hydrocote (800) 229-4937	Equal	Marginal	6	Fail	
McCloskey (800) 845-9061	Heirloom	Marginal	17	OK	
Minwax (201) 391-0253	Polycrylic	Fail	15	Slight print	
M.L. Campbell (716) 873-6000	Ultrastar	Marginal	20	OK	
Sherwin Williams (216) 566-2000	Kemvar W	Pass	20	OK	
Wood-Kote (503) 285-8371	Liquid plastic	Pass	22	OK	

Two benchmark finishes

Solvent-based nitrocellulose lacquer		Pass	21	Fail	
Solvent-based polyurethane varnish		Pass	22	OK	

Nitrocellulose lacquer and polyurethane varnish are considered the solvent-based standards in the finishing industry. Because you may be more familiar with these two finishes than you are with waterborne finishes, we've included them here as a point of reference.

Solvent resistance (30 max.)	Sanding	Appearance	Best applicator	Remarks/ Dry time
3	Moderate	Fair	Spray	Good color/ 2 hours
1	Difficult	Fair	Spray or brush	Very thin/ 2 hours
10	Difficult	Poor	Brush	Looks plastic-coated/ 3-4 hours
16	Moderate	Poor	Brush or spray	Blue tint/ 45 minutes
2	Easy	Very good	Spray	Lacks color/ 30 minutes
8	Very difficult	Very poor	Brush	Severe fish-eyes/ 1 hour
2	Moderate	Fair	Brush	Low gloss/ 1 hour
9	Easy	Excellent	Spray	Looks like nitro-cellulose/ 30 minutes
8	Easy	Very good	Brush or spray	Easy to brush/ 2 hours
0	Easy	Excellent	Spray	Cold water destroyed film/ 30 minutes
12	Difficult	Fair	Brush	Good color/ 1-2 hours
16	Moderate	Good	Brush	Lacks color/ 2 hours
6	Moderate	Good	Spray	Rubs out nicely/ 45 minutes
30	Moderate	Very good	Spray	Off-gasses formal-dehyde/ 45 minutes
18	Difficult	Poor	Brush	Poor leveling/ 2-4 hours
9	Moderate	Excellent	Spray	Industry standard
27	Difficult	Very good	Brush	Very durable, but looks yellow

The areas on the chart in this color indicate professional-grade finishes designed for spraying. Unshaded areas indicate over-the-counter, hardware-store finishes designed for brushing. There are three finishes that are recommended for both spraying and brushing.

recommended for spray application. The other half are suitable as general-purpose, brush-on finishes.

Adhesion is the most important consideration—Many projects are stained, so it's critical that a waterborne finish adhere to oil-based stain (see the photo at right on p. 33). After all, the main job of a finish is protection. If a finish doesn't stick, the rest of its attributes are meaningless. I avoid any finish that fails in adhesion. If a finish adheres marginally, I would seal stained areas with fresh, de-waxed shellac before I used that particular topcoat.

Resistance to stains, solvents and heat depends on the project—Not all finishes are appropriate for all projects. Tabletop finishes should provide good resistance to food stains and should be washable with standard cleaners. I used a stain-resistance test to determine how well each waterborne finish withstood 11 com-

Stain resistance
Place one drop of the following household products on the panel: milk, mustard, grape juice, lemon juice, olive oil, Windex, Fantastik, Spic and Span pine cleaner, ammonia, black shoe polish and hot water (140°F). After one hour, wash the panel with water, and inspect the finish. If a patch shows no stain or damage, it receives two points; if it has slight dulling, it gets one point; if it has severe damage or a stain, it gets no points. Add up the points (22 is the maximum).

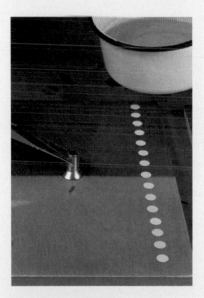

Heat resistance
Heat several large flat-head bolts in boiling water. Set a bolt (about 200°F) on each panel, and allow them to cool to room temperature. Then remove the bolts.
   Rate the finish "okay," if a bolt shows no sign of damage. If the bolt leaves a slight impression or sticks to the finish, the finish fails the test.

(continued on p. 37)

Solving waterborne finish problems

Although it's true that waterborne finishes are easy to use, they are not problem-free. However, by knowing a few corrective tricks, you can overcome most of their shortcomings.

When you first apply a waterborne finish, don't be alarmed if the finish looks milky. As it dries, and the water evaporates, a clear film of finish will form.

Reducing bubbles and micro-bubbles: Bubbles are the most common drawback to using waterborne finishes. Bubbles are caused by the surfactants (compounds added for stability, flow and leveling). Manufacturers try to counteract the bubbles by mixing in defoamers, but the defoamers deactivate over time. The older the finish, the more bubbles. To control bubbles in old (one year or more) cans of finish, I add a small amount of solvent (no more than 1½ oz. per gallon). I use lacquer thinner, mineral spirits or even

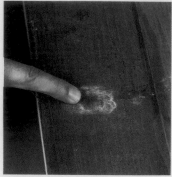

Watch the humidity—Applying waterborne finishes in high humidity and low temperatures can interfere with proper film formation. That was the case with this finish.

milk. (Fats in milk are chemically similar to defoamers.)

Another bubble problem, micro-bubbles, is particular to certain fast-drying waterborne finishes designed for spray application. Micro-bubbles form when high-pressure air from a spray gun is forced into the liquid finish. This trapped air forms tiny voids in the film. Micro-bubbles are not so noticeable in a dull or semigloss finish, but they show up as a white haze in high-gloss finishes. To eliminate micro-bubbles, reduce the atomization pressure. Lowering the pressure can cause another problem—orange peel (poor leveling). Eliminating both micro-bubbles and orange peel is

a balancing act. Sometimes, I add a waterborne finish retarder (in a pinch, you can use a 50:50 mix of lacquer retarder and water) to minimize micro-bubbles.

Applying level, blemish-free coats: When brushing on a waterborne finish, use long, even strokes, as you would with shellac. Keep the brush angle at about 30°. Avoid back-and-forth motions—they're more suited for house painting. Use a long-bristled, tapered-and-tipped nylon brush or a good foam applicator. Work quickly as you brush, and maintain a wet edge. This should reduce sanding.

In preparation for a waterborne finish, don't use a tack cloth. It contains an oily substance that will cause fish-eyes (so will some stearate-coated sandpapers). I wipe down my projects beforehand and between sanding stages with a cloth dampened with mineral spirits. If you're spraying, make sure you have a de-oiler. Also, don't use steel wool between coats. Small metal shards left by the steel wool will rust and ruin your finish.

Eliminating grain raising: Grain raising, though still a problem with waterborne finishes, is not as bad as it once

was. One way to get around the problem is to wet the wood and then knock down the fibers with sandpaper before you finish. But there is an easier way. Waterborne-finish manufacturers have introduced non-grain-raising (NGR) sealers. Apply a thin sealer coat, let it dry and then scuff-sand the surface. Nearly all the finishes in this article have accompanying sealers.

I almost always use a sealer with waterborne finishes. Compared to nitrocellulose lacquer, waterborne finishes usually are colorless and without depth. Scaling (I like super-blond shellac) before you apply the waterborne finish can dramatically improve the appearance. Tinting with NGR stain is another option.

Watching the temperature and humidity: The ideal application condition for most waterbornes is around 70°F and 50% relative humidity (RH). Temperatures below 50°F and/or humidity above 85% RH can severely compromise film integrity (see the photo above). In fact, either condition can prevent the finish from forming a film at all. Heating or dehumidifying your shop will cure both problems. Or you can wait for a better day. —*C.M.*

---

mon chemicals (see the top photo on p. 35). The higher the number, the better the stain resistance. Finishes with a rating of 15 or higher should stand up well to everyday use. If you have a house full of teen-agers, you may want to use a finish with a higher rating.

Heat resistance also is important for dining-table finishes. While it's probably not a good idea to take a hot casserole dish from the oven and place it on the table, it happens all the time. Heat-damaged finishes are very hard to repair. A simple test using a hot bolt (see the bottom photo on p. 35) can save you a lot of work later on.

The solvent-resistance test (see the top right photo on the facing page) is tedious. But it's worth checking out a finish's solvent resistance ahead of time. This is especially true for dressing tables or bar tops because perfume, nail-polish remover and drinks with alcohol in them contain sol-

vents that can damage a finish. This test is standard in the kitchen cabinet industry.

How it sands and looks may or may not be a concern—Sanding is an important step toward getting a nice finish. But I don't like to sand. Who does? If a finish is hard to sand (meaning that globs of finish accumulate on the sandpaper), I usually get frustrated, stop sanding and hope that the next coat will cover up the problem. It rarely does. That's why I select finishes that sand as painlessly as possible. It's rather tricky for a finish to be both durable (not brittle) and have the right feel (friction) for sanding. A good finish is neither too soft nor too hard.

Grading the look of a finish is subjective. I'm a nitrocellulose lacquer fan. As far as appearance goes, no finish can match it. I can't help but compare any finish to nitrocellulose lacquer, and the waterborne fin-

ishes were no exception (see the bottom photos on the facing page). Appearance rankings on the chart, as well as those for sandability, relate more to my preferences than to hard data or measurements. Take them with a grain of salt.

The good, the bad and the ugly

I've tested a lot of waterborne finishes in the last 15 years, and most have been pretty mediocre. I expected the same kind of results from this round of tests, too. What I found was quite different. The latest waterborne finishes have some real winners and a few big losers.

The real surprise was Hydrocote Equal. Although it was one of the best-looking finishes, it tested last overall. I even ran the tests twice to confirm my initial results. And then I used the same procedures to compare this finish to an acrylic floor polish made by Johnson Wax. The floor polish

Strikes against them—No finish was perfect, but some of them had serious faults (from left): Amity (poor adhesion), Carver Tripp (poor appearance), Deft (excessive fish-eye), Wood-Kote (poor leveling) and Hydrocote (poor stain and solvent resistance).

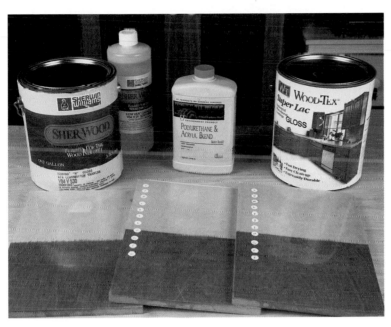

Author's favorites—Based on the tests, Minick liked three finishes (from the left): Sherwin Williams (most protective), General Finishes (best brush-on), and Wood-Tex, which is now sold as Famowood Super Lac (best to spray, best looking and best value). Sherwin Williams is shown with its catalyst.

Solvent resistance

Apply three solvents to the panels. I blended water, ethyl alcohol (ethanol) and methyl ethyl ketone (MEK) in 15 different ratios, starting with a 50:50 mix of water and ethanol and ending with 100% MEK. Space 15 dots of bond paper on the panels. Place a drop of each solution on the dots, and dry two hours. Remove the dots. A spot with no damage receives two points; slight damage or dulling of the finish gets one point; dots that stick to the finish get no points. Add up the points (30 is the maximum).

Sandability

Wrap a ¾-in.-wide strip of 400-grit sandpaper around a piece of scrap. Abrade a spot of the panel. Easy-to-sand finishes form a powder and do not load the paper. Difficult-to-sand coatings require force and gum up the paper. Moderate-to-sand finishes fall in between.

Lacquer

Waterborne

Appearance

Compare the finishes to nitrocellulose lacquer. Note the clarity, depth, color and luster. I rated finishes "excellent" and "very good" if they looked three-dimensional and warm (amber). I used "good" and "fair" for finishes that lacked color or appeared cloudy or blue. I rated ugly finishes "poor."

---

scored higher. Hydrocote does make another more expensive, more durable waterborne finish called Resisthane. This finish performed much better than the Equal. The waterborne finishes made by Amity, Carver Tripp, Deft and Wood-Kote had their share of problems, too (see the top photo). They may or may not be appropriate for your next finishing project.

But three finishes really impressed me (see the bottom photo). Kemvar W had the highest gross score. For sheer protection value, this finish is practically bulletproof. In terms of formulation, it's quite different from the others in the field because it has two parts. It's actually a spray-on, acid-catalyzed, waterborne conversion varnish designed as a kitchen-cabinet finish.

A word of caution, though. Kemvar W releases small amounts of formaldehyde gas as it dries. This finish should only be sprayed in a booth that has good intake and exhaust air flow. And it's a good idea to wear gloves and protective clothing. I also use a carbon-filter respirator.

General Finishes' EF polyurethane and acrylic blend applies easily, has excellent leveling properties, good vertical cling and looks great—a pleasant surprise in a brush-on finish. Of all the finishes, I was most impressed with Eclectic Product's Famowood Super Lac (previously available as Wood-Tex Super Lac; the manufacturer assures me that the finish in the can remains the same). This finish's color is virtually indistinguishable from nitrocellulose lacquer. It rubs out beautifully, has decent resistance properties and, best of all, has a depth not usually associated with waterborne finishes. □

Chris Minick is a finishing chemist and a contributing editor to Fine Woodworking. *He works wood in Stillwater, Minn.*

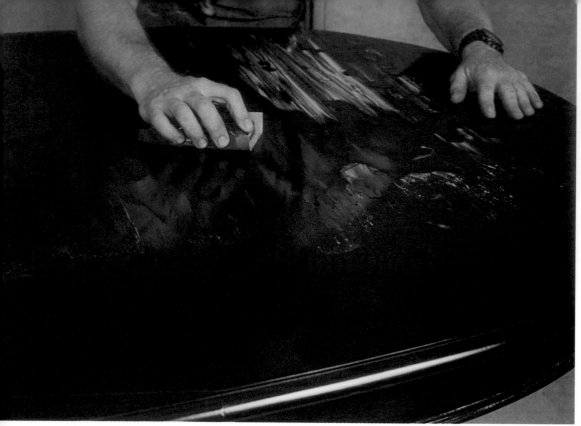

Left: Finishes are first leveled out with microfine sandpaper wrapped around a rubber block. The block is moved in long, straight strokes, about 1 ft. long. Water or naphtha is used as a lubricant. **Above:** *Polishing compounds can be removed from the buffing pad by running the pad at high speed against the end of a stick. The pad will become soft and fluffy as the compound is thrown off.* **Right:** *A power buffer, used with modern automotive polishing compounds, can be one of the most important tools in the wood finisher's arsenal. Here the author buffs out the lacquered top of a dining-room table.*

Auto-Body Tips for Fine Finishes
Swapping elbow grease for a power buffer

by Scott Lawrence

Years ago I made a horrible mistake. I had just opened my own refinishing and restoration shop and was going all out to establish a good reputation. When I was hired to refinish a dining-room table, I knew that nothing less than a flawless, mirror-perfect finish would do. After glopping on numerous coats of lacquer with a cheap, hand-held airless sprayer, I started rubbing out the surface, which now resembled a lunar landscape, with 600-grit wet-or-dry sandpaper, pumice and vast quantities of elbow grease. After a few exhausting, anxiety-filled days of backbreaking labor, the perfect finish miraculously appeared. The customer loved the hand-rubbed finish, and I was soon buried in word-of-mouth referrals, all expecting flawless finishes. Rapidly approaching nervous exhaustion, I began to search for ways to speed production and minimize labor.

To make a long story short, the method I came up with lets me rub out a tabletop, or any large finished wood surface, in an hour or so. What discovery made this possible? At some point I noticed that auto-body shops had huge lacquered surfaces to rub out to a smooth high gloss. And a customer having a $25,000 car refinished was apt to be even more fussy than my clients; so these auto-finish guys had to know some tricks. What I eventually found out was

that these tricks worked on wood, too, making it possible for me to rub out a finish very quickly with top-quality results and to make a profit on even very nasty furniture-repair problems. All I had to do was take advantage of high-tech automotive polishing compounds, abrasive pads and a high-speed, electric power buffer, like the one shown on the facing page.

This method is not without risk, as anyone who has used a high-speed buffer can tell you. The difference between success and failure is often just one inattentive second. The tool can be mastered with practice, but I recommend that your early efforts be on expendable practice pieces. You can also use the finishing compounds with traditional hand-rubbing techniques, if you don't want to risk using the buffer. For more on hand-rubbed finishes, I suggest you read Michael Dresdner's article "Rubbing Out a Finish," *FWW* #72.

Automotive products for wood finishers—My rubbing out system is based on items that are readily available at most auto-supply stores. For the initial stage, I sand the surface with Imperial Wet or Dry Color Sanding Paper, lubricated with water or naphtha. This finishing paper, manufactured by 3M Co. (Industrial Abrasives Division, 223-6N-01 3M Center, St. Paul, Minn. 55144), ranges from

From *Fine Woodworking* (March 1991) 87:70-72

orange peel, drips and other defects, let the finish cure at least a week; otherwise, the film will continue to shrink, exposing new defects as you work. I begin with 1,000-grit paper, which quickly levels the surface, but doesn't scratch the way 600-grit wet-or-dry paper does. To avoid gouging or hollowing the surface, I wrap the paper around a rubber block when sanding, as shown in the left photo on the facing page. Work carefully; any gouges you make at this stage must eventually be removed before you can achieve a perfect finish.

Ordinary naphtha from your local hardware or paint store makes a good lubricant with the 1,000-grit paper, but if you're thrifty (some say cheap) like me, a squirt bottle filled with water and a few drops of dishwasher detergent works just fine. Some finishers prefer naphtha because it won't raise the grain as water will if you sand through the finish coats. But assuming you've sprayed on two or three coats of lacquer, the 1,000-grit paper is very unlikely to cut through to the bare wood.

I level the edges of the lacquered piece first, taking short, straight strokes about a foot long with the sandpaper block. Remember, you only want to level the surface, not eliminate all the scratches, and you must be especially careful not to remove too much material at the edges, where finish layers may be thinner than at the center of the table. Once the edges are level, move on to the center section, blending the strokes from there into the edge areas. Wipe off the surface regularly to check your progress. When the surface is uniformly dull and flat, it's time to rub out the surface with polishing compounds.

Meguiar's machine glaze #1 will quickly remove the light sanding scratches left by the 1,000-grit papers. Apply a generous amount of the compound to the tabletop, smearing it evenly over the surface with the pad of your buffer. Now you're ready to buff. I generally buff out a 2-ft.-sq. area at a time, and then move onto another area. Once the whole surface is done, I make long passes over the entire top to blend the areas together. You may have to reapply the compound once or twice before the surface is free of scratches and any remaining orange peel. Generally all the scratches will be eliminated by a few minutes of power buffing. The self-cleaning compound will dry within a few minutes and can be blown off with compressed air or wiped off with a soft rag.

If you're after a satin finish, buff no further. Now switch to a gray Scotch-Brite pad (also available from 3M) backed by a rubber block and use Meguiar's #1 as a polishing compound. I find that this combination of Scotch-Brite pad and rubber block produces a smoother, more consistent rub than Scotch-Brite alone. For a bit more gloss, repeat the process with the Scotch-Brite and Meguiar's #2 or #3 compounds, which are finer than #1. Just be sure to apply consistent rubbing pressure on the block and to keep your strokes straight.

For a high-gloss finish, you must first clean the #1 compound from the buffer pad. This can be done easily by running the pad against the end of a stick, as shown in the photo at right on the facing page. The stick fluffs and separates the fibers and makes it possible for the rotation to spin off any remaining material. After removing any residue from the tabletop with a damp rag, repeat the buffing operation with Meguiar's #3 glaze. This should leave a surface that is near perfect, with perhaps just a few swirl marks at most. You can buy ultrafine rubbing compounds (sold as swirl-mark eliminators), but I find that final-buffing with a clean lamb's wool pad on the power buffer works just fine and leaves less mess to clean up. The final buffing is done with only light pressure on the tool, with the pad held at a very low angle to the surface. Be careful around the edges of the finish: the pad should rotate away from the edge at the point of contact and not into the edge.

If everything has worked as planned, you should be able to read the directions on the back of the Meguiar's container reflected in

1,000- to 2,000-grit, which makes the 600-grit paper many finishers use seem like a belt sander by comparison.

After leveling the surface with the micropapers, I switch to Meguiar's Mirror Glaze machine glazes #1 and #3 (Meguiar's, 17991 Mitchell S., Irvine, Cal. 92714). These compounds are not the heavy color coats that most wood finishers associate with glazes, but are self-cleaning polishing compounds that break down into finer and finer abrasives as they are rubbed on a surface. The Meguiar's compounds are ideal with high-speed buffers, like my Black & Decker 7-in. professional model with lamb's wool bonnet. I've found that the lower-price tools ruin your hearing and burn out in a couple of months, but they still beat hand-rubbing. And I haven't had good results with the slow-speed orbital waxer/polisher machines sold in some stores.

Rubbing out a finish—Most of the finishes I work with are lacquer, and that's the finish I'm working with on the table shown here. But the buffing method will also work with many polyurethanes, varnishes and other film finishes, too. To be sure, though, try out the technique on a test surface before you risk something valuable.

Before attempting to level out a lacquered surface to eliminate the finish surface. If you have the misfortune to notice a flaw that you missed, all is not lost; you can spot-level and buff that area and blend everything together using the same sequence as before.

Repairs with a power buffer—The power buffer is one of the mightiest weapons in the finisher's arsenal. In skilled hands, it can quickly remove serious scratches in lacquer that otherwise might have to be patched or recoated.

The trick to buffing out deep scratches is to take advantage of both the heat generated by the buffer and the thermoplastic nature of nitrocellulose lacquer, which means the material will soften and spread enough to fill in a scratch in the finish. This technique works best with a thick topcoat layer. First, you must make sure the surface being repaired is clean and completely free of

Two different colors of shellac sticks can be used to create a grain pattern in the patch area. Here Lawrence blends some dark lines into the lighter base patch with a hot knife.

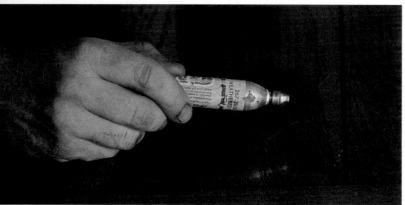

Grain patterns and lines can also be simulated with magic markers or special finisher's markers.

After the damaged area has been filled and the patch has been colored to match the surrounding grain area, the author levels the surface with microfine paper on a rubber block.

wax or oil. You can remove the wax with naphtha or a commercial dewaxer. Then, using a clean lamb's wool buffer, apply the contact area of the pad to the scratch and move the pad slowly, about an inch per second or slower, across the damaged area. Within moments, you should see the finish flowing and being forced into the scratch. Minor blistering is no problem since that can be leveled out later.

After a few passes, walk around the table and buff the repair area from the opposite direction so that you move lacquer from the other side of the scratch. Continue this process until the scratch is filled, or until your nerves can't take it anymore and you tell yourself "close enough." It's better to end up with a minor, easily overlooked crease in the surface than risk cutting through the topcoat. Level any blistering or roughness with microfine paper on a rubber block, and then buff out with Meguiar's #1 and #3 compounds until the repair area matches the sheen of the rest of the surface.

Even experienced buffer operators should try this procedure on a practice piece first, but it's a trick worth learning. It's amazing to see even a deep scratch fill up with lacquer and disappear.

Repairing wood finishes with shellac sticks—Auto-body finishing technology can be valuable to a woodworker who is faced with repairing or restoring a finish. One of the most challenging repairs for a finisher, for example, is fixing a damaged spot right in the middle of a high-gloss tabletop. The usual technique is to fill the damaged area with liquid shellac by heating one of the colored shellac sticks available from woodworking- and finishing-supply houses. You won't usually have any trouble finding a stick with the right color and you can melt enough of it with a match or a hot knife to fill the damaged area so it's level with the surrounding finish. In some cases, however, you may need two different colored sticks to simulate grain (shown in the top, left photo) or you may need to draw grain lines with a marker, as shown in the center, left photo. I got my markers from Mohawk Finishing Products Inc., Route 30 N., Amsterdam, N.Y. 12010; (518) 843-1380. But no matter how skillfully I worked, the repair usually showed somewhat until I applied automotive techniques to the problem. The microfine paper on a rubber block excelled at leveling and smoothing the repair, as shown in the bottom, left photo. For this operation, naphtha is the most effective lubricant, because this chemical levels the burn-in area faster than the surrounding finish.

After leveling out the burn-in area with microsandpaper, a very light rubbing or just a few light passes with the buffer will blend in the patch with the surrounding finish. Usually I don't find it necessary to topcoat over this repair.

When working with a polyester finish, such as so-called Euro-style black lacquer pieces, I would never rub out with anything coarser than 2,000-grit sandpaper. If you have to work regularly on polyester finishes, you might be interested in Mohawk's Gray Lapping Film, a sandpaper-like product that comes in several grades, all finer than the microfine paper. Again, wrap the abrasive around a rubber block for best results. Since polyester doesn't flow out as does nitrocellulose when buffed, the polyester finish must be rubbed out with finer and finer abrasives. After sanding the area as finely as possible, buffing with Meguiar's glaze #3 will restore the sheen to the glossiest polyester finish. I also like the fact that the Meguiar's products are about a third of the price of many compounds marketed specifically for rubbing out polyester finishes. □

Scott Lawrence is a professional furniture finisher and restorer in Colorado Springs, Colo. Photos by Gary Weisenburger.

Sealers: Secret for Finishing Success
Techniques for smooth, durable results

by Chris A. Minick

Seal first for a better finish. Sealer promotes adhesion and acts as a barrier between separate layers of finish. It can also reduce absorption of the final finish and simplify sanding between layers. Here, Minick brushes a 2-lb. cut of his favorite sealer, super-blond shellac, onto a mahogany tabletop.

Ever try to duplicate the glass-smooth finish that you saw on a fine piece of furniture? Even if you match the stain color exactly, fill the grain pores properly and use an identical topcoat, somehow your finish looks different, or it doesn't feel as smooth. The reason may be that you didn't use a sealer. Understanding why to use sealers and how to apply them will bring a new dimension to your work.

Sealers are the unsung heroes of finishing. For example, high-end furniture often has several layers of finish (usually lacquer or varnish) bonded together with sealers to form a cohesive film. But you would be hard-pressed to know that the sealers are there. When I finished the mahogany tabletop shown in the photo above, I sealed before grain-filling and

again before the final finish layer. However, when I started woodworking, I didn't see the usefulness of sealing. It looked like an extra step. Just by dumb luck, the oil-based varnish I used back then worked without a sealer. My early finishes were acceptable, but not great. With time, I began to experiment with different finishing techniques. Several peeling finishes later, I came to realize the error of my non-sealing ways.

Types of sealers

Sealers serve a variety of functions in the woodshop: They ease sanding, decrease finish absorption, promote finish adhesion, and they act as a barrier coat between separate finish layers. Sealers come in several chemical compositions, each tailored to perform a specific task (see the bottom right photo on p. 42). There are three basic sealer types: varnish-based sanding sealers; lacquer-type sealers, including thinned nitrocellulose lacquer

and shellac (super blond and orange); and vinyl sealers, which are tougher than the other two.

Sealers make sanding easier—Sanding sealers perform a dual function: They seal the wood and provide a smooth, flat substrate for the final finish. A thin coat of sanding sealer stiffens the wood fibers, so subsequent sanding will cut them off cleanly. The result is a flat, smooth ready-to-finish surface. Most sanding sealers contain metal stearates to make sanding easy. This is the same stuff used on non-loading sandpaper. The soft stearate pigments add volume to the coating. As a result, sanding sealers build fast and dry quickly, but they're relatively soft.

Resist the temptation to use sanding sealer as build coats for your finish; it's never a good idea to apply a thin, hard finish over a thick, soft one. This practice

Photo: Robert Marsala

To avoid blotchiness, seal before grain-filling. The author treated the halves of this ash board differently to show the effect of sealing the wood. The dark lower part, which was not sealed before the grain was filled, displays ghost-like smudges. The more even-looking upper part was sealed before the grain was filled.

Shellac between finish layers improves finishes. You can sand grain-filler smooth without scratching the under layers, add colored glaze coats without them bleeding, and alternate oil- and water-based layers of finish if shellac is used between layers. Here, shellac sealer helps achieve an instrument-quality finish on mahogany.

The best ways to apply common sealers are to brush on shellac, both super blond and orange (left); brush on varnish-based sanding sealer (front); and spray on vinyl-based sealers (right).

causes increased cold-checking and impact-cracking of hard lacquer finishes. To envision these phenomena, picture a thin layer of ice over soft, unfrozen mud. As you step on the ice, the mud moves, and the ice cracks. Just remember that sanding sealers are meant to be sanded down to the wood before you apply the topcoat finish. If you do this, you shouldn't have problems.

Sealers decrease finish absorption—

Finish-thirsty woods like cherry, pine and lauan benefit from a sanding-sealer coat, even if they don't need to be sanded smooth. The stearate solids in combination with the resin in the sealer stuff up the small pores and soft areas in the wood, thus minimizing absorption of the next coat of finish. This is particularly beneficial when you spray on a low-solids lacquer. But, if you use similar reasoning for stain, you can run into trouble. I've seen woodworkers brush sanding sealers on wood before staining in an attempt to eliminate unevenness on blotch-prone woods like pine. I haven't found this helpful. Instead, I use a home-brew

of linseed oil as a pre-stain conditioner to reduce blotchiness (see p. 93).

Once you've stained the wood and it's dry, you should seal in the stain layer. This way, you can sand before the next finish layer while the sealer protects the stain from scratches. This is especially helpful if you have to do some grain-filling. Fresh shellac makes a great sealer for this, as does a thinned coat of clear lacquer. But a thin coat of vinyl sealer provides even more protection from sanding abrasion because vinyl sealers are tougher. Sealing before filling the grain will also eliminate smudges that give an undesirable ghosting effect to the wood (see the photo at left).

Sealers promote finish adhesion—

Oily woods like teak, rosewood and cocobolo contain natural resins that can cause major finishing problems (see the photo at right on the facing page). Lacquers may peel from the surface or be-

come sticky after they have dried. Worse yet, some oil-based varnishes applied over these woods will refuse to dry at all. Luckily, special vinyl sealers have been developed to make the overlying finish fast, which eliminates these headaches. Vinyl sealers derive their name from the vinyl-toluene-modified alkyd resins with which they are formulated. Vinyl sealers come in a fast-drying lacquer mix for spraying or dissolved in mineral spirits for brushing under an oil-based varnish. Regardless of the carrier solvent, vinyl resins form an impervious layer between the wood and the finish, thus preventing future finish failure. For similar reasons, pigmented primers, such as BIN (William Zinsser & Co., 173 Belmont Drive, Somerset, N.J. 08875; 908-469-8100), are useful when applied under painted finishes.

When you're using vinyl sealer, pay attention to the manufacturer's instructions regarding cure time. Failure to overcoat some vinyl sealers within the specified time can lead to finish delamination. Similarly, vinyl sealers are not really compatible with water-based finishes because water-based resins will not properly ad-

From *Fine Woodworking* (July 1994) 107:85-87

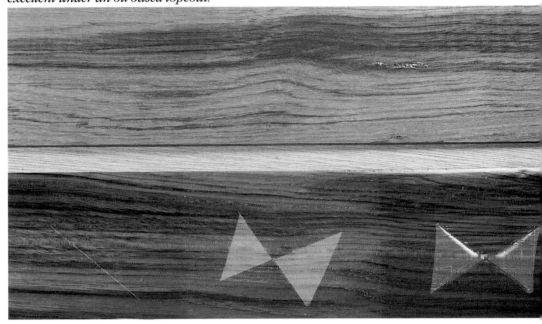

Incompatible sealer leads to a peeling finish—Always check sealer and finish compatibility first on scrapwood. As the author discovered many years ago on this butternut door, vinyl sealer and water-based polyurethane don't mix.

Sealers increase finish adhesion on oily woods like teak (an unfinished piece is at top). A water-based topcoat knifed with an X shows adhesion differences (from left below): shellac-sealed (good adhesion); not sealed (poor adhesion); vinyl-sealed (poor adhesion). But vinyl sealer is excellent under an oil-based topcoat.

here to vinyl-alkyd coatings (see the photo at right). But shellac has tremendous barrier properties and adheres phenomenally to both oil-based and water-based finishing materials. Professional furniture refinishers often apply shellac over stripped wood to seal in waxes, silicones and stripper residue that would otherwise interfere with the finish. You can buy shellac pre-mixed, but I prefer to mix shellac fresh using dry flakes and ethyl alcohol. Fresh shellac brushes or sprays on, dries quickly, seals well, is compatible with all common finishes and sands easily. That's why shellac is the sealer of choice in my shop.

Sealing between layers of finish— Sealers allow different finishes to be overlaid on the same project (for more on this, see the article on p. 13). That's why sealers became an indispensable part of my finishing routine when I started doing multi-layer finishes. For instance, my fa-

vorite mahogany finish consists of a yellow ground stain followed by grain filler, three different-colored glaze layers and two or three finish coats. Although I don't use this finish sequence often, when I do, it sure is pretty (see the top right photo on the facing page).

Here's how the sealer works: Each layer is separated from the next by a coat of shellac. The sealer over the ground stain protects it from abrasion when sanding the filler, and sealer prevents the color from bleeding into subsequent layers. The grain filler is sealed to prevent the porous filler from absorbing color from the first (rosewood) glaze coat. Sealing after this glaze layer keeps it from "walking" into the next (walnut) glaze coat. Another layer of shellac lets me use an oil-based asphaltum glaze (needed for its color) over the water-based glazes. After I seal the asphaltum layer, I brush on a water-based topcoat. This finish would not be possible without the shellac sealer coats.

A word of caution when you're layering finishes: Make sure all your base coats, topcoats, sealer coats and fillers are chemically compatible. The door in the

photo at left is a classic example of what can happen when you ignore this simple rule. I left the peeling water-based topcoat as a reminder of this lesson. Generally, it's wise to choose all your materials from the same finishing family. For instance, varnish sealer and oil-based pore filler can be used under polyurethane. The same philosophy holds true for finishes in the lacquer family and for the water-based finish family. I've had good luck combining oil-based sealers, fillers and stains with water-based topcoats, as long as I seal between each layer with fresh shellac. But the only sure way to tell if your finish layers will be compatible is to test your entire finishing sequence on scrap before you commit it to your project. A little up-front sealer testing can save hours of stripping hassles later. □

Chris Minick is a finishing chemist and a woodworker in Stillwater, Minn. He is a regular contributor to FWW.

Padding Lacquer
A quick, easy alternative to French polishing

by Mario Rodriguez

For me, French polishing is the finish of choice for the very finest furniture. When done well, a French polish has a soft but brilliant glow that brings out all the depth and color of the wood without the heavy buildup generally associated with a high-gloss finish. No other finish even comes close.

I've taught French polishing for years, and for beginners, it can be a nerve-racking juggling act. The ingredients of a French polish—shellac, oil and pumice—must be applied at the right time and in the proper amounts. The addition of each can improve the finish dramatically—or destroy it. Padding lacquer is an amazing one-step mixture of dissolved shellac, lubricants and nitrocellulose resins. It produces a surface virtually identical to that of a traditional French polish, without the risks. It still requires a lot of elbow grease, but because it's a premixed formula, you can concentrate on applying it and not worry about maintaining a delicate balance of ingredients. There are several brands of padding lacquers from which to choose (see the sources box on p. 46). I haven't found significant differences among them.

In addition to being convenient and easy to apply, padding lacquer dries quickly, so you don't need a special finishing room. It can even be applied on-site, eliminating the need to bring a piece of furniture back to the shop for finish repairs. And because shellac is the primary ingredient in a padding lacquer, it can be applied over other finishes. Finally, padding lacquer has a variable sheen. The more or less sanding you do will increase or decrease its gloss.

Surface preparation

For more formal furniture pieces, which generally look best with a high-gloss finish like a French polish, I scrape the wood until I have a fairly flat, uniform surface (see the photo at left below). Then I sand with 220-grit and 320-grit sandpaper (see the photo at right below).

After wiping the surface with a dry rag, I wash it down with denatured alcohol. This raises the grain slightly and allows me to see sanding scratches and any other flaws (see the top photo on the facing page). If I want to fill the pores slightly for a smoother finish, I wet-sand with worn 320-grit wet-or-dry sandpaper and denatured alcohol. If I want a glass-smooth, nonporous finish, I use a filler (for more, see the box on p. 46). For a moderately porous, more natural-looking finish, just dry-sand with 320- and 400-grit sandpapers once the denatured alcohol has dried.

Applying padding lacquer

When using padding lacquer, all you need is a 6-in. square of lint-free cotton. Old T-shirt scraps work great. Just make sure that there aren't any creases or seams in the center of the pad because they can mar your finish.

I pour a small amount of padding lacquer into the center of my cloth and let it soak in a few seconds. Then with a small, circular motion, I begin to rub the polish vigorously into the surface (see the center left photo on the facing page). Initially, the surface will

SURFACE PREPARATION

1. Scrape the surface until it's flat and even in appearance.

2. Sand with the grain using 220- and then 320-grit sandpaper.

1

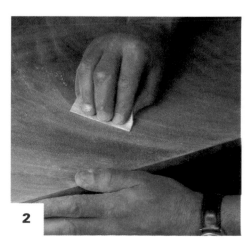

2

Photos: Vincent Laurence

APPLYING
PADDING LACQUER

3. Check for sanding scratches and other flaws by flooding the surface with denatured alcohol. This also raises the grain slightly, so follow up by sanding with 320- and then 400-grit sandpaper.

4. Quick, circular motions bring up a shine. Move the pad in tight circles in a small area, applying a good deal of pressure. The surface will be hazy at first, but after just a minute or so, a shine will start to come up. Apply less pressure as the shine increases.

5. Work just a few square inches at a time, blending adjacent areas. Apply more pressure on unfinished areas.

6. Polish the whole surface lightly. Take a clean rag, apply just a little padding lacquer and rub very lightly. The rag should just skate across the surface. Do this until the whole surface has a uniform sheen.

3

4

5

6

Pore filler gives a glass-smooth surface

Pour it on, smear it around. You don't have to be fussy when applying wood filler—just fill all the pores. Move the rag around; then use a scraper.

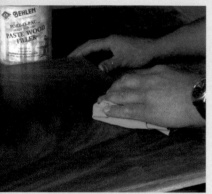

Filled pores, satin sheen— Paste wood filler dries to a satin sheen even before padding lacquer is applied. The filler dries rock-hard, so wipe the surface clean.

Like a mirror—With its pores filled, this crotch mahogany panel takes on a finish that's a dead-ringer for French polish—a warm but brilliant sheen.

In traditional French polishing, pumice helps fill the pores in the surface. Padding lacquer has no pumice, so the pores don't get filled appreciably, except by the padding lacquer itself. The result, depending on how much sanding you've done, is a relatively open-pored surface.

To get a glassy-looking, nonporous surface with padding lacquer, I use Behlen's pore-filling compound called Pore-O-Pac paste wood filler (see the sources of supply below). Pore-O-Pac is available in six shades.

Applying the filler couldn't be easier. I pour some on the surface I'm going to polish and wipe it all around with a rag (see the top photo). Then I use a scraper like a squeegee, moving the filler across the wood in all directions. This works the filler into the pores.

I let the filler remain on the surface between 30 minutes and one hour before wiping it off. This filler dries rock-hard, so it's important to clean the scraper and the surface you're filling. Otherwise, it will take a belt sander to remove it. I use a clean rag and keep wiping until the rag comes off the surface without any residue.

I wait 24 hours for the surface to dry, and then I fine-sand with 320- and 400-grit sandpaper. After sanding, I wipe down the surface with a rag soaked in denatured alcohol.

I let the surface dry and start applying the padding lacquer. A brilliant gloss will start to come up almost immediately (see the photo at left). —*M.R.*

haze and the cloth will drag a little, but with firm, steady pressure, an attractive shine will quickly start to appear. As I move from one small area to another, I carefully overlap my applications for uniform coverage (see the center right photo on p. 45).

A second coat can be applied almost immediately. As you build up the polish, though, you should extend the time between coats for the best results. When I get to my fourth and fifth coats, I usually wait between 12 and 24 hours.

Feathering out the finish

Even with very careful application, some areas will have more of a sheen than others, and the overall surface may look splotchy. You'll want to go over duller areas and make the surface as uniform as possible.

Then put a small amount of padding lacquer on a clean rag, and apply it over the entire surface, using a broad, circular motion. Bring the cloth just barely into contact with the work surface—almost glancing over it. This will eliminate any small streaks or blotches and leave a consistently brilliant, thin film (see the bottom photo on p. 45).

Repairing mistakes

As easy as padding lacquer is to use, I do run into small problems from time to time. These problems usually appear as rough crater-like patches. If they're not too severe, I simply pad over them. The application of new material usually will soften the area and vigorous rubbing will level it out. If this doesn't do the trick, I'll let the panel dry overnight, scrape or sand the damaged area flush the next day and then repolish. After a coat or two, blemishes will disappear completely.

Finishing on the lathe

I often use padding lacquer on lathe-turned objects, including table pedestals, spindles, cabinet knobs and tool handles. Here the application is even easier. Sand to 320-grit with the object spinning on the lathe. Then raise the grain with alcohol, and sand again with 320- and then 400-grit paper. You can apply the padding lacquer a little more heavily on the lathe, but don't use so much that it's spraying off the workpiece. Use gentle pressure on the rotating workpiece, and watch an incredible gloss develop. ☐

Mario Rodriguez teaches woodworking at the Fashion Institute of Technology in New York City and at Warwick Workshops in Warwick, N.Y. He is a contributing editor to Fine Woodworking.

Sources of supply

The following companies sell padding lacquers and/or fillers.

Behlen's Qualasole, a padding lacquer, and Pore-O-Pac, a paste wood filler, are distributed through:

Garrett Wade, 161 Avenue of the Americas, New York, NY 10013; (800) 221-2942

Woodworker's Supply, 1108 N. Glenn Road, Casper, WY 82601; (800) 645-9292

Behlen's Qualasole and Constantine's own Pad-Lac, another padding lacquer, are available from:

Constantine, 2050 Eastchester Road, Bronx, NY 10461; (800) 223-8087

#77 Lubricite, a padding lacquer, is available from:

Industrial Finishing Products, 465 Logan St., Brooklyn, NY 11208; (718) 277-3333

Two-Day Lustrous Oil Finish

A technique to turn four coats into a smooth, beautiful finish in just 48 hours

by Sven Hanson

Building a lustrous oil finish in just two days is easy with the proper techniques. Preparation (sanding) and a smooth stroke, applying the right amount of finish, is the key.

Wood finishing is a repository for so much voodoo lore that some procedures should list chicken blood as an ingredient. But it can be done easily. I'll give you the basics and a plan for applying four successive coats of oil in 48 hours, using a clean rag to wipe clean oil onto a clean surface with just a bit of fine sanding between coats. The fourth coat comes out so smooth (see the photo above) that abrasion, wax or oil is necessary only to fine-tune the level of gloss desired. Really!

At first I made the natural mistake of assuming that if a surface looked smooth or felt smooth, it was ready for finishing. But when a board passes beneath the planer blade, the blade's rotation causes variations in cutting angle and height. Unless you smooth that cornrowed surface, it will reappear in your finish.

So you sand. But if you start with too rough a grit and don't get those sanding scratches out, you'll see swirls, especially if you apply an oil stain. Although they are hard to see, these scratches are visible in the unfinished or unstained piece.

Reducing the need to sand

Thorough sanding devours the hours, so I try to reduce the need by keeping sharp blades on my cutting tools and buying smooth, flat lumber. But understanding some sanding basics can really speed up things. Start with the finest grit that will do the job because a fresh piece of 100-grit, for example, cuts deeper than 150-grit. So I skip the 100-grit, except on bad tearout, and begin with fresh 150-grit paper, which also helps with reducing swirls.

My first sanding typically begins with a 150-grit belt on my belt sander. I like the belt sander because, in the hands of the skilled, you can create and maintain flat surfaces, and even a gorilla can't get swirls. Before I move on to 220-grit and finer orbital sanding, I thoroughly blow off the work surface and bench to remove the accumulated 150-grit. Then I sand with moderate pressure for the majority of the time and finish off every area at one-half pressure. This lets each grit of sandpaper remove some of its own scratches. To be sure that I sand evenly, I make a series of parallel

Water rubdown makes for smoother finish—The author raises the grain with water and then sands until the grain no longer raises (right). This procedure also helps reduce stain blotching.

A hair dryer speeds up the grain-raising process. After wetting the wood enough to darken the surface (below), a hair dryer quickly gets the surface sufficiently dry to sand.

pencil lines across the surface to be sanded. As the lines disappear, I can tell exactly where I have sanded, as shown in the top photo on the facing page.

All woods improve in finishability with a light water rubdown before a final gentle sanding (see the photos above). This, by the way, is the first step in a blotch-free stain job. Serious smoothing calls for repeating this step until water no longer raises the grain. With some woods, the grain will continue to raise until hit with a first coat of finish, which raises the grain and locks it in place to be sheared off in the next sanding.

Oiling the wood

Protected by cheap vinyl lab gloves and working in a well-ventilated space, I begin oiling the wood. Many "oil" finishes are actually rubbing varnish. They're alkyd based, reduced with paint thinner, with lots of hardeners added. These "oils" offer the ease of application of oil combined with high solids for fast build and a

hard drying finish that can be built up to a bright, protective surface. My favorite finish is Waterlox because it embodies all these features, is easy to use and usually is available at hardware stores.

I flow on a good wet coat with any absorptive rag. But don't use steel wool because it breaks down and darkens the pores of the wood. It also leaves behind steel fibers beneath the finish that can react with water and acids in wood, causing black splotches.

As the oil first goes on, I always spot a few flecks or streaks of glue. I immediately scrape them off with the back of a freshly sharpened chisel dragged across the surface like a scraper. (Hey! This isn't the top of a Steinway.) It usually blends right in, but when it doesn't, I sand the still-wet repair with a scrap of my usual 220-grit sandpaper.

Cleanliness doesn't matter for the first coat. The pores are full of dust, and some finishers actually sand the oily surface with wet-or-dry paper to make dust to fill the grain. Vacuuming just wastes time. Because of dust, fibers and the breaking of the finish film over the wood's pores, you can't create a sealed finish in one coat.

I lean or hang up the oil-covered workpiece, and when the first coat loses its gloss, I return to add more finish, usually in less than an hour. This wet-over-wet second coat needs only half the amount of finish as last time.

As with the next coat or two, I try to apply just enough finish to leave a temporary gloss without causing runs or drools. After 30 minutes, which can be shortened by warm breezes and sunlight, I wipe the oil down, not off. By using a rag that contains heavy traces of oil in it, I avoid scouring the finish out of every pore. The rag leaves almost as much oil as it picks up. Think of it as "feathering off," like leveling the surface with a fine china-bristle brush. This is the essence of my fast-build system.

Hot air beats down beads

Oil stains and finishes have one nasty habit: beading up. You can apply finish and wipe it down to perfection, but when you return to see it in the morning, a constellation of tiny beads of soft finish has formed above the surface.

I beat the beads back by blasting them with hot air from my old hair dryer. The warm air lowers the viscosity of the oil, so it can

Pencil lines are a guide for even sanding—The author pencils parallel lines across the workpiece before sanding. As the lines are sanded away, he sees just where and how much needs to be sanded (left).

Building an oil finish—After the initial coat, the author lightly feathers on three succeeding coats (below) in just two days to build a heavy, durable finish. Buffing with wax will help protect the finish after the oil has hardened.

penetrate better. The heat also speeds up the cross-linking process, so the oil cures faster. I hang up the work and check on it an hour later to wipe down any beads that might have formed in spite of my best efforts. It's then left to dry overnight. If you try to work it any sooner, you'll just soften the uncured oil and remove as much as you apply.

Day two, final coats

Next morning, I lightly sand with 220-grit or 320-grit sandpaper. This is the most important, and often the only, sanding required. Just a light pass will shear off the wild hairs, cut open the bubbles and knock down the few beads that popped up. Don't fear this step. If you give every square inch a light swipe or two with a folded piece of used paper, easy on the corners, then it's done.

Now you cleanliness freaks can sweep the shop, blow the dust off the walls and vacuum the work and the work surface. Don't worry about the dust in the air. The dust that will ruin your finish will come from the work surface, polluted finish, a dusty brush or rag, or fall out of your hair or sweatshirt.

After dusting myself off, I change into a fresh shirt and apron and put on a clean dust mask. I blow off and then wipe the surface with a tack rag, making sure to clean out mortises, rabbets and around-the-corner areas where your once-clean rag can find fresh dust.

I filter the finish through a painter's filter or a clean muslin cloth. And I round up a well-worn but clean cotton sweat sock from my wife's sock drawer to use as an applicator.

I dampen the sock in clean finish and begin applying it to the difficult areas where two or more planes meet. I work from there to the outer, more visible, parts. Forget flooding and wiping off, and think of the process as brushing. I apply the amount of finish I want to remain on the work, spread it evenly, and then feather it all flat, as shown in the bottom photo. I stroke the molded edges and cross-grain parts first and finish wiping with the grain on the broad, flat parts. I try to complete the massage while the finish is still slightly liquid, so it can pull itself flat as it cures.

As I hang up the work, I'm often so amazed by the dazzling surface that I think three coats make a good enough finish. But no! Normally, after six hours of setting up, the finish has pulled tightly

around microscopic swales and hillocks of wood pore and fiber. The flatness tells me I need another coat to fully protect the wood.

If you sand, use 320-grit paper. Barely caress every visible square inch of the work. Clean up and then apply the finish just like the last time. Take the afternoon off.

I promised you a lustrous finish in 48 hours, and you've got it. Four hours later, the piece will be ready to assemble or move with careful handling. I give it the fine-old-furniture feel by waiting a few days for the oil to fully cure. Then I apply a coat of paste wax with a superfine, non-abrasive pad and buff to a satin sheen.

Virtually every finish manufacturer specifies waiting before giving a final rub. A harder finish is less susceptible to damage and will rub out faster and more evenly. Wax topcoats require maintenance but provide extra protection from liquids and abrasion. □

Sven Hanson is a woodworker and professional carpenter in Albuquerque, N.M.

Its finish all but destroyed, *this barrister's bookcase top is about to be reborn. The author fills large holes and gouges with auto-body filler and then presses shellac into the smaller cracks with an electric burn-in knife.*

To darken a high spot *(below), the author dabs a bit of powdered stain onto the surface of the finish and then quickly polishes over it.*

Though not the most practical finish *for a surface subject to wear or possible contact with liquids, a French polish is a beautiful, authentic antique finish (right).*

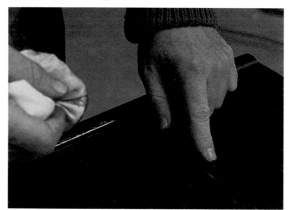

French Polishing for Restoration Work

Modern padding finishes update an age-old technique

by Scott Lawrence

From *Fine Woodworking* (May 1992) 94:46-48

The subject of French polishing almost always provokes strong opinions among finishers—some swear by it and some swear at it. This disparity of opinion is due to the finish's great beauty coupled with its fragility. Possessing little durability and having almost no resistance to common household spills, heat or solvents, it is not a practical finish for most new furniture or cabinetry. It is unsurpassed, however, for repairing and restoring antiques because it captures and preserves the age marks and patina, rather than obliterating them as is typically the case when an antique is stripped and refinished.

Even a severely degraded finish can be brought back with a French polish through the use of powdered aniline stains and a shellac stick of the appropriate color. I keep a full range of both on hand whenever I'm working on a restoration. The shellac stick allows me to fill any nicks, gouges or checks, and the powdered stains allow me to restore color to a worn or faded finish and even to match a replaced part to the rest of the piece. A word of caution: The technique I describe is legitimate for most antique restoration work, but if you are asked to restore a museum-quality antique, you should consult a conservator before taking any action.

French polishing is the building up of a shellac film that's applied with a cloth pad soaked in either a shellac/alcohol mixture or a modern, premixed formula consisting of shellac and some other solvent (such as ethyl acetate or methyl isobutyl ketone). Lubricated with a few drops of oil, the dissolved shellac builds quickly and dries as it's applied, allowing a finish to be built in one session. Although simple in theory, mastering the technique requires a fair amount of practice. If the pad is too wet, it will tend to dissolve the finish you've already put down; if too dry, the pad will stick to the finish and leave cloth prints. Even when modern, premixed formulas are used, the beginner is advised to develop the technique on an expendable piece or two. For more on the basics of French polishing, see the sidebar on the following page.

Materials

Traditionally, French polish consisted of various formulations of shellac, alcohol and a tiny amount of oil to lubricate the pad. Although traditional finishers always have delighted in discovering ever more obscure and exotic variations on this basic formula, the modern, premixed padding finishes will give virtually the same results with much less hassle (see the sidebar at right). The techniques discussed in this article were developed for use with the modern finishes, but they can be adapted for use with traditional French-polishing materials.

Modern padding finishes can be roughly categorized as high-build, general-purpose or topcoat formulas. High-build padding finishes, such as Mohawk's Lacover or Star's Lac-French, are the best choice for filling and smoothing a cracked, worn or scratched surface (see the sources of supply box on p. 52 for addresses). This high-build formula will fill and level all but the most severely degraded finish. I use this type of padding finish for all steps of a restoration except the final one and sometimes even then.

General-purpose padding finishes can be used where less build-up is required. I carry a small bottle of this formula in my touch-up kit for on-site finish repairs that don't require a high degree of stain resistance (such as table legs and the sides of case goods). Behlen's Qualasole, Star's Wil-Pro and Mohawk's Rapid-Pad are all good general-purpose padding finishes, although each possesses slightly different characteristics.

Topcoat finishes such as Mohawk's Golden Rapid-Pad or Star's Starlite are formulated to flow out smoothly with a minimum of streaking, which makes them the best choice for final topcoating of large surfaces such as tabletops or desktops.

Cleaning and preparing the old finish

I've never followed the common practice of cleaning an antique with water and detergents. Naphtha does a fine job of cleaning the finish's surface of old wax, dirt and polish, without harming either the wood or the finish as water and harsh alkaline detergents often do. I simply sponge on naphtha and blot up the crud with paper towels. When the paper towels come off the surface clean, I'm done. In severe cases, I'll gently scrub the piece first using 3M's Scotch-Brite pads and naphtha. Another advantage of using naphtha to clean antiques is that it evaporates within minutes, so restoration work can begin almost immediately. But if you clean with detergents and water, you have to let the piece dry overnight.

Right after cleaning is generally the best time to repair any gouges, chips or dents. I do this with an electric hot knife and the appropriate color of shellac stick (available from Mohawk, Behlen or Star). I prefer the electric hot knife over other types because it's more convenient when I have to make on-site repairs, and the heat it generates is most consistent. I slice a bit of shellac off of the stick, smear it into the damaged area and smooth it as best I can (see the top left photo on the facing page). Then I sand the repair smooth with #320 or #400 wet/dry sandpaper moistened with naphtha. Any graining or blending of the repair will be done later.

Next, I usually stain and seal any bare or badly worn areas with a glazing stain made up of either powdered aniline stains or artists' oil colors mixed into clear Watco oil finish. This oil-base stain penetrates and stains worn and bare areas and wipes off the darker, already-finished sections, without obscuring the grain. If the area to be stained is large, I wipe the stain on with a rag, but for smaller areas and when blending in details, I use an artist's brush. If you have rebuilt any missing parts, you can also use this same oil-stain mix to begin matching the new wood to the existing finish. Try to match the color to the lightest color in the old finish. You will darken and "age" the new part in subsequent steps.

Once the oil stain has dried thoroughly (48 hours or so), you can distress the new section to match the general condition of the piece. Observation is the key to realistic distressing. Rounding over of exposed edges, bump marks on legs and little dings where silverware and plate rims might have left slight impressions on a tabletop create a truer feel than wholesale abuse. Don't overdo it—excessive flyspecking, chain marks and rasping look phony. Think about how the piece was used, and distress accordingly. Reapply the oil stain to distressed areas, if necessary; then let the piece dry.

Building a new finish

Except in the rare instance an antique needs only a new topcoat, you must first rebuild the finish, filling in the countless scratches and scuff marks that have accumulated over the years. I rebuild the finish with high-build padding formula, adding a touch of powdered stain if I need to further doctor the color. I like to use a clear glass ashtray (available at the finest hotels and bars) to mix padding formula and powdered stain; I look for both a proper color match and the right degree of transparency given the piece I'm working on.

I apply the padding finish in circular or figure-eight strokes to the damaged area until I've built up a new layer of finish about as thick as the old one. With a very thick finish that has been severely degraded (cracked, peeled or crazed, for example), it will be necessary sometimes to build up a new film on the repaired area, sand down the adjacent old finish until the two surfaces are roughly level, and then apply a coat of the padding finish to both sides. This coat can be lightly sanded to remove any padding marks, and a final coat can be applied with the grain to blend the two areas.

With open-pored woods, such as oak, walnut or mahogany, I like to "grain" any repairs that I've burned in using a shellac

stick and a hot knife. I score the repair slightly with the edge of a chisel or a glass cutter and try to connect these lines with grain lines on either side of the repaired area to create the effect of grain running uninterruptedly through the repair. Then I rub a little dark oil stain into these grain marks until they match the color of the surrounding wood grain. Done carefully, this faux graining will make your repairs disappear. Let the piece dry overnight before proceeding.

Next, I do any final color glazing or streaking to blend in areas that have been patched extensively. I lightly brush the freshly padded surface of the repair with a dab of powdered stain on a fingertip of my left hand; then I quickly pad over it to dissolve the touch-up powder into the finish and to seal it (see the bottom photo on p. 50). This process will leave a subtle streak of color in the surface, simulating a contrasting streak in the wood or completely disguising a repair under the predominant wood color.

If the restored area still looks too light or new, now is the time to darken it, using layers of glazing made up of powdered stain and padding formula mixed in your "souvenir" ashtray. Pad on the mix using long, straight strokes running with the grain. The ability to match for color and for a realistic degree of opacity is a skill that will come only with experience. But I can tell you that a finish that is too clear will make an area stand out as new and that a finish that is too opaque will render your efforts muddy and lifeless. Remember that you are trying to recreate many years of aging—don't try to reproduce this in one quick application of glazing.

When you have blended in the restored area to your satisfaction, the entire surface (preferably the entire piece) should be topcoated with one of the light-bodied padding finishes (see the large photo on p. 50). Use a fairly dry pad at first so you don't smear your previous work. Once you've sealed the surface, you can work with a slightly wetter pad, using long, straight strokes. When you're first experimenting with the finish, play with variables such as the moistness of the pad and the pressure and/or speed of your strokes. The only hard-and-fast rule is *not* to let your pad come to a stop while on the finish surface; always keep the pad moving until it's completely removed from the surface.

Should your restored finish be too glossy for your (or your client's) liking, it can be rubbed down with #0000 steel wool after a few days. You can also put a coat of high-quality wax over a French-polish finish to give it a bit more protection. Don't use a liquid wax, however, since they often contain solvents or water, which could damage the French-polish finish. Should your newly restored piece become scuffed or scratched, don't worry. It can be easily repaired using the same materials and techniques as described above but in much less time than a full restoration. □

Scott Lawrence is a professional furniture finisher and restorer in Colorado Springs, Colo.

Sources of supply

Modern padding finishes, shellac (in many forms), alcohol and other solvents, and powdered stains are all available from the following manufacturers and distributors.
Mohawk Finishing Products Inc. (also manufactures the Behlen line*), Route 30 N., Amsterdam, NY 12010; (518) 843-1380
Star Finishing Products Inc., 360 Shore Drive, Hinsdale, IL 60521; (708) 654-8650
Wood Finishing Supply Co., Inc., 100 Throop St., Palmyra, NY 14522; (315) 597-3743
* H. Behlen and Bros. finishing supplies are available through retailers only.

French polishing: the short course

Here are the basics of French polishing in a nutshell: Make an egg-sized ball of clean cotton cloth. Saturate with finish compound—either the traditional shellac-and-alcohol mixture or one of the modern, premixed formulas. The pad should be damp but not wet. Squeeze out the excess. Then wrap the pad tightly with another clean, lint-free cotton cloth. Make sure this cover cloth is free of wrinkles on its bottom surface, or it'll streak the finished surface.

If you're using the traditional shellac-and-alcohol mixture, sprinkle a few drops of linseed or mineral oil onto the surface to be polished. This will lubricate the pad, allowing it to move freely without sticking. (This step is not necessary with the premixed padding finishes.)

Apply pad to wood with circular strokes. Start this circular motion in the air before the pad comes into contact with the surface. Gradually pad out the entire surface, using slightly overlapping strokes. Repeat this process until the desired film thickness is achieved; then finish with overlapping straight strokes running with the grain.

When using the shellac-and-alcohol mixture, you must wipe the entire finished surface with a fresh pad that's been slightly dampened with alcohol. This will remove any remaining oil from the surface and burnish the shellac film to a smooth, glossy sheen.

For more on French polishing, see *Fine Woodworking on Finishing and Refinishing* and George Frank's article from *Fine Woodworking* #58 in *The Best of Fine Woodworking—Finishes and Finishing Techniques*. —S.L.

Mix Your Own Oil Stains

*Simple recipe uses artist's pigments
to get exactly the right tone and color*

by Tom Wisshack

I'll be the first to admit it. There's a real purity to a "natural," unstained wood finish, a real virtue to letting the wood's true figure and color come through. But if you are refinishing, restoring or reproducing a piece of furniture, well, a "natural" finish is something that you just can't afford. Color, tone and patina take years, sometimes decades, to develop on "naturally" finished pieces. In almost 20 years of refinishing and restoration work, I have developed a way to get the right color and patina in a matter of hours.

My technique for coloring wood is better than either aniline dyes or commercial stains because of the control I have over tone and depth of color. Also, the stains are largely reversible. I make my own oil stains with turpentine or paint thinner, linseed oil, Japan drier and artist's oil colors.

The turpentine serves as a solvent, diluting the pigments in the artist's oil colors; the linseed oil acts as a binder to

Stain can bring out the best. The author's table, veneered with crotch mahogany and built with cherry legs, received just one light coat of his home-made oil stain. After observing the natural colors already in the wood, he mixed a stain that accentuated them and gave the wood a head start on developing a patina.

An infinite range of color choices is one good reason to make your own oil stains. A sample board illustrates the subtle colors possible using artist's oils for your pigments:

A. *The first section is natural Honduras mahogany with just one coat of linseed oil.*

B. *Section B has a light coat of the author's homemade oil stain applied to it. The stain consists of turpentine, linseed oil, Japan drier and just a bit of burnt-umber oil color.*

C. *More umber has been added to the same stain to produce the tone in section C.*

D. *Cadmium red and yellow are added to the same stain to heighten the colors already in the wood.*

E. *Finding section D somewhat too red, the author added a little green to neutralize the red and to bring the tone back to brown.*

F. *A little black adds depth to the stain.*

G. *The mixture was thinned in half with turpentine to yield the natural-looking result in section G.*

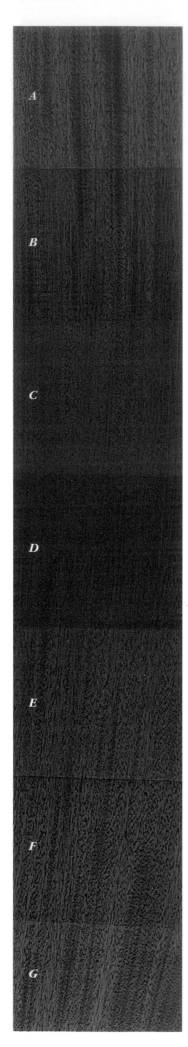

keep the ingredients in solution; and the Japan drier ensures that the oil colors will dry within a reasonable amount of time (some dry much slower than others).

One exception is that I substitute copal painting medium (available in art-supply stores) for the linseed oil if I'm working on an antique. The reason is that linseed oil will tend to darken most woods over time. The copal works just as well as a binder. When working with an antique, I take another precautionary step. I also seal the surface prior to staining with shellac before applying any stain, so the stain can be removed entirely at a later date if more work is to be done on the piece.

The key to my stains—the secret ingredients—are the artist's oil colors. What makes them so special are the quality of the pigments used and the fineness of the grind. Artist's oil colors are generally ground much finer than the pigments used in commercial stains, which are often the same as those used in paints. Because the pigment particles are so fine, the resulting stains are much more transparent than commercial stains, letting more

of the wood's figure and grain show through. And artist's oil colors are permanent and more fade-resistant than off-the-shelf wood stains.

Mixing the stain

I mix the liquid ingredients in a glass jar. For a small batch of stain, I'll start with about a pint of turpentine or thinner, one-third cup linseed oil and three or four drops of the Japan drier. I mix the artist's oils separately on a small sheet of glass (my palette), and then I add the mixed pigments to the liquid mixture a little bit at a time until I get the depth of color I'm looking for. I adjust the mix of pigments to get the tone I'm after (see the photo on the facing page).

I'm looking for a *very* dilute stain, on the order of a tenth or so as concentrated as a commercial product but with the consistency of low-fat (2%) milk. The advantage of such a dilute stain is that I can control it by applying it in two or three coats rather than all at once, deepening the tone while still retaining a semitransparent surface. Additionally, if the color is not quite right, I can adjust it repeatedly to alter the tone without ending up with a muddy, murky mess.

The maximum amount of artist's oils I add to the 1-pint solution is about one-third of a standard-size tube, or a little

From *Fine Woodworking* (January 1995) 110:49-51

Getting the color right—Mix artist's oil colors separately on a sheet of glass, and then add them to a mixture of turpentine or paint thinner, linseed oil and Japan drier until you have the tone of the pigments you want. Copal painting medium should be substituted for the linseed oil whenever you don't want to darken the wood, such as when refinishing an antique.

less than half an ounce. This can vary, depending on the intensity of the colors used, so you'll have to experiment. But even the finest quality artist's oils will give you an opaque finish if you get too heavy-handed with them. More light coats are better than fewer heavy coats.

Because these stains are so dilute, it's rarely necessary to seal new wood prior to staining. An exception is pine, which may appear blotchy regardless of how dilute the stain is. A penetrating sealer, such as one of the commercially available Danish oil finishes or a thinned solution of tung oil, eliminates this problem.

Applying the stain

I generally brush on the first coat of my homemade stain, let it stand about 20 minutes and then wipe it off. Leaving the stain on the wood for more or less than 20 minutes will not dramatically alter the amount of color the wood absorbs but how you wipe off the stain will. A brisk rub leaves only traces of the stain on the wood's surface. Gently wiping in circles and then with the grain will leave considerably more stain on the wood. Subsequent coats can be applied with a cloth.

If you don't like the way the stain looks on the wood, usually you can remove most of it with steel wool and naphtha or paint thinner while the stain's still wet. After the wood has dried, you can try again.

Sealing in the stain

After staining, I like to allow at least three or four days (a week is even better) before applying a finish. This allows the stain to dry thoroughly, minimizing the chance of it bleeding into the finish. An additional precaution I often take is to use a dilute coat of dewaxed (the most refined version, also called blond dewaxed) white shellac as a sealer between the stain and whatever I decide to use for a finish. The shellac will isolate the oil stain so that practically any finish can be applied without problems. Or you can just use the shellac itself as the finish.

Sometimes I'll also "spice" the white shellac with orange shellac. I add it in small increments to give the surface an amber tone that's reminiscent of an older piece. Whatever finish you use, though, be sure to refer to the can or the manufacturer's instructions to make sure it's compatible with the shellac sealer. □

Tom Wisshack makes and restores fine furniture in Galesburg, Ill.

Quick, custom oil stains from Japan colors

by Mario Rodriguez

When building an antique reproduction or recreating a missing component, an important and difficult part of the job often can be the precise matching of the original's color. It's almost impossible to achieve this with the application of a single coat of stain even if you mix your own stains. The task often requires several coats, with successive coats used to deepen or adjust the previous application of color. My system of alternating a light coat of lacquer between coats of stain gives me unparalleled speed, flexibility and reversibility.

For my stains, I use Japan colors suspended in turpentine. Japan colors are highly concentrated basic pigments, usually in an oil-based solution, and are available in a variety of colors. A ½-pint generally costs from $7 to $12.

I can custom mix practically any shade I need by combining two or more colors, and I can control the intensity and opacity of the stain by varying the proportion of Japan colors to turpentine. I have used this technique to alter harsh or unnatural colors from commercial stains. Garish reds and oranges, for example, can be changed to cooler browns and rusts with a light wash of green. I've also warmed up plenty of dull gray-brown walnut pieces with a light red-orange wash.

I mix my stains by pouring a little more turpentine than I need into a glass jar, and then I add the Japan colors to the turpentine. I check the color and intensity of the stain on a sample board and adjust accordingly. Usually, I apply the color with a rag to eliminate lap marks. But I use a brush when I have to get the stain into tight areas.

After the stain is completely dry, I spray on a light coat of lacquer to act as a sealer or barrier coat. To apply the lacquer, you can use a conventional spray rig, an HVLP (high-volume, low-pressure) unit or even aerosol spray cans.

When the lacquer dries, another coat of stain can be applied to darken or change the color without disturbing the previous layer of stain. If the second coat of stain doesn't achieve the color or effect you want, simply wipe it off and try again. □

Mario Rodriguez teaches woodworking in New York City, and he is a contributing editor to Fine Woodworking.

A flawless finish—
Hand-rubbing
eliminates surface
defects, which
can mar even care-
fully applied film-
forming finishes.
The author's three-
step approach in-
cludes sanding out
surface imperfec-
tions, leveling the
surface and then
polishing to a
uniform sheen.

Rubbing Out a Finish

This vital last step is the difference
between ordinary and stunning

by Jeff Jewitt

Photos except where noted: Alec Waters

A cured finish rarely looks or feels blemish-free, no matter how carefully you applied it. Bubbles, dust and debris can lodge in the finish as it dries and are especially noticeable on gloss finishes. Rubbing out a finish eliminates blemishes, so it should be the last step in finishing any piece of furniture. Surprisingly, few finishers I know do it. No doubt, some fear having to abrade a finish film that's only thousandths of an inch thick. Taken in steps, though, rubbing out a finish need not be a terrifying process.

Any film-forming finish will rub out: hard finishes, like nitrocellulose lacquer, flexible ones, like polyurethane, and even waterborne finishes, which can be challenging to polish (see the photo at right).

Rubbing out is a three-step process of removing imperfections, leveling the surface and polishing to a consistent sheen. I always use gloss finish because it can be buffed. Satin-formulated finishes contain silica flatteners that impede light reflection, so they can't be rubbed out to a gloss (for more on this, see the sidebar on p. 59).

Prepare the work surface and the finish

If you're finishing an open-grain wood like mahogany or oak, fill the pores first (see the article on pp. 119-121). If you don't, light-colored abrasives will lodge in the pores and will be visible. If your wood is textured (from a handplane, for example), sand or scrape the surface flat before you put on the finish. Otherwise, you risk rubbing through high spots and exposing the stain layer or bare wood. In situations where you can't flatten the surface (inlaid furniture and hand-tooled antiques, for example), you'll have to rub gently with steel wool. The wool acts like a cushion, so it's not as likely to shear off the high areas.

Rubbing out removes finish, so be sure to start with a thick coating. Solvent-release finishes, like shellac, lacquer and some waterbornes, fuse into a single film once they're applied. With these finishes, I generally apply six coats.

By contrast, coats of reactive finishes, like oil varnish and polyurethane, do not melt into one another. If you rub too much, you'll go through the top layer (see the bottom photo). Most reactive finishes have a higher solids content, so I usually apply only three coats, and I make sure that the last coat is not thinned.

Fully cured finishes buff up better and faster than finishes that aren't. Shellacs, lac-

How you apply it doesn't matter. These three panels, two mahogany and one walnut, are buffed to a gloss. From left, the finishes are sprayed-on nitrocellulose lacquer, brushed-on rubbing varnish and waterborne acrylic lacquer, which also was brushed on.

quers and two-part finishes should cure at least a week. Oil-based varnishes and polyurethanes should cure at least two weeks. If the finish is gummy and loads up your sandpaper, let it dry longer.

Keep in mind, too, that soft or flexible finishes do not rub out as easily or to as great a shine as hard, brittle ones. It's like the difference between polishing the sole of your shoe compared to polishing brass.

Sand imperfections

The first step of rubbing out is using abrasive papers to dry-sand or wet-sand defects from the cured finish. If the finish is in good shape, you can skip this step. Dry-sanding can be dusty and tedious, but at least you can tell what you're doing to the surface. Stearated aluminum-oxide paper works well for this, though it will clog fairly quickly on hard finishes like lacquer and shellac. Several new papers are available that have precise, uniform grit sizes. Although they are more costly, 3M's Microfinishing paper and Meguiar's Finesse paper (available at most auto-supply stores) are worth trying. They cut much more efficiently.

Wet-sanding is fast, but the slurry can give you a false sense of finish thickness. It's easy to sand through to the sealer or to the color coats. Wipe the surface, and check your progress regularly. Rub very lightly near the edges of flat horizontal surfaces where the finish is likely to be thinner.

I prefer wet-sanding with traditional wet-or-dry paper, and I use water with a dash of dishwashing soap as a lubricant. I usual-

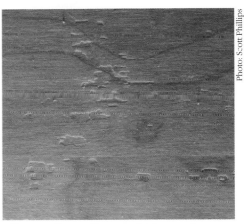

Witness lines show rub-throughs—Separate coats of reactive finishes, like water-based polyurethane, remain distinct, so be careful not to rub into an under layer. Witness lines, which look like feathery rings on this piece of birch, are the result.

Level with abrasive papers. Wet-or-dry paper backed by a cork block makes a flat abrasive pad for leveling (below). Keep the surface wet while rubbing crisscross over the middle of the panel. Squeegee off the slurry to check your progress.

SATIN FINISH

After leveling, use steel wool. For the finish to have a satin sheen, the author uses 0000 steel wool, soapy water and either thinned paste wax or Behlen's Wool-Lube to polish the surface.

GLOSS FINISH

For a gloss look, use pumice and rottenstone. Sprinkle on pumice and then wet and rub the slurry over the whole surface. Wipe this off, and follow with rottenstone.

ly sand the finish with 400-grit, but I'll go to 320-grit if there are big hunks of debris to remove. I wrap the paper around a cork block and sand enough to knock down the tops of dust pimples, so they're even with the rest of the finish. On curved surfaces, I use my hand as a backer. When the imperfections are gone, the surface is speckled with alternating dull and shiny spots.

Level with finer abrasive papers

Leveling establishes a consistent scratch pattern on the finish. I level with 600-grit, but if the surface is rough with brush marks or orange peel, I start with 400- or 320-grit. Wrap a clean sheet of wet-or-dry paper around your block, and squirt some soapy

water onto the surface (I use a plant mister). Sand all the edges first. Don't worry about the grain direction.

Next, work the center of the board in manageable sections using a crosshatch pattern (see the photo above left). Rubbing from opposing 45° angles ensures complete leveling. Now rub with the grain. As you sand, keep exposing clean, fresh grit. Change to new paper often. Finishes can gum up and clog paper quickly.

Wipe away the slurry with a rubber squeegee, and look for shiny spots under backlighting. Squirt on more water, and rework areas that are still shiny, but don't overdo it. To avoid making hollows, feather each area into the rest of the surface.

You can leave very small shiny areas because they won't be too visible once the whole surface is buffed. Rub shiny spots near the edges with dry steel wool until they're dull like the rest. When you're satisfied, switch to the next finer grit and repeat. Continue on to 600-grit.

Polish with steel wool or powdered abrasives

The last step is polishing, and you have a choice here: satin or gloss. When I want a satin finish, I rub out with 0000 steel wool or synthetic steel wool lubricated with soapy water and Behlen's Wool-Lube (or paste wax thinned with mineral spirits). When I want a gloss finish, I use traditional powdered abrasives—pumice (powdered volcanic glass) and rottenstone (powdered decomposed limestone) mixed with water or oil. Pumice is sold in grades from 1F (coarse) to 4F (fine). Rottenstone is finer than pumice and is sold in one grade.

For a satin sheen—Squirt some soapy water on the finish, and apply a generous dab of Wool-Lube to a wad of steel wool (unravel it, and fold it into quarters to make it last longer). You can also use a gray Scotch-Brite nylon pad or equivalent grade of synthetic steel wool. Rubbing back and forth with the grain, make nine or 10 slightly overlapping passes. Use two hands for firm, steady pressure (see the photo on p. 56). Wipe away the slurry to make sure you're creating a uniform scratch pattern. You may have to let the slurry dry to see if you've got it right. If you want a silky feel to the surface, let the slurry dry on the surface, and then buff it off just like wax. When backlighted, a satin surface should look like brushed metal.

For a gloss sheen—Skip the above step, and continue wet-sanding up to at least 800-grit. I take it to 1,200-grit. Now sprinkle on some 4F pumice (see the bottom right photo on the facing page), and wet it with water or rubbing oil. Wad up a clean, dry cotton cloth and, working in whatever direction you want, polish every square inch of the surface. Use lots of pressure, and replenish the pumice and water as the slurry dries. Let it haze over, and then wipe it off with a damp rag. Switch to rottenstone and do the same.

Turnings, carvings and moldings

To rub out intricate surfaces, like turned legs or carved aprons, polish with 0000 steel wool and thinned wax. The finish in these areas is just too thin to polish to a gloss. Don't rub too hard, or you'll cut through the finish on sharp details. To avoid a light-colored wax residue on dark finishes, use dark-colored wax. For moldings, wrap some 600-grit wet-or-dry paper around a sanding block that's shaped to match the convex or concave curve of the molding. Rub with steel wool and wax. When the wax is dry, it can be buffed so it approximates the sheen of the rest of the piece. □

Jeff Jewitt repairs and restores period furniture. His book, Hand-Applied Finishes, *was published by The Taunton Press in 1996.*

Sheen is a measurement of reflection

Finish manufacturers measure sheen using a gloss meter, a device that reads how much light is reflected off a surface. Tests for finishes containing flatteners measure light reflectance at 60°. When the angle of incidence (incoming light) equals the angle of reflection (outgoing light) and at least 80% of the light is reflected, the sheen is considered gloss (see the top drawing below). Semigloss finishes reflect between 70% and 80% of the light; satin finishes reflect 35% to 70%; flat, matte and eggshell finishes reflect 15% to 35%.

But you don't need a gloss meter. A simple visual test can be used instead (see the photo above). A finish that gives a clear reflection, with clean, distinct outlines is gloss. If the reflected image is readable, but fuzzy, the sheen is semigloss or satin. When little or no light is reflected or the reflection is no longer distinguishable, the sheen is eggshell or flat.

Scratches from polishing influence light the same way that flatteners added to the finish do. Both the size and the depth of the scratches affect the interference pattern, or scattering, of the light. As a general rule, the scratch pattern left from 400-grit abrasive paper produces a dull or flat luster. Finishes abraded to 1,000-grit appear satin. Those scratched with 1,200-grit and higher produce sheens ranging from semigloss to gloss.

Interestingly, when you lower your viewing angle on any surface, the sheen appears more glossy. That's because you're seeing less diffused light. —*J.J.*

How sheen affects light

Sheen is a measurement of how much light reflects off a surface. Flatteners or scratches on a finish diffuse light, which is why satin and flat finishes reflect less light than gloss ones.

Smooth surface

When angle A = angle B and at least 80% of the reflected light reaches your eye, the finish surface is a gloss.

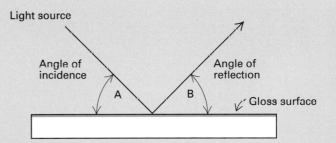

Rough surface

Scratches on a finish diffuse light. Finishes rubbed out to flat or satin diffuse more light than gloss finishes. The diffused light makes a reflected image less distinct because less light reaches your eye. Generally, the finer and more uniform the scratch pattern from polishing, the glossier the sheen.

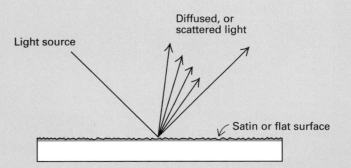

Taking the Spray-Finish Plunge

A spray system can improve finish quality and increase your productivity

by Andy Charron

My first shop was a one-car garage. What space I had was filled with tools that were absolutely necessary to make furniture. That left out a dust collector and a finishing room. As a result, getting dust-free finishes was frustrating. Brushing on shellac and varnish worked fine for small projects, but as I took on bigger jobs and built more pieces, I turned to wipe-on oils because they weren't as fussy to use. Eventually, I needed more durable finishes that didn't take long to apply.

A spray system was the answer. Spraying on finish is fast and easy. You can get into places where brushes and rags are useless (see the photo below). Spray finishes look superb, too. The coating is more uniform and the finishes between pieces is more consistent. But once I was committed to changing to spray finishes, I knew I had some research to do (see the story on p. 62).

Spray systems and finishes are better now

The variety of spray systems has increased dramatically over the last 10 years. Manufacturers have introduced small, inexpensive units that are ideal for hobbyists and small shops. Also, there have been many improvements in high-volume, low-pressure (HVLP) spray systems, particularly in terms of transfer efficiency. The price of an entry-level HVLP spray system is around $200, and there's a wide variety of systems in the $200 to $500 range. These spray systems aren't much more expensive than many power tools.

Waterborne finishes have improved as well, and as a result, the need for dangerous, solvent-based finishes has decreased. Water-based finishes are nonflammable, which means that you no longer need a spray booth to get started. Having a clean spray area, a respirator and good ventilation (I use an exhaust fan) will suffice.

Spraying gets finish in nooks and crannies. One reason Andy Charron switched to spraying is that it gets finish where other applicators won't. Here, he sprays water-based sealer on the latticework of a poplar headboard.

Spraying has benefits over other methods of finishing

1) Spray finishes are forgiving. Because a sprayed finish is built up in thin layers, small scratches and marks stay better hidden under a sprayed translucent finish than under an oil finish. Surface preparation is still important, though. This is especially true when spraying paints or opaque stains.

2) Spray finishes are fast. You can spray 30 stools or 1,000 small wooden blocks in an hour. And because the sprayer breaks the finish into small particles, each coat dries in a hurry.

Many varnishes, water-based products and sprayed lacquers will dry to the touch in minutes. Some of them can be sanded and re-coated in a few hours. Dust has a short time (while the coat is tacky) to settle on the work, which reduces the need for sanding between coats.

3) Spray finishes are versatile. Basically, any finish that can be applied by brush or by rag can be sprayed. If you use an explosion-proof booth, you can spray shellac, lacquer and other solvent-based materials. If you

And a spray system won't leave you with a pile of oily rags that can catch on fire.

Brush-on and wipe-on finishes are slow and exacting

In my furniture business, I brushed on varnishes for only a short time. Varnish was just too slow to brush and too slow to dry. And I needed excellent lighting to brush, sand and rub out the varnish.

I did stick with wipe-on oils for a while. Oil didn't require any special equipment, and I could oil in less-than-ideal conditions. I wasn't building up a thick surface film (like a varnish), so I worried less about dust and lint getting trapped in the film. Oil finishes soon became a key in my marketing strategy, too. Most of my customers liked the phrase, "authentic, hand-rubbed finishes."

Oil finishing does have drawbacks. The protection offered by an oil finish is minimal (see the article on p. 11), and an oil finish needs more maintenance than other topcoats. Surface imperfections, like scratches, stand out more than they would under a film finish. And oil finishes are time- and labor-consuming. Depending on the temperature and humidity, an oil finish can take several days to apply. It also involves a great deal of work. It's hard to get thrilled about rubbing out multiple coats of oil on 400 wooden clock frames.

Any spraying disadvantage can be overcome

As attractive as spray finishing is (see the box below), it does have a few weaknesses. Setting up a safe, efficient system takes up shop space and costs money. Besides a gun, you will need a source of air (either a turbine or compressor), hoses, filters and connectors.

Clean finish, clean gun—To get blemish-free finishes, the author filters the finish before he sprays, and he cleans the gun afterward. He often tints his paint basecoats with pigment, so the topcoat covers better.

Because spraying releases finish mist into the air, you will also need a spray area that has fresh-air circulation. If you spray solvent-based finishes, you'll need to check with your local building inspector before you set up a booth. But if you spray water-based products exclusively, you won't need explosion-proof fans and fixtures.

Unlike most brush-on and wipe-on finishes, spray finishes must be filtered and then thinned to the correct viscosity (see the photo at left). Not thinning enough can lead to lumpy finishes and "orange peel." Using too much thinner creates problems, too, like drips and sags on vertical surfaces. And it will take longer to build to the right film thickness. The result is you won't be able to get nice, glossy clear coats, and paints won't hide the underlying surface or provide good color depth. Too much thinner also lengthens the drying time, so dust becomes a problem.

Finally, keeping your spray gun clean is critical. Although cleaning does involve some effort and time, it doesn't take any longer to clean a spray gun than it does a brush.

Ultimately, spraying reduces finishing costs

Although some of the finish does get wasted through overspray, you can still lower your material costs. I've had to reject far fewer pieces that I've sprayed than those that were finished by brush or rag. And spraying saves labor costs. In the first month, I more than offset the initial expense of the equipment (about $800). Now my business couldn't survive without a spray system. □

Andy Charron runs a cabinetmaking shop in Long Branch, N.J.

---

don't have a booth, you can still spray water-based finishes. With some spray systems, you can apply water-based contact cement, which works great for laminate work.

4) Spray finishes can be precisely controlled. Spray-gun adjustments combined with proper spray techniques give you good control over how and where the finish is applied. A brush transfers nearly 100% of the finish to the work, but you have to be diligent at keeping the coat even and at the right thickness.

Even though the transfer efficiency of a spray gun is lower than a brush (between 65% and 85%), you can adjust air pressure, fan size and fluid flow to ensure light, even coats. Also,

because the atomized material flows together uniformly, there are no brush or lap marks.

5) Spray finishes are relatively easy to apply. Spray finishing is fairly basic. You can learn how to spray a simple case or frame in less time than it takes to master brushing or wiping on a finish. With a bit of practice, you can spray stains and dyes to get uniform coverage and consistent color depth. After some more practice, you can use tinted clear finishes to do special techniques, such as shading or sunbursts. Because spraying allows a greater range of finishes, your projects will look more professional.

6) Spray finishes are consistent in quality. Without a

Spray guns increase production. Charron compares the number of clock frames he sprayed (left) vs. those painted with a brush.

doubt, the best reason for investing in a spray system is the overall higher quality of finish that you can achieve.

A spray-on finish is far superior to brush-on or wipe-on finishes. The problems caused by

brushing, such as runs, drips and air bubbles, are reduced with spray equipment. And brush marks are gone. You can spray an entire piece, no matter what its size or shape, with light, even coats of finish. —A.C.

Which Spray System Is Right for You?

What's good and not so good about four kinds of sprayers

by Chris A. Minick

Mention the names Delta, General or Powermatic to a bunch of cabinetmakers, and everyone in the group will know you're talking about woodworking machinery. Mention DeVilbiss, Mattson or Sharpe to the same crowd, and you'll likely get some blank stares. Those companies are just three out of dozens that make spray-finishing equipment. Chances are, though, many woodworkers just don't know as much about choosing a spray system as they do about buying a tablesaw. Considering that a high-quality spray system costs as much as a decent tablesaw ($700 or more), it pays to be well-informed before you buy.

Andy Charron explains why he switched to spray finishing in his shop (see the article on p. 60). I'll present some equipment options—high-pressure spray guns (see the photo at left), high-volume, low-pressure (HVLP) systems and airless spray guns. But first, it would be helpful to know a little about spray-gun anatomy.

How a spray gun works

The basic principle behind a spray gun is relatively straightforward. A stream of liquid finish is forced into an airstream, which breaks the liquid into tiny droplets (atomization) and carries them to the target surface. It sounds simple, but in reality, a collection of precision parts must work in concert to pull the whole thing off.

In a standard high-pressure system, air flows from the compressor hose through a series of valves and baffles in the body of the gun and out through an air cap. The valves and baffles control the maximum atomization pressure at the air cap. The volume of air used by the gun as well as the spray pattern is governed by the size and placement of the holes in the air cap (see the drawing on p. 64).

A standard air cap for furniture finishing

An air compressor can power a high-pressure or conversion-air HVLP spray system. With either type, you'll need an oil and water filter separator, a regulator, an air hose and couplers. Choices for guns (from left): conventional touch-up, external and internal mix, two HVLP units and conversion-air touch-up.

produces a tapered (fan) pattern 9 to 11 in. long. Typically, the gun uses about 8 cubic feet per minute (cfm) of air at 50 psi.

Pulling the trigger extracts the needle from the fluid tip, which opens the orifice and allows the finish to enter the airstream. The size of the orifice and the viscosity of the finish control the amount of material sprayed. I've found that a 1mm orifice is ideal for finishing furniture. The fluid tips and needles are sold in matched sets (fluid setups). Most spray-system manufacturers have technical-service departments that will help you choose the right one.

Once the finish exits the tip, high-pressure air from the air cap blasts the stream into tiny droplets. The droplets can range from about 15 microns in dia. to 70 microns or more. The size depends on the fluid viscosity and on the equipment. Once the atomized finish is deposited, it flows together to form a smooth film. Generally, the smaller the droplets, the better the finish.

Gun composition affects the kind of finishes you can spray—A gun that has an aluminum cup and fluid passages is compatible with hydrocarbon-solvent-based finishes like nitrocellulose lacquer and oil-based varnish. But within a matter of hours, the same gun will be corroded beyond repair if it is used to apply a finish that contains a chlorinated solvent, such as methylene chloride (which is the main ingredient in many paint strippers). Even nonflammable solvent cleaner will corrode aluminum parts. Similarly, the alkaline portion of waterborne finishes can damage bare aluminum parts if the gun is not cleaned immediately after use.

As a corrosion-fighting alternative to aluminum, some low-cost units combine plastic cups and dip tubes with brass fluid-handling parts. But brass wears quickly,

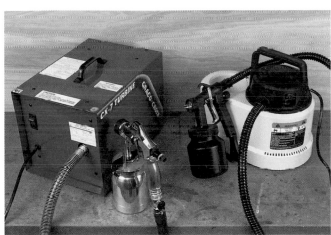

Turbine-driven HVLP systems are compact, but the hoses are cumbersome. Both the two-stage Graco/Croix unit (left) and the Wagner single-stage model spray efficiently and are portable.

Airless spray systems work well with latex paint and most varnishes, but they don't apply other finishes well. If not the right viscosity, the finish will be poorly atomized and leave a coarse, blotchy surface.

particularly if the gun is used to spray pigmented finishes like paint. The pigments act like the abrasives used in sandblasters.

Mild-steel components (especially fluid tips and needles) are also common in inexpensive spray guns. Though steel is compatible with most finishes, it has a nasty tendency to rust. One solution is to buy a gun that has a stainless-steel cup and fluid-handling parts, but that type is pricey. Those guns make sense for industrial users, but they are overkill for small shops. As an alternative, some spray guns come with stainless-steel fluid passages and a Teflon-lined aluminum cup. The Teflon lining protects the cup from corrosion and makes for easy cleanup.

High-pressure spray equipment

Early in this century, high-pressure spray equipment was developed in response to the automotive industry's need for high-speed finishing. Spray components have changed little since that time (see the top photo on p. 63). A full system consists of three main parts: a compressor (with attendant hoses, tank and pressure regulator), an oil and water separation device, and a spray gun.

The air compressor is the heart of the spray system; both the horsepower rating and tank size affect spray performance. A 3-hp compressor with an air output of 10 cfm and a 20-gal. air tank is really the minimum size.

When air is compressed, water vapor in the air condenses to a liquid. If not removed, the water that passes through the spray gun will cause all kinds of finishing problems. So an oil and water separator is a critical part of any compressor-driven spray system. The separator also removes residual oil that's used for lubrication of the compressor.

Internal mix or external mix—High-pressure spray guns are available in two types: internal and external mix (see the photo and drawings at right). The mix designation is based on where the airstream is introduced into the fluid stream.

Most internal-mix guns (air and fluid are mixed inside the air cap) produce a coarsely atomized spray. Although this spray is unsuitable for applying lacquers or other fast-drying finishes, it is ideal for applying thick, difficult-to-spray materials, like adhesives and pore fillers. Internal-mix guns consume modest amounts of air and can be powered with a 1-hp or 2-hp compressor. But they are limited to spraying slow-drying varnishes and paints.

By contrast, external-mix guns (air and

Air caps

Guns can be internal mix (left) or external mix (right). The spring, retaining ring and baffle have been removed in the external-mix gun.

Internal-mix air cap
Air and finish are mixed inside cap.

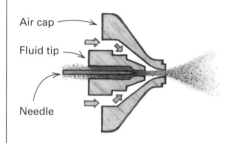

Air cap
Fluid tip
Needle

External-mix air cap
Air atomizes finish and shapes spray pattern outside cap.

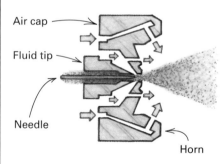

Air cap
Fluid tip
Needle
Horn

fluid are mixed outside the air cap) are versatile. They're the most common spray guns used in woodworking shops. Hundreds of fluid tip/needle/air-cap combinations are available to allow the spraying of virtually any liquid at almost any pressure. External-mix guns can be fed from a 1-quart siphon cup attached to the gun or pumped from a 1-gal. remote pressure pot when greater quantities are needed.

External-mix spray guns have two drawbacks. They use lots of air, so they require at least a 3-hp (4 hp or 5 hp is preferable) compressor. And they aren't very efficient at putting the finish on the work. Only about 35% of the finish actually lands on the target; the rest ends up as overspray.

High-pressure spray guns only make sense in a shop that has a good spray booth.

More finish ends up on your project with HVLP

High-volume, low-pressure (HVLP) spray equipment has been around a while. In the late 1950s, I painted models and birdhouses with an HVLP painting attachment that came with my mother's canister vacuum cleaner. HVLP equipment is more sophisticated now, but the underlying concept remains unchanged. To atomize the finish, HVLP systems use high volumes of air rather than high pressure. Unlike conventional spray guns, HVLP guns produce a soft spray pattern. The benefits are increased transfer efficiency, low overspray and almost no bounce-back. Simply put, HVLP spray guns put more finish on the project and less on everything else in the shop and in the environment.

Spray-equipment manufacturers have taken two very different approaches to HVLP. Some have developed turbine-driven systems and others have developed conversion-air HVLP systems, which are driven by a standard air compressor.

Turbine-driven HVLP spray systems are portable—Turbine HVLP systems use a fan (like those used in vacuum cleaners) to generate from 45 cfm to 110 cfm of air at pressures between 2 psi and 7 psi. You can buy turbines in three power levels: one, two or three stage. The center photo on p. 63 shows a two-stage turbine and a single-stage unit. Each stage, or fan section, in the turbine adds approximately 40 cfm and 2 psi of air output.

Unlike a compressor, a turbine blows out a continuous stream of warm, dry air at a constant pressure. This eliminates the need for pressure regulators and air dryers (separators). But warm air can be a problem. The metal handles of some spray guns can get uncomfortably hot.

Also, dried drops of finish tend to accumulate on the fluid tip; eventually, the finish glob breaks free and deposits itself on the freshly sprayed surface. On the positive side, turbine systems are compact, store easily and operate on 110v current.

The more stages a turbine has, the wider the viscosity range of the spray finish. When I sprayed with a one-stage turbine (a Wagner Finecoater), I had to thin the finish to get proper atomization. Thinning is the kiss of death for some waterborne finishes. When I sprayed the same finish with a two-stage turbine (a Graco/Croix CX-7) there was sufficient power to spray without thinning. I didn't try a three-stage turbine. Designed for multiple guns and high production, they're a bit pricey for me (more than $1,000).

Conversion-air HVLP spray systems are versatile—Conversion-air HVLP systems convert compressed air (under high pressure) to a high volume of air (at low pressure) by passing it through baffles and expansion chambers in the gun body. A decent gun costs $250 or more. Conversion-air guns have the reputation of being air hogs. But the latest conversion-air spray guns will operate off most 3- or 4-hp compressors. If your shop already has a compressor, it may power a conversion-air HVLP gun.

A big advantage that conversion-air systems have over turbines is that the atomization pressure at the air cap can be adjusted (between 2 and 10 psi with most guns) to accommodate a wide range of coating viscosities. I compared the two types of HVLP systems side by side (see the box below). The conversion-air system consistently produced a finer atomized finish, a higher delivery rate and a noticeable decrease in overspray.

Conversion-air spray guns work best when connected to ⅜-in. air hoses. The quick-connect fittings on the hose and the spray gun must be matched (connectors are available at most auto-paint and com-

Considering that a high-quality spray system costs as much as a decent tablesaw, it pays to be well-informed before you buy.

pressor repair shops). Use a ⅜-in. coupler; a ¼-in. coupler will negate the advantage of the larger hose.

Airless spray systems

Airless systems usually are associated with house painting rather than furniture finishing. But airless spray systems are common in large furniture factories. These commercial units operate at pressures approaching 4,000 psi. However, high pressure, high delivery and high efficiency come with a high price tag—upward of $1,500 for an entry-level unit.

Consumer-sized airless units (see the bottom photo on p. 63) still have a place in the shop. I like them for applying latex paint and oil-based varnish on certain projects. The motor size of an airless gun determines its price and its versatility. A 110-watt gun is powerful enough to spray unthinned latex paint. But with a 45-watt unit, the paint has to be thinned significantly. A motor rating of 85 watts or more usually is adequate for spraying furniture.

Unfortunately, airless spray guns produce a coarse spray pattern. So only slow-drying paints and varnishes should be applied with them. Lacquers, including waterborne varieties, tend to dry before the droplets flow together. The result is a rough texture (orange peel).

Even with these limitations, however, an airless spray system can help get you started spray finishing—and for a reasonable price (around $200). One of the best things about an airless spray unit is that it doesn't use a cumbersome air hose. It just needs an extension cord.

The choice is yours

If you're considering a spray system for your shop, take a good, hard look at conversion-air HVLP spray systems. As a bonus, you'll have an air compressor to do other things in the shop. ⌙

Chris Minick is a finishing chemist and woodworker in Stillwater, Minn. He is a contributing editor to Fine Woodworking.

Evaluating spray patterns

I couldn't resist comparing the performance of the spray systems in this article. I used a gloss, water-based lacquer (tinted black) in each spray gun. This is a demanding test when you consider I didn't adjust the viscosity. Spray patterns reveal where atomization was poor (large spots on borders) and where fan adjustments were limited (wide dispersion band). In general, high-pressure and conversion-air HVLP systems delivered fine atomization and more uniform spray patterns. Turbine HVLP and airless systems produced coarser spray patterns. —C.M.

Coarse and splotchy

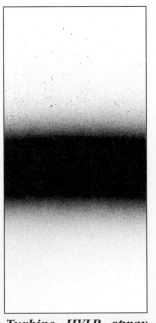

Fine and uniform

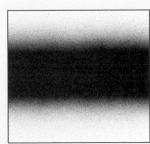

Conventional high-pressure spray (from Cal-Hank touch-up gun).

Conversion-air HVLP spray (from DeVilbiss touch-up gun).

Turbine HVLP spray (from Graco/Croix gun). Finish was thicker than recommended viscosity.

Airless spray (from Wagner gun). Finish was thinner than recommended viscosity.

Turbine Spray Systems

A high-volume, low-pressure finishing alternative

by Philip Hostetter

Until recently, one of the most common ways to apply a finish was to use a spray gun and a conventional air compressor. But another kind of spray system best known by its acronym, HVLP, has been receiving a lot of attention lately. HVLP stands for high volume, low pressure, and refers to spray systems that apply finishing materials in an entirely different way than conventional high-pressure spray systems. But there's a lot of mystery surrounding HVLP systems and their purported advantages, such as the systems' efficiency and ease of operation. Some manufacturers have gone so far as to promise that their HVLP system will cut the amount of finishing materials you use in half.

For many years, I have used compressed air and HVLP systems for applying a variety of finishes, including shellacs, lacquers (both nitrocellulose and water base) and catalyzed finishes, to the cabinets and furniture made in my commercial shop. As you might

guess, I've found that both systems have advantages and shortcomings. Anyone considering buying an HVLP system should understand its pros and cons, as well as how this system works and how it differs from compressed-air setups. The information in this article is intended to help you decide if an HVLP system is right for your finishing needs.

How an HVLP system works

Unlike a compressor and standard spray gun that apply a finish with a relatively low volume of air at high pressure, an HVLP system uses a blower and a special gun to (as the name says) apply a finish via a high volume of air at a lower pressure. A typical HVLP system consists of a turbine, a gun and a large-diameter air hose, all of which look and function somewhat differently than a compressed-air system.

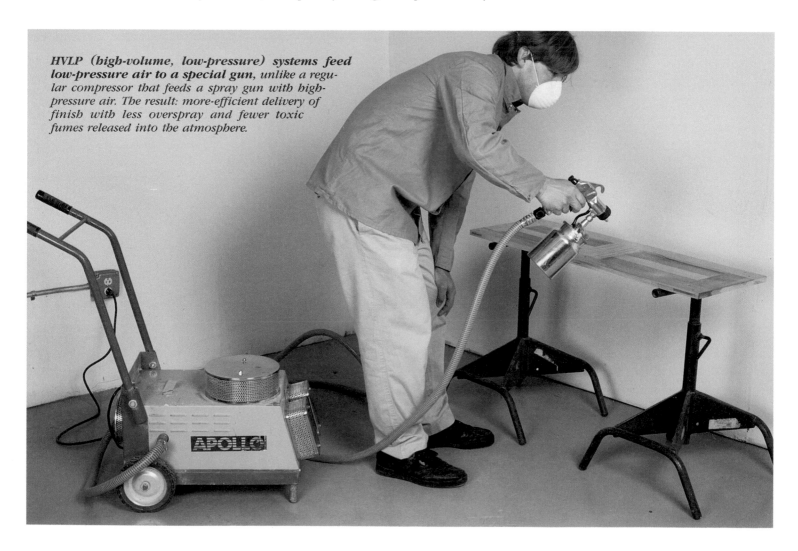

HVLP (high-volume, low-pressure) systems feed low-pressure air to a special gun, unlike a regular compressor that feeds a spray gun with high-pressure air. The result: more-efficient delivery of finish with less overspray and fewer toxic fumes released into the atmosphere.

Photos: Sandor Nagyszalanczy

At the heart of a typical HVLP system is the turbine, which pushes out a large volume of air with relatively good efficiency. For example, a small (7 amps to 8 amps), one-stage turbine unit typically produces 3 p.s.i. at 40 CFM to 50 CFM (cubic feet per minute), while a larger (10 amps to 12.5 amps), three-stage unit may deliver 6 p.s.i. at 85 CFM to 100 CFM. Each stage means the unit employs another fan, and fans working in a series are capable of generating higher pressures. An increase in motor size (amperage) produces a higher volume of air. Because they don't require heavy, bulky, steel air-storage tanks, turbine units are compact and lightweight. Small, single-stage and two-stage units are typically housed in a sheet-metal box about 2 ft. sq. Larger, multiple-stage turbines intended for the professional finisher are considerably heavier, weighing 50 lbs. or more, and have wheels for portability.

The turbine discharges air through a quick-change outlet, which accepts an air hose that connects to the spray gun. Many larger HVLP turbines have two air outlets, which allow two guns to be run at the same time. To carry the large volume of air efficiently, an HVLP hose is fairly large—about 1 in. in diameter. Since the turbine has no air-storage tank, the turbine-produced air must escape when the gun is not spraying. Therefore, an HVLP gun is called the "bleeder" type: The gun contains a valve that emits a constant stream of air whether or not its trigger is pulled.

Like a regular spray gun, the air passes through an HVLP spray gun and atomizes the liquid finish, propelling it onto the wood. Most conventional spray guns are "siphon" type: Air passes through the gun and creates a partial vacuum that draws fluid up from the cup. In contrast, an HVLP gun uses pressurized air to force fluid into the gun via a small tube from the sealed cup to the gun. An HVLP gun can be fitted with a variety of different fluid tips and air caps, depending on several variables: the desired spray pattern (a wide fan is used for spraying large surfaces, a narrow jet for detail work); the output of the turbine; and the viscosity of the finish.

Setting up and using an HVLP system is a breeze. You just plug the turbine in, connect the hose, load the gun's cup with finish and shoot. Some professional HVLP systems, like the Lex-Aire LX-75A and the Croix CX-20 (see sources of supply on p. 69 for addresses), feature a large, pressurized paint pot or tank that holds 2½ gal. or more with a feed line that runs to the gun to supply finish. Turbine units have air filters that require occasional cleaning or replacement, but no other special maintenance is usually required.

HVLP's high transfer efficiency

One of the most touted advantages of HVLP systems is their ability to deliver finish with a much higher transfer efficiency than compressed-air systems. Transfer efficiency is specified as the percentage of sprayed material that actually ends up on the workpiece as opposed to the amount that's lost as overspray. For example, if you are spraying door panels with three quarts of lacquer through a standard compressed-air spray gun with a 35% transfer efficiency, little more than *one quart* ends up on the wood. My experience has been that if you spray those same three quarts through a properly tuned HVLP gun with a transfer efficiency of 50% to 70%, about *two quarts* end up on the panels.

An increase in transfer efficiency translates into a savings in finishing materials, as well as a reduction in harmful solvent emissions to the atmosphere. Clean-air legislation in some areas of the country, such as Southern California, mandates that commercial finishers maintain a minimum transfer efficiency of 65% while spraying solvent-base materials. This percentage, which is difficult to achieve with an ordinary compressed-air system, is another reason why finishers are turning to HVLP spraying. In addition, a reduction in overspray means spray-booth filters don't need to be changed as often.

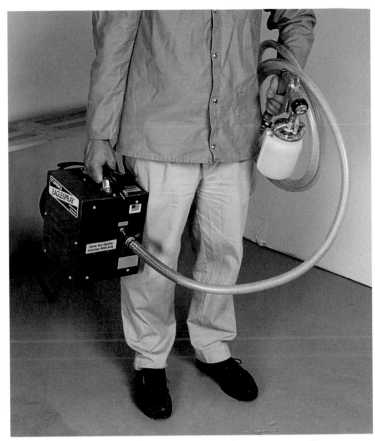

Portability is one of HVLP systems' greatest advantages. *Most small single-stage turbines, like the EagleSpray Turbo shown here, are light and have a handle so that the unit, its hose and the spray gun are easy to carry.*

Another advantage of spraying with a high-transfer-efficiency system is that it reduces spray "bounce back." This is a common finishing problem when spraying the inside corner of a closed-back cabinet, for example, where the overspray bounces back into your face in a choking cloud and settles on adjacent cabinet surfaces, leaving them rough and pebbly. HVLP guns have less bounce back because their low-pressure spray is more like a gentle mist than a forceful shower.

HVLP vs. compressed air

For the past five years, I have used an HVLP system side by side with a conventional compressed-air system as part of my woodworking business. This has given me the opportunity to see how the two systems compare. First of all, HVLP systems are very easy to set up and use, which makes them a good choice for the inexperienced or occasional finisher. Setting up a standard compressed-air system requires more experience, time and physical effort. Plus, the spray gun mix must be set very carefully to yield optimum finish delivery. In contrast, an HVLP turbine produces a preset volume of air at a fixed pressure, and people who have never sprayed a finish before usually find they get acceptable results the first time around.

One of HVLP's greatest advantages is the system's portability: Single- and two-stage units are typically between 18 lbs. and 30 lbs. (see the photo above), and most turbines either have a handle on top or wheels on the bottom. They're also wired for 110v; so you can plug them into a standard household electrical outlet. This makes HVLP a good choice for those who must spray-finish at an installation site. Further, the air that a turbine produces is warm and dry, in contrast to the chilled, damp air released by a compressor. This warm air can actually help water-base finishes dry faster

Conversion air systems: HVLP performance with a standard compressor

by Michael Dresdner

A conversion-air-system (CAS) spray gun allows a finisher who already owns a standard air compressor to spray with an HVLP gun. The Accuspray model 10, shown here, features a regulator and gauge mounted below the gun for convenient air-flow adjustment.

There is little doubt that converting to a high-volume, low-pressure (HVLP) spray system can save you money by reducing the amount of overspray; this is probably the single biggest reason for HVLP's quick acceptance by the manufacturing community. For example, when General Motors replaced its standard spray guns, it paid for the entire cost of the new equipment with the amount of money saved in paint in just *one day*. But like many other shops, GM saw no reason to tear out its extensive compressed-air system when making the change. Instead, it turned to HVLP's sister technology: conversion air systems (CAS). CAS provides a way for even small shops to adopt a highly efficient, cost-effective spray system while continuing to use existing compressors and air lines.

How CAS works: Instead of using high-volume/low-pressure air from a turbine, a conversion air system reduces high-pressure compressed air to low pressure and high volume mainly in one of two ways. The first is by using a dedicated CAS gun (like the Binks Mach 1, the DeVilbiss V2 or the Croix 711V) that has a mechanism inside that performs the conversion with a venturi tube or other device. These guns spray like HVLP guns, but connect directly to standard, high-pressure compressed-air lines. The second system, manufactured by Accuspray, features a small pressure-conversion unit that mounts directly to an HVLP gun (shown at left). This system is versatile because it can be fed from either a compressor or a turbine. A third type of conversion air system uses a wall-mounted unit, which takes in compressed air and provides an outlet for an HVLP hose that feeds a standard HVLP gun. (DeVilbiss and Accuspray manufacture these systems.) Because these wall-mounted systems are mostly intended for large production users, I won't discuss them here.

and flow out better, and it also can reduce blushing problems that sometimes occur when spraying solvent-base lacquers. I've found that I can spray lacquer with an HVLP system even on rainy days—an activity that would more than likely result in a blushed finish using compressed air and a regular spray gun.

If material costs and application time are your major criteria for selecting a spray system—as they should be if you run a production shop—HVLP systems again have the edge. I use my HVLP unit to great advantage when I'm spraying lots of large cabinets or furniture, since the high transfer efficiency allows me to spray on more finish in less time. And frankly, I like the feeling that I am doing something to reduce the amount of toxic material that's polluting the environment.

If HVLP has an Achilles' heel, it is its lack of versatility. Merely by cranking up the pressure of a compressed-air line, you can spray thick finishes (even contact cement), drive a sandblaster, blow sawdust from surfaces or run a variety of air-powered tools. An HVLP turbine, on the other hand, is designed only to spray finishes. If your shop already has a compressor, yet you'd like to use a system that has the efficiency of HVLP, you'll want to consider a conversion-air-system setup (see the sidebar above).

Finishers accustomed to a conventional system will need time to adjust to HVLP's idiosyncrasies. Since HVLP guns generally deliver a higher volume of finish, the tendency at first is to inadvertently flood panels with finish. Also, conventional-spraying veterans will feel much less recoil when pulling the trigger on an HVLP gun (due to the lower operating pressure); this can upset spraying rhythm and result in an uneven spray pattern on a large surface. One annoyance of HVLP systems is the constant drone of the turbine, which sounds quite a bit like a shop vacuum. Another irritation is the stiff, thick hose that tends to be unwieldy. Fortunately, maneuverability can be restored by attaching a special 2-ft.-long, extra-flexible "whip end" at the gun. And although most HVLP guns sport adjustment controls that are almost identical to those on conventional guns, others employ mechanisms that may be unfamiliar. For example, the width of the spray pattern (fan) on several HVLP guns is controlled by turning the air cap instead of by adjusting the more-common thumbscrew at the back of the gun.

After weighing all of HVLP's pluses and minuses, I'm still not ready to retire my compressed-air system. When it comes to very fine spray finishing, such as on tabletops and other horizontal surfaces, I still prefer my "old-fashioned" compressor and spray gun. Perhaps it's just that I'm accustomed to my old gun, but I think it produces a superior surface film, especially for gloss finishes. However, other wood finishers I've talked to say that they've achieved spraying results comparable to compressed-air guns with HVLP guns that are of a higher quality than mine.

Choosing an HVLP system

If you've decided that an HVLP system fits your finishing needs, you'll still be faced with deciding which one to buy. There are nearly a dozen manufacturers producing HVLP systems (see the list in the sources of supply box on the facing page), and most offer several models. To ease the confusion, rest assured that turbines of a given motor size (amperage) and number of stages (one, two or three) will output about the same amount of air, regardless of brand. The same cannot be said of the guns, however, which vary as much in quality as they do in price. It seems that the difference

Advantages: The greatest advantage of conversion air systems is that they are driven by a regular air compressor; no special turbine is needed. Also, CAS guns use a standard, flexible, ¼-in. or ⅜-in. compressed-air hose. This is in contrast to the thick, stiff, 1-in.-dia. hose used with HVLP systems. Also, the compressor and air line can be used to drive blow-off guns, vacuum pumps and air-powered tools—things that a turbine can't do.

Dedicated CAS guns are the non-bleeder type, which means air flow can be stopped totally when the gun's trigger is released. This makes a CAS gun handle just like a compressed-air spray gun—a real plus for the veteran finisher who is familiar with conventional equipment.

Another advantage of a dedicated CAS gun is that it can generate high pressure at the tip, up to 10 p.s.i., allowing the gun to spray much more viscous finishes than a regular HVLP gun—even adhesives such as contact cement. By the time air and finish mix at the tip, CAS guns spray like HVLP guns, and so it is reasonable to expect the same high transfer efficiency from a CAS gun as from an HVLP system.

Some CAS guns have a control valve and dial gauge at the base of the gun handle, offering adjustability for different spraying conditions, convenience and an instant readout of gun pressure. At least two companies, Binks and Accuspray, have gone a step further by adding a cup-control valve, which allows the sprayer to create separate fluid-feed and air-feed pressures. For instance, this degree of gun adjustability is great when spraying latex paints, which require high atomization pressure and low feed pressure.

Disadvantages: The largest drawback of using CAS is the compressor itself; larger compressors tend to be heavy and bulky, and hence lack portability. Also, many compressors aren't wired to run on standard 110v household electricity. Another disadvantage of CAS involves air-quality requirements. Standard air compressors produce cool, damp air, which is undesirable for trouble-free finishing. Fitting compressed-air lines with filters and moisture traps will take care of the contaminants, but warming the air involves a more costly air-line heater. Most CAS finishers I know have chosen to live with the cooler air since it's not a significant liability, especially when spraying solvent-base finishes. If you shoot water-base finishes, you may experience orange-peel problems in cold weather.

There's another fly in the ointment to using a CAS gun: Converting air from high to low pressure is inefficient. As a consequence, CAS guns generally need to be fed from a rather large compressor. CAS guns typically draw at least 10 CFM (cubic feet per minute), but they can draw as much as 17 CFM to 20 CFM—a sizable volume of air—when higher tip pressures are used to spray thick materials. Wall-mounted CAS devices that drive standard HVLP guns are even worse, since the gun bleeds air even when not in use. Therefore, it is important to consider your compressor's CFM output before buying a conversion air system. I wouldn't attempt to run a CAS gun with a compressor smaller than 5 HP.

Buying a CAS gun: Most of the better-known spray gun manufacturers (see the sources of supply box below) currently offer CAS guns in a wide range of prices. But expect to pay at least $450 for a good-quality CAS gun; more-elaborate models can top $1,000. Outfitting an entire conversion air system—gun, lines and filters—will generally cost $200 to $300 less than a comparable turbine-driven HVLP system, provided that you already own an adequate compressor.

When selecting a gun, make certain that the company you buy it from offers a complete range of tip and needle sizes so you can set up the gun to handle the range of finishes and the type of spraying you plan to do. □

Michael Dresdner is a contributing editor to FWW and a finishing consultant in Perkasie, Pa.

in cost between comparable HVLP systems is largely due to disparities in guns rather than turbine units.

As far as my recommendations are concerned, most small-shop woodworkers spraying furniture or cabinetry will need a turbine with no less than two stages, powered by a motor that's rated at no less than 9 amps. One-stage turbines, which are usually too small for most full-size finishing jobs, are a great choice for hobbyists spraying small projects or for furnituremakers and finish carpenters who want a light, portable unit for touch-up work. Some small units, like the Accuspray Series 23, come complete with an adjustable carrying strap, allowing you to tote them around a job site. Professional wood finishers or production-shop workers who plan to use an HVLP system for most of their finishing shouldn't settle for less than the power and versatility of a three-stage turbine. The three-stage unit I own, an Apollo model 1100, has two switches on top, which allow me to select between three air-flow levels, depending on the job at hand. At the highest setting, I can connect two guns to my unit, and a helper and I can finish even a big spray job expediently. Regardless of what size turbine you choose, I suggest you buy the best gun you can afford, since the gun is the most crucial component of an HVLP system. If you plan to spray water-base finishes, catalyzed lacquers or epoxy paints, choose a gun with stainless-steel fluid passages to avoid corrosion problems.

Manufacturers of HVLP equipment usually sell their systems as a complete package, including the turbine, hose and spray gun; there's nothing else to buy to get started spraying. An HVLP system should cost less than a conventional compressed-air system. Typically, single-stage HVLP systems run about $500; two-stage systems are about $700; and three-stage systems start at about $1,000. Incidentally, some manufacturers don't mention in their literature how many stages a particular turbine has; you'll need to ask. □

Philip Hostetter is the owner of The Woodshaper Ltd., a cabinet shop in New York City that specializes in architectural cabinetry and finishing.

Sources of supply

The following U.S.-based companies offer HVLP systems.

Accuspray, Inc., 26881 Cannon Road, PO Box 391525, Cleveland, OH 44139; (800) 321-5992, (216) 439-1200.

American Spray Industries (Amspray), 221 S. State St., PO Box 86, Harrison, OH 45030; (800) 443-4500, (812) 637-3215.

Apollo Sprayers International Inc., 1030 Joshua Way, Vista, CA 92083; (619) 727-8300.

Binks Manufacturing Corp., 9201 W. Belmont Ave., Franklin Park, IL 60131; (708) 671-3000.

Croix Air Products Inc., 520 Airport Road, Fleming Field, South St. Paul, MN 55075; (612) 455-1213.

DeVilbiss Ransburg Industrial Liquid Systems, PO Box 913, Toledo, OH 43692-0913; (800) 338-4448, (419) 470-2169.

Graco Inc., 4050 Olson Memorial Highway, Minneapolis, MN 55422; (612) 623-6000, (800) 367-4023.

Hood Products (EagleSpray–Kace Technologies Inc.), PO Box 513, Milltown, NJ 08850; (800) 966-5223, (908) 651-1555.

Lex-Aire Spray Systems, 34 Hutchinson Road, Arlington, MA 02174; (800) 537-2473, (617) 646-1102.

Wagner Spray Tech Corp. (Capspray), 1770 Fernbrook Lane, Minneapolis, MN 55447; (800) 328-8251, (612) 553-7000.

Vacuum Motor Turns into a Spray Rig

Enjoy the benefits of high-volume, low-pressure finishing in a compact unit

by Nick Yinger

For years, I did my spray finishing with a conventional compressor-driven setup. I was never entirely satisfied with the arrangement, and I recently built my own high-volume, low-pressure (HVLP) unit, as shown in the photo at right, to replace it. What bugs me about conventional spraying? For starters: finishing the inside of a case with a swirling cloud of overspray billowing back in my face. I can't see what I'm doing, and I wind up ingesting a big dose of chemicals no matter what kind of mask I wear. Even when I'm spraying water-based finishes, which are inherently safer, I find overspray annoying. Although they're neither toxic nor flammable, water-based finishes are expensive, so it makes even less sense to blast these precious fluids all over the booth with air compressed to 50 pounds per sq. in. (psi). HVLP spraying looked like the answer to these problems. This method promised to transfer 70% to 80% of the material from the gun to the object compared with 20% to 30% with a conventional setup. To accommodate a stream of warm, dry, low-velocity air, HVLP guns have large hoses and air passages. They use copious amounts of air—as much as 30 cu. ft. per minute (cfm) but at only 5 psi. (For pros and cons of HVLP, see the box on the facing page.)

I had a 3-hp compressor, so it seemed a simple matter to install a large, low-pressure regulator to feed 5-psi air to the gun. But there was a catch. A 3-hp piston compressor won't pump 30 cfm continuously at any pressure. The rule of thumb is 1 hp per 4 cfm of air, and we're talking about large, healthy, industrial horses not puny, underfed, home-improvement horses. Because 8- to 10-hp compressors are expensive and connecting my small compressor to a tank the size of a submarine seemed impractical, I decided I'd investigate the turbine compressors sold with HVLP guns.

I borrowed an HVLP unit from a friend and used it to finish some bathroom cabinets. It performed beautifully: almost no overspray, good atomization and good fluid and pattern control. My only criticisms were that the hose seemed cumbersome, and the handle of the gun became uncomfortably hot.

As I used the HVLP unit, I couldn't help thinking that if it acts like a vacuum cleaner, sounds like a vacuum cleaner, it must *be* a vacuum cleaner. I peeked inside. Sure enough—a two-stage vacuum cleaner turbine with an 8-amp motor! Soon thereafter, I set out to build my own HVLP turbine compressor.

Build your own HVLP unit

An HVLP machine is a centrifugal turbine compressor contained in a box with an inlet to bring air into the turbine and a plenum or outlet chamber to capture the compressed air discharged by the turbine and route it to your sprayer hose (see the drawing on p. 73). The turbines used in large vacuum cleaners are integral with their electric motors and are referred to as vacuum motors.

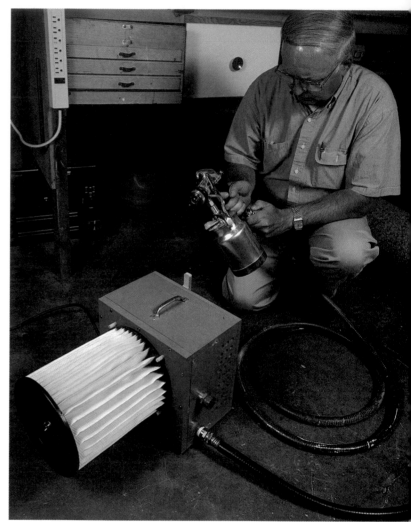

Shop-built spray unit*—*A high-volume, low-pressure unit like this one that the author built is ideal for on-site work or in the shop.

***First buy a vacuum motor*—Go to an industrial supply company, or get their catalog. I bought mine at Grainger (contact their marketing department at 333 Nightsbridge Parkway, Lincolnshire, Ill. 60069; 800-473-3473 for the nearest location); their catalog lists 45 vacuum motors, ranging from $40 to more than $280. You'll find a wide selection of features, such as bearing type, motor voltage, number of compressor stages and motor amperage. Most important for this application is *bypass*, not flow-through motor cooling. This means the motor is cooled by a separate fan. With this design, the motor won't overheat if the vacuum inlet or outlet is obstructed.

Single-stage compressors move large volumes of air but produce the lowest pressure. Two- and three-stage units supply higher

Photos: Jonathan Binzen

Conventional spraying vs. HVLP

by Dave Hughes

Okay...it's 8 a.m., and you've just entered your shop, coffee in hand. Standing before you is your latest project, nearly completed. It just needs to be lacquered. You take a deep breath, fill your spray gun, crank up the compressor, put on a particle mask and go for it. Fifteen minutes later, the atmosphere in your shop resembles that of Venus, every tool is covered with a fine white dust, the shop's out of commission for the rest of the morning and you've got a serious headache. Sound familiar? If, like most of us, you've tried to do finishing with conventional spray equipment in a small shop space, it probably does. Well, there's an alternative. It's high-volume, low-pressure (HVLP).

By now, most professional finishers have an HVLP unit in their arsenal of tools and increasingly, the units are finding favor with folks who do only occasional finishing. One big reason is that HVLP units have far higher transfer efficiency than conventional spray units. This means, simply, that most of the stuff you're spraying goes where you want it to go. A

painter friend of mine did his own little test when HVLP first hit the market. He painted one cabinet with a traditional, compressor-driven gun and an identical cabinet with an HVLP unit. When he was done, there was three times as much paint left in the HVLP cup. Where was the paint missing from the conventional gun? All over.

Aside from transfer efficiency, HVLP offers a string of clear benefits over conventional setups:

• They are compact, lightweight, self-contained, easy to set up and clean.

• The guns have a wide variety of spray-pattern settings for finishing intricate shapes as well as broad, flat surfaces.

• The low-pressure air supply is adjustable and so creates far less bounce-back of material from inside corners.

• The dry, heated air helps materials flow on smoothly, level out nicely and set up quickly. It also helps avoid blushing on cold, damp days.

• Your shop is not rendered useless for hours. (But open a window anyway.)

Drawbacks? There are a few:

• HVLP units are not really a high-production tool but are more suited for small- to medium-sized projects.

• Standard models have a rather cumbersome air hose all the way to the gun, limiting wrist mobility somewhat.

• As with any quart-gun arrangement, you can't spray upside down, and you're constantly, it seems, filling it up. (Higher priced models offer a 1- or 2-gal. pot that stands on the floor for less-restricted gun movement and less-frequent fill ups.)

• And there's that whining motor—it reminds me of a car wash vacuum.

HVLP is a definite advance for the small-shop woodworker or finisher who wants professional results. With prices starting under $500 and savings from high transfer efficiency, they're a good investment. From the money you save, stake yourself fifty bucks for a decent charcoal respirator and a pair of earplugs. □

Dave Hughes is a professional finisher in Los Osos, Calif.

High volume, low pressure (HVLP) in a small package. At 15 in. sq. and 18 lbs., the shop-built turbine-powered HVLP spray unit in the photo below is a fraction of the size and weight of the standard medium-sized compressed air setup in the photo at left.

pressure air at some sacrifice in volume but typically have more powerful motors and, hence, better overall performance. I chose a two-stage turbine with a 13-amp motor rated at 116 cfm that costs $163, an Ametek model #115962. I could have purchased a less powerful unit, but I wanted to be able to operate two spray guns on occasion, and anyway, I like overbuilt machinery. For a one-gun setup, you might try the Ametek 115757-P, which costs $63. For the rest of the parts in my HVLP unit, including the hose but not the gun, I spent less than $70.

Make a cradle for the motor—These motors are designed to be mounted by clamping the turbine housing between two bulk-

heads using foam gaskets. Make the rear bulkhead first. Cut it to size, bandsaw the circular hole and then chamfer the back side of the hole. The chamfer will ease the flow of motor-cooling air away from the motor housing. Cut the positioning ring to size, and rough out the hole with the jigsaw, leaving it slightly undersized. I made a Masonite routing template to exact size by cutting the hole with a fly cutter on the drill press. Use the routing template to finish the hole in the positioning ring.

Cut the housing sides, top and bottom to size, and make the dado for the rear bulkhead in each of them. Then drill the cooling outlet holes in the side pieces. Assemble the housing with the rear bulkhead in place, and when the glue has set, drop in the posi-

Improving sprayer output—Plastic laminate coiled in the outlet chamber acts as a fairing and increases output by lowering resistance. Weather stripping and rubber tubing form gasket seals.

Mounting electricals—Switch, cord and circuit breaker are mounted in the back panel. Holes in the side of the back chamber are for motor-cooling air. A wooden cleat holds the wound cord.

tioning ring, and glue it in place. I used screwed butt joints for the housing pieces and relied on the bulkhead to stiffen the box.

Gasket and sealant—The turbine is held in the circular rabbet created by the bulkhead and positioning ring and is isolated from the wood by silicone rubber sealant. To hold the turbine centered in the rabbet while the silicone sets, cut three 2-in.-long pieces of ⅛-in.-inside-dia. (ID) soft rubber tubing that compresses to about 1/16 in. under moderate pressure. (This surgical tubing, with a wall thickness of 1/32 in., is available in hobby shops and medical supply houses.) Lay the housing on its back, and put a generous bead of silicone in the rabbet. Lay the three pieces of tubing across the rabbet at 12 o'clock, 4 o'clock and 8 o'clock, and push the turbine down into the wet silicone. If you want the turbine to be easily removable later, spray the rim with an anti-stick cooking spray such as PAM before setting it into the silicone. Let the silicone set, and trim off the squeeze-out and tubing ends later.

Next rout the gasket grooves around the front edge of the housing, and press lengths of 3/16-in.-ID soft rubber tubing into them. Make the front and back covers, and apply the rings of ½-in.- by ½-in. adhesive-backed weatherstrip, as shown in the photo at left, and then screw on the front and back.

Holes in the box—I tried various locations for the outlet holes and found no detectable differences. But I did get better output when I installed a fairing made from a strip of plastic laminate, which makes the outlet chamber roughly cylindrical (see the photo at left). Drill one or two 1-in. outlet holes in the housing, and screw ¾-in. pipe thread close nipples into them. Attach adapters to the nipples to provide ¾-in. male hose threads.

I attached a large shop-vacuum air filter to the front cover. Four short dowels hold the base of the filter in place, and a bracket pulls it tight against the cover. The bracket consists of two threaded rods screwed into the front cover joined by a hardwood crosspiece with a bolt through its center. A washer and wing nut secure the

closed end of the filter against the crosspiece. You could also try using a large automotive filter. In that case, a Masonite or plywood disc secured by a similar bracket could hold the filter against the front cover.

Electricals—Mount the electrical parts: a heavy-duty switch, a circuit breaker with the appropriate rating for your motor, and the supply cord through the back cover, as shown in the photo at right. Then add rubber feet, a carrying handle and a cord-storage device.

> With HVLP, far more of what you spray sticks to the object you're spraying.

Nice hose—I tried three different types of hose. All were ¾ in. ID and can be equipped with ordinary garden hose threaded fittings or quick-connect couplers. The most flexible was the lightweight, corrugated type provided with most factory-built HVLP sprayers, but its rough inner surface doesn't deliver as much air as smoother types. Plastic garden hose is cheap, smooth inside and flexible when warm, but in use, the heated air causes the hose to become too soft and to kink easily. My favorite is Shields Vac extra heavy duty/FDA hose available from marine distributors. It is made of a soft flexible vinyl molded around a hard vinyl helix. It's recommended by the manufacturer for use in boat plumbing below the water line, which means it will withstand a lot of heat as well as mechanical and chemical abuse.

Gun control—You can't just hook up your old gun to your HVLP turbine. HVLP guns are designed to enable them to atomize fluids with low-pressure air. List prices for these guns start at around $250. Of the HVLP guns I've tried, my favorite is a DeVilbiss (contact DeVilbiss at 1724 Indian Wood Circle, Suite F, Maumee, Ohio 43537; 800-338-4448 for a local supplier). The current model most like mine is their JGHV 5285 that lists for $365. It has stainless-steel fluid passages and a stainless-steel needle, so water-based finishes won't cause corrosion. And much to the relief of my palms, the handle is a nylon composite that doesn't get hot in use. ☐

Nick Yinger is a professional land surveyor in Kirkland, Wash.

Shopmade HVLP unit

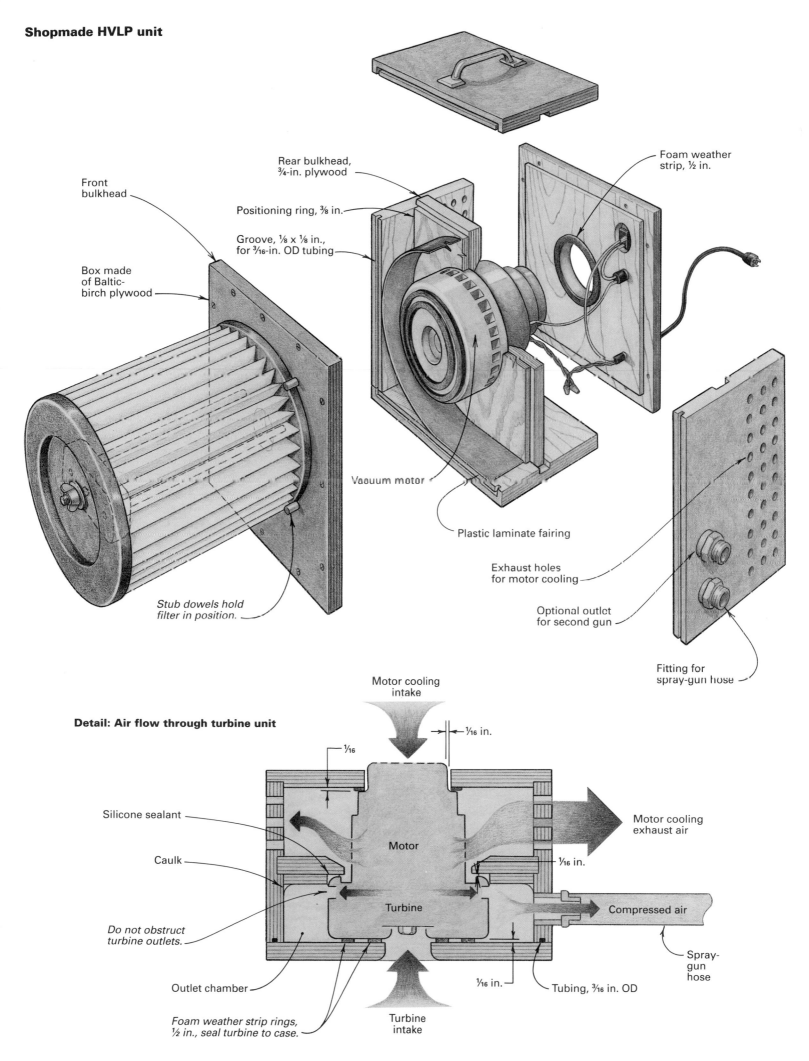

Front bulkhead

Box made of Baltic-birch plywood

Rear bulkhead, ¾-in. plywood

Positioning ring, ⅜ in.

Groove, ⅛ x ⅛ in., for ³⁄₁₆-in. OD tubing

Foam weather strip, ½ in.

Vacuum motor

Plastic laminate fairing

Stub dowels hold filter in position.

Exhaust holes for motor cooling

Optional outlet for second gun

Fitting for spray-gun hose

Detail: Air flow through turbine unit

Motor cooling intake

¹⁄₁₆ in.

¹⁄₁₆

Silicone sealant

Caulk

Do not obstruct turbine outlets.

Motor

Motor cooling exhaust air

¹⁄₁₆ in.

Turbine

Compressed air

Outlet chamber

Foam weather strip rings, ½ in., seal turbine to case.

Turbine intake

¹⁄₁₆ in.

Tubing, ³⁄₁₆ in. OD

Spray-gun hose

Removing an Old Finish

A *chemical stripper*
will do the work for you

by Michael Dresdner

Refinishing has developed a bad reputation over the years, and most people view it as a troublesome and messy task. But, there are times when it is the best, if not the only way to restore the beauty of a good but worn piece of furniture. Of course, if your table or chair is an antique and its rich patina and worn finish are part of its pedigree, you should never touch it without first checking with a museum conservator or other expert.

If you just want to spruce up the more ordinary furniture most of us live with, refinish away. Actually, the process is much less daunting than you might expect, if you remember that refinishing consists of two simple steps: stripping an old finish and putting on a new one. Once the old finish is off, you are merely at the first step of the finishing process, just as if you had built the piece yourself, and it is no harder to finish old wood than it is to work on new wood. In fact, it is often easier, since the sanding has already been done for you by the original finisher.

Choosing a stripping method

You have several options for removing a finish, but the three most common methods involve scraping it away with abrasives, melting it with heat or dissolving it with chemical solutions. For almost every case the average woodworker might encounter, I'd recommend removing the finish chemically, which is both the simplest and most controllable method and the one I'll discuss in detail. You might think it would be easy to remove a finish with sandpaper, a cabinet scraper or (heaven forbid) a piece of glass, but you'll regret it. Using glass is dangerous, and sanding or scraping makes hard work of a simple operation. In addition, sandpaper and scrapers don't know when to stop; they usually remove wood along with the offending finish.

Melting a finish with a propane torch or heat gun is even less appealing. First of all, the heat is likely to release some very harmful vapors. In addition, heat, like sandpaper, is sadly non-se-lective and will cheerfully burn wood along with the finish. In some cases, industrial polyester finishes won't budge under any chemical remover, so heat may be your only resort. But be extra careful; wear an organic-vapor mask, goggles and heat-resistant welders' gloves. Work outdoors or with the windows open, a fan blowing and a fire extinguisher handy.

In contrast, chemical removers only affect the finish and not the wood. Most commercial strippers won't harm even old veneered wood or destroy already weak glue bonds. And your local paint or hardware supplier can help you find a stripper that meets your needs fairly precisely and with a minimum of potential health hazards. I'll talk more about the different chemical removers in the sidebar on p. 76.

Tools for refinishing

In addition to a chemical stripper, you'll need some other equipment, most of which you probably already have around the shop. Those big, old splayed brushes you've been saving, without quite knowing why, are perfect for applying the chemical solution. It doesn't matter if they are clean or crusty. You'll also need a scraper or putty knife for scooping off the goo. It's a good idea to round the corners of the putty knife, so they won't dig into the wood. Gather up some wood shavings from the planer or jointer, a wooden dowel sharpened to a point in a pencil sharpener and a few stiff, nylon-bristle scrub brushes. You'll also need some coarse (0 or 1) steel wool, or better yet, some 3M Scotch-Brite general-purpose hand pads, a handful of rags or paper towels and a few containers—old steel or porcelain bowls, or even large tin cans. Then grab a stack of old newspapers, and put a drop cloth over the floor or anything else you want to keep clean.

You'll also need some masking tape to cover any unfinished areas, like the insides and sides of drawers. Before you apply the stripper, remove any hardware from the furniture, and take

From *Fine Woodworking* (March 1992) 93:84-88

enough of the piece apart so that you can work on horizontal surfaces as much as possible. Be sure to cover the screw holes for drawer or door handles from the inside with masking tape to prevent drip through.

Let the paint remover do the work

The key to easily removing an old finish is to let the paint remover do the work while you take it easy. You'll need to keep the furniture surfaces wet with stripper until the old finish is completely off. With liquid strippers, that means immersing the wood in the solution or continually rewashing it to keep it wet. Unless the piece is small, or you have extra time to kill, you'll probably find a semi-paste stripper will lighten your work load. These thick solutions flow less quickly than the liquid strippers, so they are easier to control, especially on vertical surfaces. Also, the semi-paste removers contain either waxes or clays that rise to the top and form a crust that slows down the evaporation of the active solvents, thus keeping the remover wet and active longer. That means you don't have to keep going back to rebrush the remover. In fact, if you do rebrush, you'll break up the crust and defeat its purpose.

To apply the semi-paste remover, shake the can a few times, lay a rag over the cap to block any spurts and open the cap slowly to release the pressure gradually. Pour some remover into one of your cans or bowls, and daub it all over the finish with your biggest, floppiest brush (see the photo at right). After applying a nice thick coat, *leave it alone.* Remember to take full advantage of the remover. Make sure the entire surface is wet; if you see any dry spots, go back and daub on some more paste.

Now sit down and enjoy at least a 10- to 15-minute break, but keep an eye on the stripper. If any dry spots develop, re-wet them. If you let the mixture of finish and remover dry completely before taking it off, the resulting crust will be far more difficult to remove than the original finish. After 15 minutes, scrape a small area to see

Apply semi-paste strippers with a big, floppy brush. Lay a thick coat on but don't rebrush it, or you will break the crust and allow the active solvents to evaporate. Always wear good-quality neoprene gloves when handling strippers that contain methylene chloride or alcohol.

Chemical strippers will remove paint or clear finishes without harming the wood's surface. The large photo above reveals what the author found after stripping several coats of paint from the chair in the inset photo—oak with only minor blemishes.

if the finish comes off to the bare wood (see the inset photo on the next page). If it doesn't, but the remover is still wet, leave it alone for a little while longer. When your test area shows bare wood or when your patience is exhausted, carefully scoop the goo off the wood and onto some of those old newspapers. If the wood is not completely clean in all areas—and don't be surprised if it isn't—re-wet the area with more remover immediately before it dries completely. For carved or fluted areas, grab a handful of wood shavings and scrub them into the softened finish to help absorb and dislodge it. Then take a stiff bristle brush and scrub out the loaded shavings, as shown in the top photo on the next page. In very tight corners, use the pointed dowel to clean out the recesses (see the bottom right photo). If the paint refuses to come out of the pores of large-pore wood, like ash or oak, use the stiff bristle brush to scrub the pores while the remover is still wet. In severe cases you may have to resort to a fine brass-bristle brush to clean the pores. Re-apply the remover as often as needed to make sure everything is dislodged, and give the piece a final scrub with a

Scotch-Brite pad soaked in remover just to be sure (see the bottom left photo). Then wipe off the surface with rags or paper towels.

At this point the wood should look clean, but it probably contains wax, silicone or other oils that may impede the finishing process. The wood may also contain old filler and stains you'd be better off without. The best way to remove these contaminants is with a series of solvent washes. Using a clean piece of Scotch-Brite, scrub down the wood with a liberal amount of lacquer thinner, followed by a scrub with alcohol and then one with mineral spirits or naphtha. It is not necessary to wipe off the wood in between washes. If you'd rather avoid working with these flammable solvents, scrub the surface with a solution of water and trisodium phosphate (TSP), a degreaser found in most paint and hardware stores. Just mix the solution according to the directions on the box. It is not as effective as the solvent sequence, but it is better than nothing. Finally, scrub down the wood with a solution of ammonia in warm water (about 2 oz. of household ammonia per quart of water), and then wipe off any excess liquid. During this final wash, the wood should look clean

Methylene chloride strips best, but there are other options

Identifying an old finish is a lot like determining what species is what in a mixed pile of lumber—it's easy if you've had a lot of experience, but frustrating for a beginner. Most finishes look pretty much alike to a neophyte, so rather than having anyone agonize over identifying a finish and selecting a stripper specifically for that finish, I recommend buying a good, wide-spectrum commercial remover that contains enough methylene chloride (a powerful stripping agent) to be classified as non-flammable.

Generally, you'll find a wide variety of removers at any good paint or hardware store. Most of these products fall into one of four general categories.

Paint and varnish removers: These strong solvent mixtures will remove a wide range of finishes and are the ones I recommend most often, especially if the identity of the old finish is not known. Some of these are flammable and most smell and produce annoying and harmful fumes. Most are poisonous if swallowed and contain solvents you should avoid getting on your skin. They're sold both as thin liquids and heavy-bodied semi-pastes, which I prefer because they cling better to vertical surfaces and stay wet longer.

One common thread among these removers is methylene chloride, a very fast and effective solvent. An interesting feature of methylene chloride is that adding it to a flammable solvent mixture can make the mixture non-flammable. Another curious aspect of methylene chloride is that as a stripper, it works from the bottom up rather than from the top

down. This means that once the remover is put onto the surface, it drops down through the coating and softens it at the wood line, allowing most finishes to peel off in sheets rather than turning into sticky gunk. That can translate into less material waste and easier disposal. When working with these materials, observe the safety precautions outlined in the sidebar on p. 78.

Wood refinishers: A refinisher is a thin, watery mixture of common finish solvents, usually alcohol, toluene and acetone, which dissolves shellac, lacquer and some varnishes but has little effect on most paints and polyurethanes. To see if the material will work on your finish, apply some refinisher to a small, obscure spot, and see if it melts the finish. If the refinisher turns the old finish into a liquid, you have a few options: move the finish around with rags or abrasive pads to "re-knit" an old checked or cracked surface, remove most of it and leave only the barest sealer coat, or keep washing down the wood until the old finish is completely gone. Admittedly, leaving only a partial finish that still looks good will take some practice. Because refinishers contain only solvents and no waxes, they leave the wood surface clean and ready to refinish. On the down side, refinishers are very flammable, create lots of solvent vapors, evaporate quickly and generally smell awful.

"Safe" strippers: The new so-called safe strippers utilize solvents that are considered to be much safer than their

predecessors, but they are not as effective on all types of finishes. Some manufacturers specify that their material works on only one class of finish, such as oil-based materials; others offer two or more different formulations to cover all the bases. Generally, these strippers are thick, slow drying and non-flammable; they have very little odor and won't burn or harm bare skin. (One company offers a product so gentle to the skin that it can be used as a hand cleaner.) The fumes that do come off are regarded as safe so that work can be done indoors. The trade-off is that these strippers work slower than methylene chloride or harsh solvent mixtures and frequently cost more. But they are the ideal choice for people who are particularly sensitive to hard solvents or people who must work indoors.

Caustics: Certain types of paint, such as milk paint, won't respond to most solvents but can be softened with strong acids or alkalies. Caustic strippers, like lye, were the most common type before methylene chloride mixtures were developed, but they have virtually died out along with the milk paints that necessitated them. Some people still like the idea of using lye to remove paint, but it can burn and discolor wood if it's left on too long, soften some glues and seriously raise the grain of old wood. More importantly, it will seriously burn skin and eyes, and the fumes are antagonistic to the nose, throat and eyes. Take precautions and, above all, keep your wits about you and watch where the lye splashes. Better yet, select another method. —M.D.

After waiting 10 or 15 minutes, use a plastic scraper to see if the finish will come off to the bare wood (inset photo above). If there are several coats of paint, as there are on the chair shown here, you may have to remove the goo, and apply another coat of the stripper.

In hard-to-reach places on turned or carved parts, rub a handful of wood shavings into the softened finish to help remove the residue. Then scrub out the shavings with a stiff bristle brush (large photo above).

Scotch-Brite pads are ideal for scrubbing down the wood with a final coat of stripper, as shown at right, and for washing the surface clean with lacquer thinner after all the finish has been removed.

A sharpened dowel is handy for cleaning stripper and finish residue from very tight corners, as shown in the far right photo.

and the color should be somewhat uniform. If the water wets the wood unevenly or leaves splotchy areas, not all the residue has been removed. Go back to the paint remover and repeat the stripping- and rinsing-solution sequence outlined above. When the wood is clean as a whistle, let it dry overnight.

Cleaning up

That sludge you've collected on the newspapers, rags, steel wool and paper towels is considered toxic by most communities, and shouldn't be treated as normal trash. Check your local regulations before disposing anything. Your community may have a special collection site for used oil, paint and solvents. If it's going to end up in a landfill, let the residue dry completely prior to disposal. The residue will become hard and crusty, which is less damaging than the solvent-laden sludge. Before the residue hardens, you can clean your brushes, putty knives and even the Scotch-Brite with lacquer thinner, but disposing of the dirty lacquer thinner will be regulated just like the sludge.

Removing stains

Even though the wood is now free of finish, it may still be marred by both intentional and accidental stains, which you may want to remove. Intentional stains are whatever dyes or pigments the first finisher applied to the wood; accidental stains are the various water rings, ink spills, uneven sun fading and other marks of age and use. Many people feel that these accidental stains add character and history to furniture and should remain under the new finish, but for the most part, these are the same people who believe that old furniture should never be refinished. Though not all stains and discolorations can be removed, there are ways of dealing with some. First, let's deal with the intentional stains.

Wood stains are either pigments or dyes. Most, if not all, of the pigments should have been removed by the solvent scrubs; whatever is left now is likely to remain forever. But most aniline dyes can be denatured by using either commercial decolorant solutions or chlorine bleach, which is sold in grocery stores as laundry bleach. These bleaches are generally rather weak concentrations (usually a 5% solution), so they will work slowly and require several applications to remove the dye. You can make a stronger solution by mixing swimming-pool chlorine (sold under various names) into water. The label on the pool treatment will indicate the percentage of active ingredient, usually 65% to 85% of either calcium or sodium hypochlorite. Get the highest percentage available. Add the white crystals to a glass jar of hot water; let them sit a few minutes and stir occasionally. Keep adding the pool treatment until no more will dissolve and a layer of white residue settles to the bottom of the jar. Wear rubber, protective gloves, and use a synthetic sponge to flood the wood surface with the warm mixture; then let it dry overnight. In the morning, you'll see a layer of dried crystals on the wood, which should be washed off to remove the stain. A second wash will be even more effective.

Oxalic acid (sometimes sold in liquid form as deck brightener) is often effective on water rings and ink stains and on "silvered" weathered wood. But it works best for quickly and completely removing the blue/black iron stains often found when oak and other high-tannin woods contact iron hardware or nails. Make sure you remove the nails or hardware before bleaching, or you may create new stains as the wood dries. If you can't remove the nails, countersink them, and putty over the holes before you apply the oxalic acid.

Both stain removal processes require a lot of water, which often raises the grain of the wood. Although it is usually not necessary to sand wood when refinishing, it will probably be necessary after stain removers are used. Use a very fine sandpaper (220-grit or finer) and scuff-sand quickly and lightly. For turnings and carvings, use Scotch-Brite pads instead of sandpaper. □

Michael Dresdner is a finisher in Perkasie, Pa. This article was adapted from his book, The Woodfinishing Book, *published by The Taunton Press, 63 South Main Street, PO Box 5506, Newtown, Conn. 06470-5506.*

Fresh air and common sense reduce refinishing hazards

Every paint-remover manufacturer suggests that you work in a well-ventilated area, but few explain what that means. I think the ideal situation is a shady area outside in 75° weather with a light breeze, but ordering good weather is difficult. If you can't strip outdoors, open the windows, and turn on a fan to bring in fresh air and to carry off any contaminated air. Unless you've chosen a so-called safe remover, stripping furniture is not a wintertime activity. Ventilation is particularly important with methylene chloride. When you inhale the fumes, your body metabolizes them to carbon monoxide. This is not good for anyone, but it can be particularly dangerous to heart patients who should avoid the chemical totally. Goggles are good to protect your eyes from splashes, and good-quality neoprene gloves are essential to protect your skin. Both alcohol and methylene chloride can be absorbed through the skin, and methylene chloride in particular will carry with it heavy metals, such as the lead often found in old paints. Also, if you're working with flammable compounds, avoid sparks and flames.

Even if you're working outdoors on an ideal spring day, I'd suggest closed shoes (not sandals), long pants, long sleeves and a plastic apron to protect against splashes. Buy extra-long gloves, and turn the ends up into a cuff when you put them on. That way, when you lift your hands, the paint remover will run into the cuff and not down your arm. (Remember, some of these chemicals can burn sensitive skin.) Finally, use common sense; if the smell of the stripper starts to sicken you or makes you dizzy, *stop*, get some fresh air and a new game plan.

When working with dry bleach crystals, wear a nuisance-type dust mask when you handle the irritant and when you subsequently sand the wood. Though neither chlorine nor oxalic bleaches are severe caustics in solution, gloves and goggles are always in order. Most bleaches will "eat" natural fiber brushes and rags, so use synthetic sponges and brushes (nylon or polyester).

If these warnings have you wondering whether refinishing is really worth all the trouble, you have one other alternative. Look in the yellow pages and find a commercial furniture stripper to handle the job. But make sure the company specializes in wood stripping because outfits that work mostly with metals frequently use caustic strippers, and these may loosen glue joints and play havoc with the wood grain. —M.D.

Spray-Finishing Done Right

Getting a blemish-free finish is easier than you think

by Andy Charron

Quite a few woodworkers I know are un-enthusiastic, even fearful, about spray finishing. They believe the equipment is too mysterious, too costly and too hard to master. In fact, just the opposite is true. There are many simple-to-operate, reasonably priced spray systems out there (see the article on pp. 60-65). It took me less time to become proficient with a spray gun than it did to master a router. Best of all, the finish from a gun is often so smooth that I don't have to rub it out. Following sound spraying principles and knowing how to use the equipment helps me produce virtually flawless finishes.

Where to spray

The best place to spray is in a booth where a powerful exhaust removes overspray and dust from the air. If you're spraying solvent-borne finishes, you really have no other choice than to use an explosion-proof spray booth. But they're costly. You don't need explosion-proof equipment to spray waterborne finishes, and they're getting better and better (see the article on pp. 32-37). You only need a place that is well-ventilated and clean. If you have the floor space, you can build a spray room that has an exhaust fan and intake fil-

Spraying takes a bit of practice. Surface preparation, finish consistency and technique all are important.

ters to ensure a steady supply of clean, fresh air. No matter where you plan to spray, check with your local building officials first.

Careful preparation is essential

How you prepare the surface is just as important as how you spray the finish. Sand the entire piece thoroughly (see the photo at left on p. 80). For stained work, I usually raise the grain with a damp cloth, let the surface dry and sand with 220-grit before I spray. For waterborne finishes and dyes, I sand to 180-grit and spray a light coat of dye stain or finish. This raises the grain and stiffens the fibers, making them easier to sand with 220-grit.

Spraying paint or pigmented lacquers is more involved. Opaque finishes highlight tiny imperfections (see the article on pp. 88-91). They often require at least two rounds of filling, sanding and priming before the wood is ready to be sprayed.

Thin the finish to a sprayable consistency

Life would be easier if you could always pour finish straight from the can into a spray pot and begin applying it. But occasionally, you'll have to thin it. Which thinner you use and how much you add will depend on the material you're applying, the spray system you're using and what the piece will be used for. Some manufacturers do a lousy job of providing thinning information. If the appropriate thinner is listed on the label, use it. Because some cans of finish say that the contents don't need to be thinned, they don't list a thinner. If this is the case, you generally can thin the finish with the solvent that's recommended for cleanup.

Finding the correct viscosity—The viscosity of a finish is a measurement of its resistance to flow. Thinning a finish lowers the viscosity, which allows it to be broken into smaller particles (or at-

Sprayed finishes are only as good as the surface below. *The author primed this bookcase and now sands it with 220-grit paper in preparation for spraying on a tinted waterborne lacquer topcoat.*

omized) more easily by the spray gun. The finer the atomization, the smoother the appearance.

Thinners can eliminate common spray problems (see the box on pp. 82-83) like orange peel, but if used improperly, thinners actually cause problems. Waterborne finishes are especially sensitive to thinning. Overthinning can prevent the finish from forming a clear, hard film.

Some spray-gun manufacturers recommend finish viscosity for a particular needle/tip combination. This information may be given as a ratio or a percentage of thinner and finish. The viscosity also may be given as the number of seconds it takes to empty a certain size viscosity cup. Viscosity cups have small holes in the bottom, which let liquid drain through (see the photo at right on the facing page). Appropriately sized cups are available from most spray-system makers.

Room conditions are a factor—Temperature and humidity dramatically affect how much thinner to use in a finish and how it will spray. Low temperature and high humidity are not especially conducive to spraying. Even if you follow all the labels exactly, you may have to adjust the amount of thinner you add. You can keep records of how much thinner you need for different conditions. After a while, you'll get a feel for this.

SPRAY THE LEAST VISIBLE AREAS FIRST

Before spraying, make a dry run through the whole process. To help prevent you from overcoating or missing areas, visualize and then practice the sequence of spray strokes. Although the order in which you spray parts of a piece may vary slightly, there are a few rules of thumb worth following: Start with the least visible areas, such as drawer bottoms and cabinet backs, and work your way to those parts that will be seen. For example, spray the edges of tabletops, doors and shelves before the tops. This minimizes the overspray on the most visible surfaces. Working from the inside out holds true for case pieces, too, as shown in the series of photos at right. Always work from the wettest edge, so you can easily blend areas you've just sprayed. Where possible, move the gun away from your body, toward the exhaust fan (assuming you have one). This will help prevent overspray from settling on previously sprayed areas, and it will give you an unclouded view, too.—*A.C.*

1 *Spray overhead corners, and then fill in the inside top.*

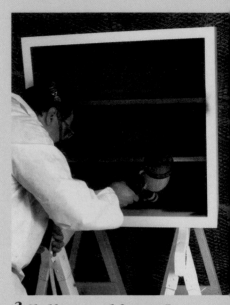

3 *Shelf tops and fronts—Remember to overlap strokes.*

5 *Do the exterior cabinet sides and front corners.*

From *Fine Woodworking* (March 1996) 117:71-75

2 *Coat interior back and sides. These areas won't be highly visible when the piece is finished.*

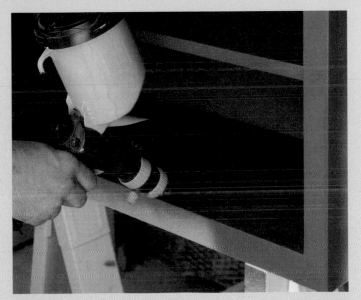

4 *Finish the face frame. Begin with the inside edges, and then move to the front of the case.*

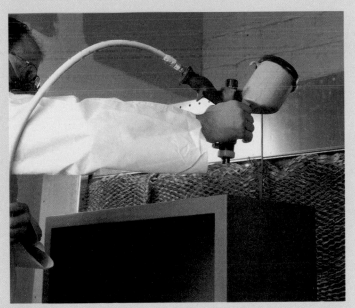

6 *Spray the top. By leaving the top for last, the most visible part of the case isn't marred by overspray.*

Straining the finish and filling the pot

Your finish and your equipment should be as clean as possible because a speck of dirt or dried finish could ruin the job. To remove impurities, pour the finish through a strainer or filter (available at paint-supply dealers). As an added precaution, you can install a filter on the end of the dip tube that draws finish from the pot, or put an in-line filter near the gun. To keep the air that comes from the compressor dry and clean, I run the line through a canister-type separator, which filters out water, oil and dirt before they get in the hose supplying air to the gun.

Check the finish with a viscosity cup. A stopwatch and the recommended viscosity cup show whether thinner must be added. Once thinned, the finish is passed through a filter.

Selecting suitable fluid tips and air caps

The fluid tip in a spray gun controls the amount of finish that gets deposited on a surface. In general, lighter finishes require a small tip. Thicker materials (or those with a higher percentage of solids) require larger fluid tips. The air cap in a spray gun controls the velocity of the air, which governs how finely the fluid is atomized. Air caps with smaller holes cause the air to leave the gun at a higher velocity, thus producing finer atomization. Air caps are matched with fluid tips to give optimum performance.

Most guns come equipped with a standard setup appropriate for several finishes. The setup includes a fluid tip that's about .050 in. dia. and a corresponding air cap. The standard setup will produce acceptable results with most finishes, but sometimes it's worth trying other combinations of fluid tips and air caps.

In a turbine-driven high-volume, low-pressure (HVLP) system, the amount of air feeding the gun is constant, so adjustments to the air pressure can only be done by changing air caps. If you are using a waterborne finish with a turbine and a bleeder-type (constant air flow) gun, make sure that the nozzle stays clean. These guns are prone to blobs of finish drying on the air cap and then blemishing the work.

Adjusting the gun

Spray guns come with adjustments for air and fluid. The type of finish being sprayed, the size of the object to be coated and the speed of application all play a role in deciding how to control the fluid and air. I always test my fan pattern and finish delivery rate on scrap wood or cardboard so that I can make adjustments before I actually spray the piece.

Turbine-driven HVLP systems—Adjusting a turbine-powered spray gun is a simple process: no matter what type of gun you own, the idea is to start air flowing through the gun first, and then introduce finish slowly until it flows continuously and evenly. The gun should apply a full, wet coat with no heavy spots or misses. From this point, you can open or close either knob to obtain the best spray rate and fan pattern.

If you want to spray a lot of material in a hurry, open the fluid control more. If you are coating large surfaces, widen the fan pattern. If you're trying to achieve a fine finish or you're spraying small items, you'll have more control of how much finish is applied and where it lands by restricting the fan and fluid. But remember, how you set one knob affects the other. For example, if you increase the air flow without adjusting the fluid, the finish may be too fine. Conversely, opening the fluid control without widening the fan can cause runs and sags. At the ideal settings, the finish will coat evenly and flow together well.

Compressor-driven systems—With high-pressure spray guns and conversion-air HVLP guns (both powered by a compressor), you have the ability to control the air pressure entering the gun in addition to adjusting the fluid rate and fan shape. Getting all three adjustments coordinated can be a bit tricky and takes some trial and error, but being able to regulate the air pressure at the gun allows more spraying options.

Develop a spray strategy

Regardless of the size and shape of the object you're spraying, the main thing to keep in mind is that you want to spray an even coat over the entire piece. Always spray the finish in several thin coats rather than one heavy one. Lighter coats are less likely to run, dry faster and make sanding between coats easier.

If the pieces you are spraying are so small that the air from the gun blows them all over the place, try placing them on a piece of screen or wire mesh. I prefer spraying small parts with my turbine HVLP gun because the spray is softer. A good production tip for spraying many small pieces is to put them on a lazy Susan and spray several at once (see the photo above). Rotate the turntable as you spray, so you don't build up too heavy a coat on the pieces.

Position large work on sawhorses or a stand so that the height is

Turntable for even, quick coats—After arranging trophy bases on a lazy Susan, the author sprays with an HVLP gun.

comfortable. You shouldn't have to bend, reach or otherwise contort your arm or body while you're spraying. You should be able to turn and move the work easily. I sometimes support the work on stickers or points (blunted drywall screws work well) to make sure that the bottom edge gets good coverage.

Spraying uniformly

To maintain even spray coverage, there are a few things to remember. Grip the gun firmly, but not so tightly that your hand gets tired or uncomfortable. Point the nose of the gun so it's perpendicular to the work surface, and hold the gun at the same distance from the work on each pass. Move the gun parallel to surfaces, not

Correcting spray-finish troubles

Fine Woodworking contributing editor Chris Minick found big improvements in his finishes when he switched to spray equipment. But the transition wasn't painless. Here's his list of common spray problems and, where they're not obvious, the solutions.

Orange peel

1) **Atomization pressure too low:** Increase pressure and adjust fluid.
2) **Spray gun too far from work:** Maintain 6- to 10-in. gun distance.
3) **Coating viscosity too high:** Thin to correct application viscosity.
4) **Not enough coating thickness for proper flow.**

Blush or cottoning

(Right half shows blush)
1) **High humidity:** Dehumidify shop, or add retarder to finish.
2) **Improper thinner:** Use only recommended thinner.
3) **Moisture in spray equipment:** Install water separator in air line.

White spots

1) **Water contamination in spray equipment:** Install water separator in air line.
2) **Water on work surface:** Dry work surface before spraying.

Sags and runs

1) **Coat too heavy:** Decrease fluid flow to spray gun.
2) **Spray gun too close to surface:** Maintain 6- to 10-in. gun distance.
3) **Thinning solvent drying too slowly:** Use faster evaporating thinner.
4) **Drafty spray room.**

Plan for drying—The author uses racks to cure his spray-finished items. The area is warm, dry and dust-free.

in an arcing, sweeping motion. Begin your stroke 6 in. or so before the gun is over the wood, and continue the same distance beyond the other side. Trigger the gun a split second after you start your motion, and keep spraying until your arm stops. As you spray across the piece, move your arm steadily and smoothly without changing speed.

For most HVLP guns, hold the gun about 6 to 8 in. from the surface. This will let you spray a full, wet coat with minimal overspray and decent coverage. Move the gun at about the same speed you would a brush. Each pass should overlap the previous one by about half. When spraying small objects or tight places, reduce the flow and move the gun closer. To avoid clouds of overspray and

bounce back, work from inside corners out. Use more wrist action, and trigger more quickly. On large areas, increase the flow, pull the gun back an inch or two and make passes in opposite directions. I lightly spray across the grain to make a tack coat. Then I immediately spray with the grain.

In situations where your spray passes intersect, such as the stretcher-to-leg joint of a chair, release the trigger a bit sooner than you normally would. This will feather out the finish. If overlapping passes still give you a problem, mask off adjacent areas.

Drying and cleaning up are critical

It's easy to forget that once you spray a piece, the finish needs a warm, dry and dust-free place to cure. If you don't have a separate drying area (see the photo at left), production in your shop can grind to a halt. Even if you have a designated area, storing a number of wet cabinets, doors, drawers and trim pieces can be a problem. I use a system of racks to dry components and store them for short periods. Plywood trays, slipped into old baker's racks, come in handy when I have to dry lots of small pieces. When I'm drying round or odd-shaped items, like balusters, I hang them on an overhead wire from swivel hooks. Each piece can be rotated and sprayed and then hung in my drying area.

I have made it a ritual to clean my spray gun thoroughly while my work is drying. After cleaning the parts with the solvent recommended on the finish container, I dry them with compressed air. Then I coat all the fluid passages with alcohol and let it evaporate before I store the gun in its case. □

Andy Charron writes about woodworking and builds custom cabinets in Long Branch, N.J.

Fat edge

1) Corner profile too sharp: Slightly radius 90° edges.
2) Drafts on one side of workpiece.
3) One side of workpiece warmer than other.

Cratering

(Solid chunk in center)
1) Solid contaminant (usually from non-loading sandpaper) lowers surface tension: Sand defect, and wipe entire surface with mineral spirits.

Fisheyes

1) Silicone or wax residue from paint stripper or old finish: Wipe surface with mineral spirits; mist coats (let each dry) to trap contaminants.
2) Oil in spray equipment (usually from compressor): Install oil separator in air line.

Microbubbles

(Haze, waterborne finish only)
1) Coating is drying too fast: Add retarder to finish.
2) Defoamer deactivates in waterborne finish: Don't use waterborne finish that's more than 1 year old.
3) Atomization pressure too high.

Sample photos: Boyd Hagen

Milk Paint
Making an udderly timeless topcoat

by A. Richard Fitch

C ows' milk has been used to produce paints since the dawn of history. Milk curd (casein) materials were used by artisans of ancient Egypt, China, Greece and Italy. Ancient Hebrews are known to have used milk curd for house painting and decoration. In the 12th-century treatise *The Various Arts*, the preparation and use of milk paint is described in some detail. Casein, or milk-base, paints have been used continually since then—by renaissance craftsmen to produce their superb masterpieces, in post renaissance Europe, in Colonial America, and during the 19th and 20th centuries in the United States and Europe. In fact, the first U.S. paint patent issued in 1865 (U.S. patent 50058) covers a casein product. Casein paints reinforced with tung oil were used for decorative purposes at the 1933 Chicago Century of Progress Exhibition. Surprisingly, U.S. government specifications still included both an exterior and an interior casein paint as late as 1945. And if you add to this long history the fact that milk paint meets the currently fashionable criteria of "all natural" and "environmentally safe," you can easily see why its use for decorative painting has captured the fancy of many contemporary painters and decorators.

The charm of a milk-paint finish is largely dependent on its rath-er coarse, unsophisticated surface. This characteristic surface produces a pleasing decorative effect on walls in old homes, and it is quite appropriate for unpretentious so-called "use furniture." American colonial, Shaker and Country style furniture are prime prospects for milk painting (see the photo on the facing page). Milk paints may also be used on a variety of plaster, masonry and wood surfaces. Over time, milk paint develops tenacious adhesion to porous surfaces and becomes water-resistant and insoluble in most solvents. In addition, because of its low cost, milk paint is often used as a primer under oil paint.

Milk and casein paints are categorized as types of distemper. Distemper is a British term for paints made from either animal glue or milk protein. In the United States, these products are often called calcimine. Casein, a small but commercially important part of cows' milk, is produced by allowing or causing skim milk to sour and precipitate curd. Commercially, this souring may be accomplished by the addition of mineral acid to skim milk. The curd is then separated from the whey (or liquid), washed to remove butterfat and dried. Granulated casein can then be rendered soluble in water by adding an alkali, such as lime, ammonium hydroxide or potassium hydroxide, to the mixture. This solution is then

Photos: Jim Boesel

Milk paint is a good choice for Country style furniture, such as the cherry, hinge-top bench above. The author is sanding through the green topcoat and revealing some of the red undercoat to give the piece an antique look.

Yes, milk paint really is made with milk. Casein, or milk curd, is used commercially for making paints and adhesives. All you need to make your own milk paint (left) is skim milk, lime, chalk or whiting, boiled linseed oil and some pigment if desired.

mixed with inert pigments, like chalk, whiting or certain types of clay, and color pigments to make milk paint.

For painting furniture and other purely decorative renderings, lime is generally the preferred alkali because of availability, easy handling and the reputation for superior resistance to water. Alkali-proof pigments must be used in the preparation of lime-and-casein paints. A comprehensive discussion of pigments and their various characteristics is beyond the scope of this article, but generally, red or black iron oxides and yellow iron hydroxide are excellent pigments for milk paint. Earth colors, such as umbers, siennas, Venetian red and yellow ocher are also good, as are titanium dioxide, chromium oxides and lampblack. Ultramarine blue and toludine red can also be used. As a rule of thumb, you can trust pigments used to color cement for patios or stucco.

Making your own milk paint

A few years ago, my son, David, was restoring the painted surfaces in an 18th-century house in Pennsylvania when the owners asked him to use milk paint in some of the rooms. In order to satisfy the request, he referred to an old book published in the late 18th century called *The Painters and Varnishers Guide* by P.F. Tingry, a

Recipes for homemade milk paint

Most of the ingredients in the following formulas are available from large suppliers of art materials or paint and decorator-supply stores. Slaked, or hydrated lime, is available as a soil supplement at garden-supply stores. Calcium carbonate, also called whiting, can be substituted for Spanish white in the first recipe. If you don't live near a large paint store, you can mail-order calcium carbonate, casein and alkali-proof earth pigments that are compatible with lime from Johnson Paint Co. Inc., 355 Newbury St., Boston, Mass. 02115; (617) 536-4838.

P.F. Tingry's formulas

The first two recipes are taken directly from P.F. Tingry's *The Painters and Varnishers Guide,* second edition published in 1816 by Sherwood, Neely and Jones, Patternoyster Row, London, England.

Painting in milk (makes about ½ gal.):

skimmed milk—4 lbs.; oil of poppy (or linseed) or nut oil—4 ozs. lime, newly slaked—6 ozs.; Spanish white—3 lbs.

Put the lime into a clean bucket and having poured over it a sufficient quantity of milk, add gradually the oil, stirring the mixture with a wooden spatula; then pour in the remainder and dilute the Spanish white (whiting) as follows: The Spanish white is carefully strewed over the surface of the liquid. It gradually becomes impregnated with it and falls to the bottom. When the white has fallen to the bottom, it is stirred with a stick.

The paint may be colored with various coloring substances employed in common painting. The above quantity will be sufficient to give a first stratum to a surface of 24 sq. yds.

Resinous painting in milk:

For painting outdoor objects, add to the preceeding composition for painting in milk, 2 ozs. of each of the following:

slaked lime; linseed oil; white burgundy pitch (or rosin)

Put the pitch into the oil, which is to be added to the liquid milk and lime, and dissolve it in a gentle heat. (As an alternative, use 4 ozs. of linseed oil and eliminate the pitch or rosin.)

Formula to meet U.S. government specifications for exterior casein paint (makes a little more than 1 qt.):

whiting and color pigment—2 lbs. (combined)
lime—4 ozs.; casein—4 ozs.
water—2½ lbs.; boiled linseed oil—3¼ ozs.
a. Mix thoroughly and sieve dry ingredients.
b. To use, mix 1 qt. cool water thoroughly with dry powder (use mechanical mixing if available). Don't make foam and bubbles.
c. Add oil slowly while stirring constantly.
d. Allow the mix to stand 20 to 30 minutes before use.
e. Adjust consistency with remaining water.

Notes

When making the paint, color pigment can be used to replace 10% to 30% of the whiting, depending on the oil absorption and the strength of the particular pigment. To tint basic white milk paint, mix dry pigments with water to make a light, smooth paste and add it to the paint while stirring vigorously. Distemper paints change color drastically when dry, so always check color after the sample is dry. To extend the usable life of these paints, the older formulas recommend the addition of ⅛ oz. of either oil of cloves or pine oil for each pint of milk.　　　　—D.F.

Milk paint will lighten as it dries, as illustrated by a fresh brush stroke alongside a dry sample of the same color (above).

To show the effects of antiquing with milk paint (left), the author made this step-by-step sample panel. From left to right: bare cherry; one coat of red milk paint (Tingry's interior formula); a coat of green over the red, which is then sanded through a bit; and a strip on which the raised panel edges were rounded over with sandpaper before the first coat of paint, the green topcoat was sanded clear through to the cherry in one corner, and then a coat of varnish was applied to darken the paint.

professor of chemistry, natural history and mineralogy at the Academy of Geneva. In his book, Tingry enumerated two formulas for milk paint, one for interior use and the other for exterior use (given in the sidebar on the previous page). David purchased skim milk from a local dairy, lime from a garden store, and pigments and whiting from a paint and decorating supplier, and mixed up a large batch of milk paint. The job was a complete success, and the owners were thrilled to learn that the milk in their paint came from the dairy farm right down the road. David's only complaint was that the paint had to be stirred fairly often to prevent the pigment from settling.

I also followed Tingry's recipes to prepare the milk paint for the test pieces and furniture shown in the photos in this article. The basic formula given in the first recipe in the sidebar is for interior painting. Tingry's second recipe is for exterior use and calls for the addition of a little more lime and oil as well as some pitch or rosin. The third formula in the sidebar, which meets U.S. government specifications, is very similar to Tingry's exterior formula except that it is based on mixing commercially prepared casein with water, instead of using skim milk for the liquid. Because of the addition of the extra oil in the exterior formulas, the milk paint will dry with a darker, glossier look than the flat, chalky look of the interior formula. When mixing in the pigment, bear in mind that the color of milk paint lightens a great deal after it is dry, as shown in the above photo at right. If it is stored for a long time, milk paint made from skim milk may develop an ammonia-like odor, which indicates the degradation of the casein. It is best to use milk paint within two days.

If you want to use milk paint for a project but don't want to make your own, dry milk-paint compound that is ready to mix with water is available from The Old Fashioned Milk Paint Co., PO Box 222, Groton, Mass. 01450. This product can also be purchased from Constantine, 2050 Eastchester Road, Bronx, N.Y. 10461 and other finishing sources listed in mail-order catalogs. A 6-oz. can of milk paint from The Old Fashioned Milk Paint Co. is $7.95. It will make about 1 pint of paint when mixed with water, and 12 colors are available. The company also offers a natural gela-

tin that can be applied between coats of paint to produce a crackle finish. Just like homemade milk paint, this powered milk paint is a child-safe, lead-free finish. However, it may differ slightly from the paint made from Tingry's formula thanks to casein containing less butterfat and to pigment blends of controlled particle size.

Surface preparation and distressing

Milk paint works best on clean, porous surfaces such as unfinished wood, plaster or masonry. It can also be applied over flat latex paint. But if you are going to apply milk paint over other paints or most primers, the surface must have good porosity, which can be achieved by sanding thoroughly with 100-grit or 120-grit paper. When in doubt, apply milk paint over a small area. If it beads up, more sanding is required.

As with all finishing, preparation is of prime importance. If you want a smooth finish, you must paint on a smooth surface. Sand thoroughly, especially endgrain areas; 120-grit paper is a reasonable choice for most purposes, although you may use finer grits on more refined furniture designs. In addition to being smooth, the surface must be clean and free from contamination.

Most Country furniture and other simply designed pieces are enhanced by physical distressing. Believable distressing requires some imagination and some logic. Start by rounding sharp edges and drastically altering sharp corners (as shown on the far right in the above photo at left). You must consider each piece of furniture individually. What areas of the piece receive the most abuse? Logical areas are at or near knobs, locks, handles, feet and lower legs, exposed edges, corners and tops of drawer fronts. If you wish, you can take the distressing a step further by making minor changes in the configuration of turnings or by inflicting dents, scratches, burns and other signs of attrition. Any effect that could normally be caused by accident or hard use is fair game. The degree of physical distressing is somewhat controlled by the style and type of furniture involved. For instance, pine or other softwood pieces are prone to more radical distressing than those made of oak, maple or cherry. Most antique hardwood furniture is in surprisingly good condition. Furniture normally used in the kitchen or pantry will usually show more severe natural distressing than furniture used in halls, bedrooms or parlors. In all instances, discretion is called for—you must distress, not destroy.

Applying milk paint

Once the project is well prepared and distressed if desired, the rest is relatively easy. First, mix up the milk paint to a proper consistency. According to Tingry, the paint should " …run or drop from the brush in a thread when taken from the pot. If the color does not form a thread, it is too thick." Then you just apply this paint as you would other types of paint. Use a synthetic fiber or foam brush—a bristle brush is not recommended. Two or three coats are usually required to ensure good color and film strength. Allow the paint to dry overnight if possible, but in a pinch, two to four hours of drying time between coats will usually suffice.

At this point, if you like the color of the paint, leave it alone. If you want the color to be deeper and stronger, you can wipe on Danish oil, tung oil sealer, or a 50-50 mix of boiled linseed oil and mineral spirits. As shown in the photo below left, a large variety of interesting colors can be achieved by wiping on gel stains after the milk paint has dried. You may also finish your project with conventional wipe-on or brush-on oil-base varnish, polyurethane or water-base finish, to add greater depth of color and better durability, especially on pieces for use outdoors.

Decorative techniques

Although milk paint has a matte, somewhat primitive look that is itself completely adequate as a finish, it may also be used to produce many of the decorative effects common on 18th- and 19th-century furniture that are now enjoying a resurgence of popularity. Some of these effects are sponging, spattering, stippling and dry-brush graining. All of these effects are best accomplished with a relatively dry and stiff brush or sponge, which should be blotted on newspaper each time after it is dipped into the paint, to avoid applying too much color (see the top photo below right). Because of the coarse nature of the paint, sponging several coats with different colors will result in a stone-like texture (see the bottom photo below right). If some areas aren't to be painted, such as the molded area around the field of a raised panel, they should be shellacked before the adjacent areas are painted and then cleaned off carefully with shellac solvent after the paint has dried.

I would like to make a prediction. I think the renewed interest in milk paint may well carry its use for decorative purposes right up to the 21st century and beyond. Certainly a useful product that offers us a link with our past and pampers our environment is a strong candidate for survival. □

Dick Fitch is a painting and finishing consultant for The Bartley Collection in Easton, Md.

A stiff sponge can be used to apply different colors over one another to achieve a stippled or mottled finish (shown top right). When applied this way, the coarse texture of the milk paint has a stone-like quality, as you can see on the painted particleboard tabletop shown bottom right.

Stains can be applied over milk paint to increase the range of colors. Below: This whole panel was painted red and then mahogany stain was applied on the left and fruitwood stain on the right. The panel was then varnished.

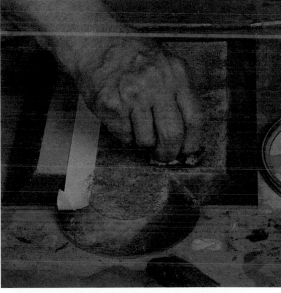

Better Painted Furniture

Use automotive filler and primer to level the wood, aerosol cans to paint and clear coat it

by Chris A. Minick

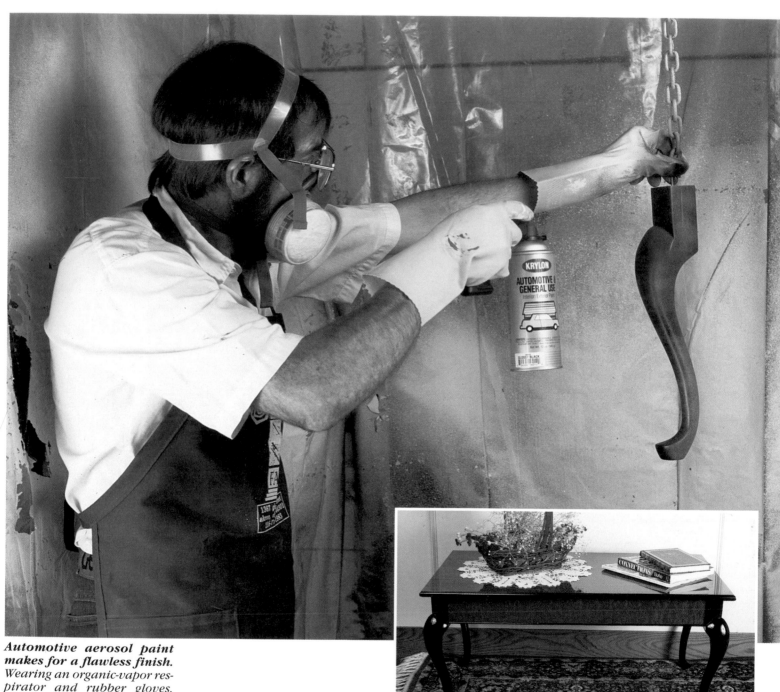

Automotive aerosol paint makes for a flawless finish. *Wearing an organic-vapor respirator and rubber gloves, Chris Minick sprays a cabriole leg in a number of light coats. By hanging the leg from a chain, he can rotate the leg as he fills in missed areas. The spray booth is a U-shaped drape of 4-mil polyethylene hung from his garage rafters. Minick leaves the doors open for ventilation.*

Paint showcases furniture's wood and form—*Painted maple legs emphasize the lines of the author's highly polished coffee table. The black tabletop edges, bottom apron bead and corner legs make an attractive frame around the ribbon-striped-mahogany veneer top and quilted-mahogany veneer apron. The underside of the table is also painted.*

Photos: Alec Waters

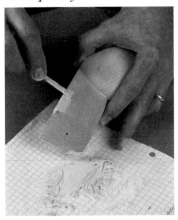

"If it works, don't mess with it," sums up the attitude that many woodworkers have toward finishing. Learning about a new finishing technique can be complicated and confusing. So it seems easier to stick with an old standby like tung oil, or stain followed by varnish, even though it may be merely adequate. If that's your habit, you may have overlooked an important class of finishes—paint.

Paint is a versatile medium because it can be used as a design accent to emphasize the lines of a piece, or it can be used to draw attention to handsome woods in furniture (see the bottom photo on the facing page). A painted finish also lets you use up those too-good-to-burn pieces of scrapwood. But don't be mistaken. Paint cannot cover up poor workmanship or shoddy surfaces. A painted finish requires better preparation than a clear finish. Fortunately, there are some products that make the whole process relatively painless.

If I have to paint a fairly large project or one that needs a special color, I use a good latex paint and an airless sprayer. But for most items, especially the ones that require a professional-looking paint job (such as the coffee-table leg in the top photo on the facing page), I use ordinary aerosol spray cans for priming, painting and clear coating. Auto-parts stores have a marvelous variety of colors and types to choose from. And automotive fillers and putties are superb too.

Learning from automotive finishers

Folks working in the automotive industry are constantly refining paint finishes, due to the meticulous demands of car finishes (see the box at right). That's the main reason I buy many of my furniture-finishing products, including fillers, primers and paints, from my auto-parts store. And given the fact that paint is more easily scratched and more difficult to repair than most clear finishes, I borrow another technique from automobile finishers: I clear coat my painted finishes. Before I buy anything for a project, though, I think through my whole painting strategy.

Planning your paint job

Painting, like any finishing technique, can be frustrating when some unexpected problem arises halfway through the process. The best way to eliminate surprises is to test all your materials and practice new techniques on scrapwood. After all, you wouldn't cut dovetails the first time using prized wood for your project. So you should treat paint-finishing the same way. Paint decisions for a piece of furniture must be made before the first board is cut.

Because my furniture pieces often combine painted elements as well as stained and clear-coated portions, it's easier to finish each component separately, then assemble them. Though this requires careful planning of the construction and care in final assembly, it eliminates complicated masking and leads to better finish results.

When choosing stock for your project, think about which com-

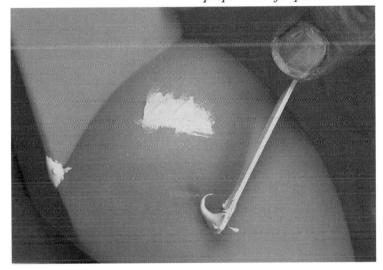

Why new car finishes work on wood

Furnituremakers may question the wisdom of using automotive finishes on wood. After all, aren't car finishes brittle—meant for relatively immobile surfaces like metal instead of dimensionally unstable substrates like wood? Although that argument was true in the past, it is no longer accurate. Automotive primers, aerosol paints, clear-coat finishes and touch-up paints have changed because car components have changed. The latest materials, such as high-impact plastics and composites, are used to manufacture car bumpers, trim and door panels. So paint makers have had to reformulate their coatings to accommodate increasing flexibility. This flexibility allows woodworkers to use car-finishing products on wood, which is notoriously unstable. If you don't care to use finishes from the auto-parts store, you can use most general-purpose aerosol primers, paints and clear coatings to get equally stunning results.

—C.M.

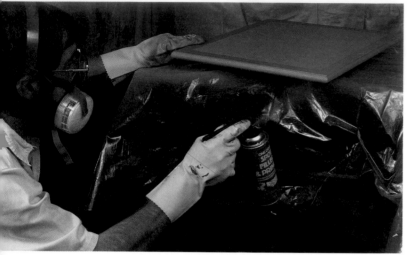

ponents will require special needs. For example, if you decide that certain parts must be real smooth, then maple, poplar and birch are good wood choices. However, if you want to show a bit of wood texture through the paint, then open-grained woods, such as oak and ash, are more appropriate. I wanted smooth, glossy black legs on my coffee table that would enhance the figured-mahogany veneer top and apron. In addition, I wanted the legs to be hard to guard against knocks. For these reasons, maple was the logical wood choice. But as far as the painting goes, the wood used is irrelevant, really, as long as you are careful with the under-paint treatments.

Preparing surfaces and equipment

The key to getting flawless painted furniture is meticulous surface preparation. The monochromatic nature of paint dramatically magnifies minor flaws that would otherwise go unnoticed under a clear finish. Small tearouts, hairline cracks in knots, stray sanding scratches and other seemingly minor defects must be filled and smoothed before painting. This may sound like lots of dismal work, but if you follow car surface-preparation steps, you can reduce the drudgery.

Sanding and filling—All parts should be thoroughly sanded to at least 180-grit and inspected under a strong light; then use auto-body fillers to level off any voids. These polyester fillers (familiar brands include Bondo and White Knight) work exceptionally well at repair because they tenaciously stick to raw wood, cure quickly, sand easily and accept most kinds of oil-based and latex primers and paint. Best of all, they don't shrink. On the down side, they smell bad and have a short working life once mixed, usually less than 15 minutes.

For the coffee-table legs, I filled dents and nicks with two-part auto-body filler (3M's 2K Lightweight putty). I even built out an edge that had been clipped off on the bandsaw (see the top photo on p. 89). I also filled in the knots. No matter how sound they look, knots always have cracks that show through the paint. Knots often contain resins, too, especially in softwoods. So once the filler in the knots had cured (about 30 minutes), I sanded them flush and spot-sealed the knots with shellac just to be safe. Finally, to make the edges of the medium-density fiberboard (MDF) top perfectly smooth, I used some spackle (see the story at left).

Setting up a makeshift spray booth—I don't have a paint booth in my home shop, so before I prime or paint, I set up a crude but effective painting area in my garage (see the top photo on p. 88). Ventilation for my plastic spray booth is provided by a box fan that draws outside air through an open rear door and exhausts it through a partially opened garage door. I also use a good organic-vapor respirator to protect myself when I'm using aerosol cans to spray primer and high-solvent lacquers.

Priming and puttying—Primers serve the same functions for painted finishes as sealers do under clear coats. Primers seal in resins and extractives that may discolor the paint, provide a uni-

Use spackle to fill voids in edges

*Spackle fills voids in medium-density fiberboard—*After masking off the veneered top of his table with paper and acrylic adhesive tape, the author rubs wallboard spackle onto the MDF edges. The spackle adheres well, dries quickly and sands beautifully.

The medium-density fiberboard (MDF) edges of my coffee-table top posed a unique finishing problem for me. Because the top was veneered, I needed a way to hide the MDF core. Edge-banding with solid wood was an option, but that didn't fit my design. I ruled out veneer as well because of the shaped edge that I wanted. So I decided to paint the edges black, like the legs. But first I had to prepare the surface of the MDF for primer.

MDF absorbs finish like a sponge, and the small pits in the core must be filled or they will show through the paint. A few finishers tackle this problem by using glazing coats; this technique requires real skill. Large furniture manufacturers solve the problem by spraying on two-part edge filler/surfacer, but it is expensive, hard to find and requires specialized spray equipment. I avoided all this by wiping a coat of wallboard spackling compound (made by DAP) on the exposed MDF edges (see the photo above). The spackle sands easily, fills the pits and provides a good base for the primer. To save yourself some work, mask off the top and bottom of the tabletop before you start spackling the edges.   —C.M.

For a high-gloss finish, rub out the clear coats with liquid automotive polishing compound. As a finishing touch, Minick buffs out the clear-lacquer topcoat (one of five) on a coffee-table leg.

finer than 320-grit. While you're sanding, be careful not to cut through to the wood, or you will have to re-prime. The object of this final sanding is to level and smooth the surface but still leave some tiny scratches in the primer. This slight texture, called tooth, makes a better bond between the primer and topcoat.

Painting, clear coating and rubbing out

Aerosol paint cans are available in different colors, gloss levels and brands. I have had good luck using both Plasti-kote and Krylon on furniture. Aerosol paints that are low-gloss sand easier than high-gloss ones, but I prefer the high-gloss variety because their higher resin content adds to the durability of the finish. You shouldn't be overly concerned about the actual glossiness, however, because the final sheen of the project will be controlled by the clear coat.

To start painting, I mist a tack coat of paint over all the primed area. Then I spray several light coats to fill in the blanks until the entire surface is covered with a level wet coat. Continued painting at this point will result in runs or sags. Let the solvent evaporate for five minutes or so, and then lay on another coat the same way. Two or three coats are usually enough to provide sufficient color build on a well-primed substrate.

For the tabletop's edge, I overcoated the spackled and sanded edge with the same automotive primer and paint that I used for the legs. The only differences were that I masked off the top and then used a lazy Susan to hold the work (see the top photo on the facing page).

The clear coat is the final touch that sets apart an average paint job from a real showstopper. Clear coats not only protect the paint from occasional dings but also add depth to the finish, which is more suitable for fine furniture. In addition, clear coats unify components by providing a consistent sheen over the entire piece. And clear coats are easier to rub out and repair than paint.

For peace of mind, I usually choose my clear finish from the same resin family as the paint. I used an aerosol automotive clear acrylic on my table project, but any good clear lacquer will work. For the tabletop edges, I clear coated the paint with Pratt & Lambert #38, which is the same varnish I used on the mahogany-veneered top and apron. Four or more clear coats may be needed to achieve a good film thickness (3-4 mils). Remember, some film will be lost when rubbing out, so compensate for this. Make sure that your paint is completely dry before you clear coat. I like to wait several days.

For rubbing out clear coats to a high luster, I like to use liquid automotive buffing compounds (not paste compounds). I've found that car buffing compounds are easier to use than those carried by most wood-finishing-supply places. Both 3M and Meguiar's offer good compounds for polishing. Meguiar's has several formulas with different abrasive levels for hand-rubbing or power buffing. Let the clear coats dry a day or so, and then buff out to whatever sheen you desire (see the photo above). □

form non-porous base for the color coat and highlight any defects that were missed in the filling process. Aerosol primers are sensible to use if you're painting relatively small areas. I often use automotive high-build, scratch-filling primers under pigmented-lacquer paints. High-build primers are easy to apply, sand like a dream and fill in tiny nicks and pits in wood. Adhesion tests in my shop show that automotive primers are completely compatible with high-solvent lacquers, but marginally compatible with oil paints and not at all with latex. When I buy primer at the store, I pick up several different brands of cans and shake each until I hear the little agitator ball dislodge. I pick the can that takes the longest for the ball to loosen because, generally, this means the primer contains a higher percentage of solids. Primers with more solids do a better job and are easier to sand.

Allow the primer to dry thoroughly (it should powder easily when sanded), and then inspect the piece carefully. You'll be surprised at the number of imperfections that will appear on your supposedly smooth wood. You must fill the tiny defects, or they'll show through the paint. Don't use the two-part auto filler this time, though, because it won't stick to the prime coat. Instead, use an automotive glazing putty, which is designed for application over primer (see the bottom photo on p. 89). 3M's Acryl-Blue Glazing putty suits my needs, but any non-shrinking brand should work.

Sand the primer and dried putty smooth. Next apply a final coat of primer. Then sand again—this time to at least 220-grit but not

Chris Minick is a finishing chemist and a woodworker in Stillwater, Minn. He is a regular contributor to Fine Woodworking.

Changing the Color of Wood

A primer on modern stains

by Chris A. Minick

Gel stains are great for vertical surfaces like cabinet sides because, unlike liquid stains, they don't run off.

W hy would anyone want to stain a piece of furniture or cabinetry and cover up the natural color and figure of beautiful wood? While few of us would even consider staining flame-grained mahogany or burled walnut, not all of us can afford to build every project from first-rate cabinet hardwoods. Most woodworkers I know often employ cheaper woods, such as pine, poplar and birch. And the appearance of such plain woods can be enhanced by staining.

In addition to giving inexpensive woods a richer color, stains are indispensable for matching the color of new woodwork to existing wood furnishings or for evening up natural color variations in boards glued up into wider panels. A judiciously applied coat of stain can even lend a subtle color contrast to bring out the spectacular grain of a highly figured exotic species.

But don't expect to get a perfect staining job by picking up the first can of stain you see on the shelf at your local hardware store and sloshing it on. To get good results for a wide range of staining situations, you need to know the characteristics and qualities of different types of stains, so you can choose the best one to obtain the desired effect. Good stain jobs also depend on proper surface preparation and application technique, so the wood receives the stain evenly. A further assurance of success comes from making stain samples to test the color before applying the stain.

Pigmented stains

Most stains used in modern woodworking shops can be divided into two broad cate-

Photos except where noted: Sandor Nagyszalanczy

gories according to colorant type: pigmented stains and dye stains. Pigmented stains are suspensions of finely ground colored minerals (mostly iron oxides) mixed into a solvent-based solution. Pigmented stains color the wood when pigment granules lodge in the natural crevices and grain pores on the surface of the wood. This quality makes pigmented stains a good choice for accentuating the grain of ring-porous woods like oak and ash. Unfortunately, the pigment particles will also lodge in sandpaper scratches and boldly reveal a poor sanding job. Pigment particles are opaque; therefore, they resist fading well. They also act like thin paint to obscure the delicate figure of wood like fiddleback maple, making them good for covering up unattractive inexpensive species or plywood.

Most of the stains you'll find on your local hardware store's shelves are pigmented, oil-based stains. The solvent, or vehicle, used in these stains is mineral spirits, and stains also contain a binder (usually linseed oil or an alkyd resin) that acts like a glue to hold the pigment particles on the wood. Without the binder, the dry pigments would simply rub off. The oil binder is the reason you must apply a seal coat, such as shellac, before using a water-based topcoat over an oil-based stain.

Dye stains

Unlike pigmented stains with color particles suspended in a liquid vehicle, dye stains are mixtures of synthetically derived colored powders that are completely dissolved into solution. The color in a dye stain never settles out, so dye stains don't require extensive stirring. Also, unlike pigmented stains, which are made from a limited range of earth tones, dye stains are available in a wide range of hues, including brilliant primary colors. They are ideal for color-matching applications because you can combine exactly the colors you need to make the stain yellower, greener or bluer.

Dye stain solutions penetrate deeply into the wood matrix, coloring each individual cellulose fiber, accentuating the subtle grain patterns in figured woods. However, dye stains won't bring out the contrast in non-figured open-grained woods like butternut and oak, creating a monotone look I don't care for. Dye stains are not as fade-resistant as pigmented stains, so care should be taken to keep dye-stained wood out of direct sunlight.

Dye stain powders come in three main varieties based on which solvent they're mixed with: water-soluble, oil-soluble and alcohol-soluble dyes. Even though dye stains are often referred to as "aniline" dyes, modern dyes contain no aniline. The name is an unfortunate holdover from 19th-century Germany, where the dyes were first developed from derivatives of aniline (a toxic petroleum-based liquid that's a suspected carcinogen). Rest assured that modern synthetic dye powders are safe to use in the shop.

Water-soluble dyes have the greatest penetrating power of all common wood stains. The deep penetration creates the illusion of depth associated with high-quality furniture. Water-soluble dyes are also relatively resistant to fading, so I prefer them over all others dyes for staining fine hardwoods. And, in case you sand through the finish, water-soluble dyes are more repairable than other wood stains.

Powdered water-soluble dye stains are easily prepared in the shop. Merely dissolve the dye crystals in warm water, let the solution cool to room temperature and it's ready to wipe on the wood. No stinky or hazardous solvents are needed, and cleanup is in warm soapy water. The only real complaint about water soluble dyes is that they raise the wood's grain when applied. But this is easily remedied by wetting the wood before final sanding.

Oil-soluble dyes are closely related to water dyes but are dissolved in a hydrocarbon solvent—usually glycol ether or lacquer thinner. These dyes are often sold pre-mixed as "NGR" (non-grain-raising) stains, so called because the solvent base does not fuzz the grain when applied to raw wood. Oil-soluble dyes form the bridge between pigmented stains and dye stains, giving woodworkers the best of both worlds. But the relatively poor penetration and poor lightfastness of NGR stains somewhat limits their use for fine furniture.

Alcohol-soluble dyes are primarily used for tinting or special effects that can be applied with a spray gun. They dry too fast for any other application method. This feature makes alcohol-soluble dyes popular with production furniture finishers. In the small shop, they're normally used only for touch-ups or finish repairs.

Though they are harder to apply evenly

Stain conditioner prevents a blotchy look

I spent the better part of two months building my first major woodworking project: an Early American-style pine corner cupboard. But when I applied the stain, my would-be masterpiece was instantly transformed into a blotchy mess (even though I carefully followed the directions on the can). I've since learned to eliminate the blotchy stain problem by applying a pre-stain conditioner to the raw wood before applying any solvent-based stain. The stain conditioner evens out the absorbability of the wood, allowing it to take color more uniformly.

Stain controllers made by Minwax and McCloskey are available at most hardware stores, but I home-brew my own conditioner that works fine and costs a lot less. Simply dissolve 1 to 2 cups of boiled linseed oil into 1 gal. of mineral spirits. Brush a heavy coat of the mixture over the entire project, making sure porous areas are kept wet. After 10 minutes or so, wipe off the excess, and follow your normal finishing routine.

Pre-stain conditioners work best on resin rich woods like pine (see the photo at left) cherry or birch. But regardless of species, any parts with lots of exposed end grain (raised panels for instance) will benefit from this treatment, but make a test sample just to be sure. —C.M

Pre-conditioning wood prevents blotchy staining. The author's shop-brewed wood conditioner, applied only to the top half of this pine sample before staining, ensures that all areas of the grain will absorb stain evenly.

than water dyes, alcohol-dye stains have one major advantage over all other stains: They're perfect for tinting or shading wood to create special finishing effects. The best example of this shading technique is the sunburst finish commonly used on guitar bodies.

Any type of dye stain can be a little hard to find locally. The best way to buy them is from woodworking supply catalogs. Woodworker's Supply (1108 North Glenn Road, Casper, Wyo. 82601; 800-645-9292) has a finishing supply catalog that has a complete selection of all types of dye stains. If you don't like to order through the mail, try regular fabric dye from your local grocery store; it's basically a dye stain. A pre-mixed, water soluble dye gel made by Clearwater Color is available from Garrett Wade Co. (161 Avenue of the Americas, New York, N.Y. 10013; 800-221-2942). This product is good for staining vertical surfaces, such as cabinet sides, because the thick gel doesn't run down and make a mess (see the photo on p. 92). Bartley's makes a pigmented gel stain, which is available at hardware stores.

Chemical stains

While certain woodfinishers advocate the use of chemicals for changing wood's color, I'm thoroughly against it for several reasons. First, most chemicals used for wood coloring are strong oxidants or are highly caustic and dangerous if they come in contact with your skin. Further, some chemicals, such as potassium dichromate are very poisonous and potentially fatal if ingested. Worse, potassium dichromate looks like a bright orange-colored kiddie drink when mixed in solution.

The second reason to avoid chemical colorants is that they are unpredictable. They create color by reacting with chemicals naturally present in the wood, and results can vary, even in different sections of the same board. Worst of all, these chemicals can deteriorate (oxidize) the clear finish applied over them! Given the low cost and convenience of modern wood stains, there are plenty of reasons to steer clear of chemical colorants.

Mixing different stains together

If you don't see the color you want on the manufacturer's chart, you can often mix stains from different cans in various proportions to achieve the desired color. The catch is that not all stains have the same vehicles (water, oil, alcohol); some types can be mixed and others can't. Further, all oil-based stains will mix with all other oil-based stains regardless of brand. To be

Sludge settles out of a pigmented stain because the color particles are in suspension. The particles are not dissolved in solution as in a dye stain.

Photo: Susan Kahn

Stains can be mixed or applied in layers. Solvent-compatible stains can be mixed together in the can and applied at once, here over cherry (left sample). Note the difference in the right sample showing the same three stains applied one at a time (from top to bottom): unstained cherry, yellow, reddish mahogany and medium-brown dye stains.

safe, you can always restrict yourself to the same brand name and type. The same goes with water-based stains. Manufacturers sometimes mix two different types of stains together, say, an oil-based pigmented stain and an oil-based dye, for certain colors or special applications. But I'd avoid this practice because it usually brings out the bad qualities of both types and minimizes the good ones.

If you're unsure about the vehicle type of a stain, there are a couple of simple tests you can do. First, smell the stain before it's stirred. It's probably an oil-based pigmented stain if it smells like mineral spirits, and there's a layer of sludge on the bottom of the can (see the photo at left). In contrast, if a drop of stain in a glass of water dissolves, the mixture is probably a water-soluble dye stain. A drop of oil-soluble dye stain will just sit on the surface of the water.

Layering stains for better effects

If you are trying to match an existing finish of a commercially produced piece, chances are the original stain was applied in *layers* rather than all at once. Even if you mix exactly the right shade and hue of color in the can, sometimes the results just aren't satisfying on wood. It is not uncommon for commercial finishers to apply a brightly colored dye stain first to bring out the grain, followed by a wood-toned pigmented stain to even up the color. In practice, I often stain the wood initially with a yellow dye stain before applying additional layers of reddish or brownish stains (see the photo at left). I find this tends to bring out the inner figure and heighten the luster of woods, such as cherry, mahogany and walnut.

Another advantage of layering is that it allows you to mix different stains, even if they're not compatible. Nine times out of ten, you'll get away with it. Even if there's a problem, you can try changing the order in which the stains are applied (save any oil-based/self-sealing stains for the last layer). For a dramatic effect, try applying a dark stain to an open-grained wood (such as oak or ash); then lightly sand before applying a lighter-color stain. The dark color remains only in the open grain while the lighter stain colors the surrounding areas, creating a high-contrast effect. Again, experimenting will show you the true effects, and perhaps you'll discover a color effect you couldn't have gotten out of a can. □

Chris A. Minick is a product development chemist and an amateur woodworker in Stillwater, Minn.

From *Fine Woodworking* (July 1993) 101:66-69

Getting the stain on the wood

There's more to getting a good stain job than just choosing the right color. The final results are determined by how well the wood is prepared (including sanding), choosing the best application method and testing the stain before committing it to your precious workpiece.

Surface preparation

While the degree of surface preparation of raw wood for a clear finish demands fairly standard practices, surface preparation for staining may vary depending on the stain and the wood you choose.

Water-soluble dye stains raise wood's grain and should be applied only after wetting the wood with plain water and sanding the fuzz away after it dries (the grain will not raise again during staining). With pigmented stains, the wood surface *must* be evenly sanded and free of stray scratches; otherwise, the pigment will show scratches (see the top photo). This is especially true on close-grained woods that tend to show scratches anyway. Sand using successive grits, from the roughest to the finest (at least to 180-grit), not skipping more than one grit size between passes. Be especially careful with orbital sanders. Pressing too hard or moving too quickly causes swirl marks that will show up later. Resanding after scratches show up during staining is twice as much work. Certain resinous woods, such as pine, will take stain unevenly even if they've been perfectly sanded, so treat such woods with a pre-stain conditioner, as described in the sidebar on p. 93.

If you're working with dense woods, such as hickory, the degree of sanding affects the amount of pigmented stain the wood accepts, hence the darkness of the final color. It's best not to sand maple with finer than 180-grit paper. Otherwise, the pigment will have no place to stick and the color will look washed out. It is better to switch to a dye stain, which will give you the desired color regardless of how smoothly the surface has been sanded.

Application

There are few restrictions in the way most stains can be applied to wood. You can use a brush, a sponge or a lint-free rag. But avoid paper towels or loosely woven cloth rags that might snag on open-pored woods such as oak. If you own a spray gun and a compressor, spraying can be a time-saving way of applying dye stains to large surfaces, and it's the only way to get an even finish with fast-drying, alcohol-soluble dyes. Avoid spraying pigmented stains. The abrasive pigment particles can damage the delicate (and expensive) nozzle on your spray gun, literally sandblasting it from within.

Pigmented stains should be thoroughly stirred before application to get the pigment particles that have settled to the bottom of the can back into suspension. Otherwise, you'll end up with a considerably different color (see the bottom photo). Because they are true solutions, dye stains can be applied without stirring (I shake them anyhow, just to be sure). Wear gloves and a respirator when applying any solvent-based stain, just as you would for application of a clear wood finish.

The length of time you wait before wiping the excess stain off is relatively unimportant; the final color of the wood is controlled by the concentration of dyes or pigments in the stain formulation. To darken a pigmented stain finish, apply a second coat. To increase the color intensity of a dye stain, increase the concentration of dye powder mixed with the solvent. Incidentally, if you accidentally sand through a dye stain during finishing, apply the original dye solution to the damaged area. The color match will usually be perfect, and the repair will be undetectable.

Test the color first

Examining and evaluating your staining results on raw wood is usually misleading. All stained surfaces look muddy when dry. Dye stains in particular change color considerably once topcoated with a clear finish. Also, different topcoats will change the final color and sheen of the piece in different ways. The best way to avoid surprises is to create one or more test panels before staining the workpiece. First, be sure to use the same species of wood as your project—different wood species take stain differently. After applying stain to your test panel, follow your normal finishing procedures, applying all the coats of stain and clear finish, then waxing and buffing your samples. Second, make your samples from larger boards, not small pieces of scrap. I like my test panels to be 4 in. to 5 in. wide and at least 18 in. long. I've found large sample panels to be indispensable for accurately judging the finished appearance of the project. I save the test panels that look good for reference, with complete finishing instructions written on the back. The ones I don't like are used to heat my shop. —*C.M.*

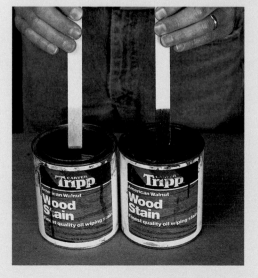

Pigment particles lodge in sanding scratches, revealing a poor sanding job. Proper surface preparation requires careful, even sanding, using successive grades of grit, coarser to finer.

Stirred vs. unstirred pigmented stains can be vastly different in color. Therefore, always mix thoroughly if you are applying stain right out of the can.

For Vibrant Color, Use Wood Dyes

Aniline dyes enhance figure, even out tones

by Chris A. Minick

Getting consistent colors—*Exact measurements and careful record keeping are important for duplicating colors. Wood dyes usually are a blend of colors, visible as dye powder dissolves in water (above) and in filter paper (right).*

Aniline dyes are a good product with a bad name. Their nasty reputation is a holdover from the days when these versatile coloring agents were highly toxic. It's a misnomer not much different from golfers still calling their drivers "woods," even though many modern golf clubs are made of metal. Woodworkers still know dyes by the name "aniline," even though modern wood dyes no longer contain the chemical.

First used in the textile industry in the mid-1800s as a substitute for natural dyes, aniline-derived dyes worked fine, but they faded quickly and were soon replaced by more light-fast synthetic colorants. Unfortunately, the term *aniline dye* stuck. It is still used to distinguish transparent wood stains from their pigmented cousins.

Dyes are useful for special finishing effects, like layering (adding depth) and toning (applying tinted finish). Probably the best use for dyes is evening out differences in color, like those between sapwood and heartwood.

Dyes can work miracles on figured wood (see the photos on the facing page), but they aren't magic. For example, when an uninteresting piece of wood is dyed, it will just become an uninteresting, colored piece of wood.

You can buy premixed-liquid or gel wood dyes or mix-it-yourself powdered dyes. I mostly use powdered dyes, which have an indefinite shelf life. Dye is classified by the solvent that dissolves it. The three classes are water-soluble, oil-soluble and alcohol-soluble dyes (see the sources of supply box on p. 100). Each type has finishing advantages.

From *Fine Woodworking* (September 1995) 114:72-76

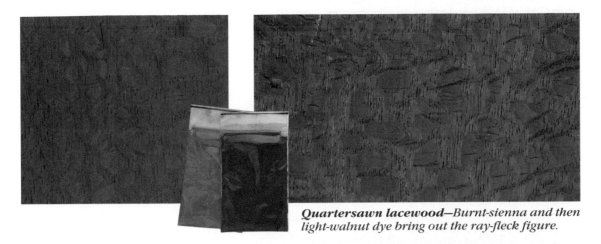

Quartersawn lacewood—Burnt-sienna and then light-walnut dye bring out the ray-fleck figure.

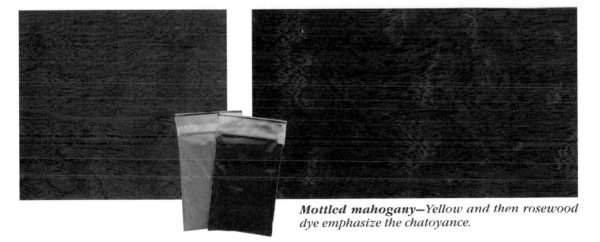

Quilted bigleaf maple—Scarlet red and then cherry-brown dye highlight the undulating figure.

Mottled mahogany—Yellow and then rosewood dye emphasize the chatoyance.

You can even use ordinary fabric dyes. Brands like Rit can be found at department stores, but you'll have to mix or layer several colors to get more natural wood tones. Powdered fabric dyes sometimes have fillers, so I buy the premixed-liquid type. They're fairly inexpensive, so they're good for experimenting.

Dyes are less hazardous than many household cleaners, but you will still need to handle dyes carefully:

• Use a paper mask when mixing the dye.
• Wear rubber gloves, so you don't absorb the dye through your skin.
• Keep dye powders and solutions away from children and pets.
• When a dye is mixed with a flammable solvent, store it properly.
• If you get dye on your clothes, wash them separately.

Differences between pigments and dyes

What distinguishes dye stains from pigment stains is the size of the particle that's doing the coloring. Individual colorant particles in a dye solution are exceedingly small—there are more than 10 million trillion per quart. In comparison, the particles in pigment stains would look like boulders.

Pigments are suspended when in solution; dyes dissolve totally in solvent. The tiny size of dye particles explains why dye stains are so transparent and why they penetrate wood so deeply. Pigments stay near the surface of wood where they lodge in wood pores, which emphasizes the pores and any blemishes like sanding scratches. Dyes color everything similarly. Even end grain can be dyed so that it looks like the rest of the wood.

Water-soluble dyes have lasting color and clarity

Water-soluble dyes are the most versatile of the three wood-finishing dyes. Water-soluble dyes are easier to use, easier to repair and are more light-fast than the other two types. The exceptional clarity and penetration of water-soluble dyes help make figure come alive. Laboratory experiments confirm that water-soluble dyes penetrate the wood about five times deeper than alcohol-soluble dyes. The deep penetration and chemical structure of water-soluble dyes account for their superior fade resistance. (The story on p. 98 gives a general explanation of how fading occurs.)

To mix water-soluble dyes, I use a gram scale to weigh the water and dye powder (see the photo on the facing page). Keep track of dye brands, colors and concentrations every time you use them. If you ever have to match a color, a mixing logbook will save you hours of making up sample stain boards. Once the dye is mixed, sponge the wood with the solution until the wood is thoroughly wet. Wipe off the excess before it dries. (Leaving wet dye stain on wood for a long time will not darken the color any further.)

Because water raises wood grain and makes the surface fuzzy, water-soluble dyes do the same. Fortunately, there is a simple solution to this. I flood the wood with clear water after I have sanded to 180-grit. After the wood dries overnight, I knock down the raised grain with 220-grit sandpaper. Once the grain has been sanded flat, the dye stain will not raise the grain again.

Blotch-prone woods like cherry and pine don't fair any better with water-soluble dyes than they do with solvent-based pigment stains. To minimize blotchiness, I substitute a hide-glue size for the initial coat of clear water. Make the glue size fairly dilute (by weight, I use one-part hide glue granules to nine-parts water). If you use pre-mixed hide glue, you'll have to dilute it as well. Once dry, the size accepts the dye stain evenly. This only works with hide glue, though. I once ruined a butternut desk by trying white-glue size.

Oil-soluble dyes can customize stain color

Most woodworkers have used gallons of oil-soluble dye over the years and don't even know it. Pigment-stain manufacturers often include oil-soluble aniline dyes in their stain formulations to add a little life to an otherwise dull stain. (To learn more about the uses of pigment and dye in stains, see the article on pp. 92-95.) Oil-soluble dyes will dissolve in common shop solvents, like mineral spirits or VM&P naphtha, but they dissolve most completely in lacquer thinner.

Once dissolved in solvent, oil-soluble dye can be added to linseed oil, Danish oil or varnish to make a custom color. In solution, oil-soluble dyes can also be added to a can of pigment stain to modify the color. One problem with oil-soluble dyes is their lack of clarity. Because of their muddy look, I don't like to use oil-soluble dyes on raw wood. But I still keep a full array of colors in my shop for tinting varnishes when I'm toning areas of furniture.

Alcohol-soluble dyes tint shellac, lacquer

Comedian George Burns once asked a clothing-store clerk what the shrink-resistant label on socks meant. She replied, "The socks will shrink, but they really don't want to." The latest alcohol-soluble dyes, touted as "fade-resistant," are somewhat analogous to this. I've found that most of these alcohol-soluble dyes will fade, but they really don't want to. They do have a place, though. Furniture restorers like them for tinting shellacs and solvent-based lacquers in touch-up work.

Alcohol-soluble dyes can be dissolved in methanol (wood alcohol) or ethanol (grain alcohol). I like ethanol because it's the least toxic of the two. Alcohol-soluble dyes dry very rapidly, so they can leave lap marks when brushed or wiped on. Spraying is really the only acceptable way to apply them to large surfaces. Because most alcohol-soluble dyes fade quickly, I find little use for them in my shop.

Non-grain-raising dye stains save sanding

Dye stains that do not raise wood grain are called NGR (non-grain raising) stains. Although NGR stains are technically not a separate class of dye stains, many woodworkers view them as such. But here's the rub: Some brands (the bad ones) are just oil-soluble dyes dissolved in solvent. They give wood the bland look of oil-soluble dyes. Good brands of NGR stains, like Behlen's Solar-Lux (see the sources of supply box on p. 100), are water-solu-

---

Dyes go deep but still fade

Pigments tend to obscure wood's fine details. By contrast, dyes are more transparent, which lets the wood show through. Instead of muddying subtleties in figure, dyes enhance them, as shown in the photo at right.

Even though dyes penetrate more than pigments, dyes fade more. Fading is a form of photochemical degradation. Though ultraviolet light plays a part in fading, intense visible light is mainly responsible.

Visible light is composed of seven colors: red, orange, yellow, green, blue, indigo and violet. White light is a blend of all these colors. A red dye stain looks red because the dye absorbs the other colors and reflects only the red.

Dyes are large, organic molecules primarily composed of atoms of carbon, hydrogen, nitrogen and oxygen. The arrangement of these atoms within each molecule dictates how a dye responds to light.

Quite often, enough light energy is absorbed by a dye molecule to initiate a photochemical reaction, which changes the arrangement of its atoms. Photochemically changed molecules usually are colorless. Because of this, the color becomes more dilute; therefore, the dyed wood appears lighter—faded. Pigments produce color the same way as dyes, but they are more immune to fading.

Alcohol-soluble dyes fade the fastest. The alcohol-dyed half of the sample shown in the photo at right faded from a nice walnut color to swamp-green in less than two months under fluorescent lighting. Water-soluble dyes fade the least (see the unfaded portion of the photo at right). Oil-soluble dyes fall somewhere in between.

Even though the fading of dyes is inevitable, don't let it prevent you from using them. If you use a fade-resistant dye, your project should remain the same color for decades. —C.M.

Pigment (top) vs. dye stain

Faded (top) vs. unfaded

ble or organic dyes that, through a chemical sleight of hand, offer decent clarity and penetration without making the wood fuzzy. If you drop some NGR stain in clear water and it dissolves, it's a good one.

NGR stains made with water-soluble dye still lack the depth of penetration of water-dissolved dyes, so they look a little flat by comparison. There are rare occasions, though, when a water-soluble dye is impractical. Intricately carved areas, for example, can't be sanded easily after a water-soluble dye has raised the grain. For these situations, I'll use an NGR stain. I make my own by mixing concentrated powdered dye with hot water and then diluting the solution with lacquer retarder from James B. Day & Co. (1 Day Lane, Carpentersville, IL 60110; 708-428-2651). A volume ratio of one-part dye solution to three-parts retarder is about right.

Adjusting dye color to suit the wood

Customizing the color of a dye stain is easy. All dyes within a solvent class can be intermixed. For instance, any two water-soluble dyes can be mixed or layered to produce a third color (see the top photo at right). Likewise, colors within the alcohol-soluble and oil-soluble families of dyes can be blended.

Dye colors are not always consistent from one supplier to the next or even from one batch to another from the same company. Luckily, you can modify the color slightly by adding small amounts of liquid dye-tinting colors. I use Dayco brand (carried by James B. Day & Co. and most professional paint-supply stores).

You can also tint dye to get that special color you want. A dull-looking walnut can be livened up, for example, by adding a bit of red tint. Adding green to a cherry dye

stain (which is often too red) will cool the overall color to a more natural cherry tone. Conversely, dyes that are too blue can be warmed by adding orange dye.

Color intensity (how light or dark a dye stain is) is controlled by the amount of solvent in the dye solution. So if your dye stain is too light, just add more dye powder. I add a little black India ink to my dye stains when the standard color is a little too bright and needs to be toned down a shade or two. India

ink is not a dye, but rather a dispersion of very fine lamp-black pigment that imparts a neutral gray tone to dye solutions. Incidentally, quarter-sawn walnut stained with India ink makes a decent substitute for ebony.

Special effects: layering, shading and toning

Woods with large, open pores like oak look a little strange when stained with dye. The areas between the grain lines color evenly, but the open pores do not. Dyed oak

usually lacks contrast between the earlywood and latewood bands.

I solve this problem by layering a pigment stain over a dye stain. I start with a yellowish-brown, water-soluble dye, seal it with shellac (let it dry) and then wipe on walnut-colored pigment stain. The shellac prevents the walnut stain from coloring the areas between the grain lines. But the pigment does color the open pores. The result looks like antique oak.

The basic idea behind layer-

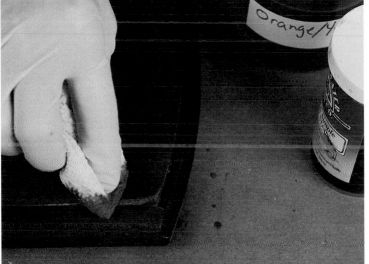

Use dyes for finish touch-ups. The author stains a sand through on a mahogany tabletop. After he applies an orange-red dye, he'll seal the repair with shellac. Once that's dry, he'll wipe on the rosewood dye and seal it in preparation for a topcoat.

Giving wood a new look—To give butternut a rich, two-tone look, dye the earlywood and latewood separately. With ring-porous woods, coloring between grain lines is easy.

Dyes are great for special color effects. After building a case for his son's electric guitar, the author custom-finishes the lid. Successive bands of color create a sunburst effect.

ing is to create distinct depths of color within the wood. Layering different dye stains produces an effect that cannot be achieved any other way. Dye-layered finishes look particularly stunning on wooden instruments.

One of my favorite layered finishes is for mahogany. I start by applying a bright yellow dye stain to all surfaces. This first layer, called a ground stain, highlights the figure deep in the wood and evens the color of the separate boards that make up a piece. The next layer is a coat of rosewood dye stain made by Clearwater Color Co. (Highland Hardware, 1045 N. Highland Ave. N.E., Atlanta, GA 30306; 800-241-6748). The rosewood dye gives the wood a rich, reddish-brown hue. The topcoat of finish can even be tinted to bring out other highlights. The timing of the dye applications is critical to getting distinct layers. For instance, I apply the second dye when the ground-stain looks dry but feels damp. The second dye does not penetrate as deeply as the first, so two layers of color are formed.

As I mentioned, certain dyes are soluble in finishes. Oil-soluble dyes can tint oil finishes and oil-based varnishes. Alcohol-soluble dyes can tint shellac and lacquer. Water-soluble dyes and NGR stains can tint waterborne finishes. Because all these dye-tinted finishes are transparent, two fancy techniques, toning and shading, are possible.

Toning is applying a tinted finish to an entire piece to alter the overall color slightly. Shading is more of a decorative effect that's achieved by selectively applying a tinted finish to highlight areas of a piece. Shading the center of a tabletop darker than the edges, for example, gives the table a worn, aged look.

You can improve your dyeing methods with different applicators. With small brushes, for example, you can color in areas of wood or add detail, as shown in the bottom photo on p. 99. With a spray gun, you can cover large areas or add zones of color (see the photo above).

But the best advice for using dyes, no matter how you apply them, is to experiment with a dye stain on scrap until you're happy with the color. If you absolutely hate the results, don't despair. You can sponge on full-strength chlorine bleach, and the color will disappear. □

Chris Minick is a finishing chemist and a contributing editor to FWW. He works wood in Stillwater, Minn.

Sources of supply	Water-soluble dyes	Alcohol-soluble dyes	Oil-soluble dyes	NGR stain
H. Behlen & Bros., 4715 State Highway 30, Amsterdam, NY 12010; (518) 843-1380	✓	✓		✓
Furniture Care Supplies, 5505 Peachtree Road, Chamblee, GA 30341; (800) 451-0678	✓	✓	✓	✓
Garrett Wade Co., 161 Ave. of the Americas, New York, NY 10013; (800) 221-2942	✓	✓		✓
Homestead Finishing Products, 11929 Abbey Road, N. Royalton, OH 44133-2677; (216) 582-8929	✓	✓		
Lee Valley Tools, 1080 Morrison Drive, Ottawa, Ont., Canada, K2H-8K7; (800) 461-5053 (U.S.)	✓			✓
Olde Mill Cabinet Shoppe, 1660 Camp Betty Washington Road, York, PA 17402; (717) 755-8884	✓	✓	✓	✓
Woodcraft, 210 Wood County Industrial Park, Parkersburg, WV 26102; (800) 225-1153	✓			
The Woodworkers' Store, 4365 Willow Drive, Medina, MN 55340; (800) 279-4441	✓	✓		
Woodworker's Supply, 1108 N. Glenn Road, Casper, WY 82601; (800) 645-9292	✓	✓	✓	✓

Glazes and Toners Add Color and Depth

Layered finishes allow correction, enhancement

by David E. Colglazier

Many woodworkers assume they're committed to store-bought stain colors. For some finishing jobs, though, a one-time application of stain just won't do. But by adding colored finish layers at the right time, you can alter or compensate for an existing color as you go, getting exactly the right result. Two finishing products, glazes and toners, will let you do this.

Glazing and toning can add depth and color to a finish or adjust the hue to get the look you're after. I rely on both methods in my antique-restoration work because there's no other finishing process I'm aware of that can bring such subtle refinement or dimension to a finish. Despite their similarities, glazes and toners are used differently.

Glazes rely on an applicator to add texture or simulate grain detail. It helps to think of glazing as painting (see the photo below) because you're covering, or at least partially obscuring, a base color of some kind. Glazes usually go on just before the topcoats so that you won't disturb or cover up the brushstrokes.

Toners are generally not manipulated with a brush or rag after

Glazing transforms color and adds detail. *Glazes are colored finish layers applied over a sealed base, like this painted cabriole leg. Glazes stay workable long enough for blending and texturing.*

> *I rely on both glazing and toning in my antique-restoration work because there's no other finishing process I'm aware of that can bring such subtle refinement or dimension to a finish.*

they are applied. Think of toning as applying thin layers to alter the overall color of a piece. Spraying is best.

Glazes and toners are great for refinishing, restoration and color matching, but they aren't for every job. They require more artistic skill than other finishing methods. With glazing and toning, you need to know how to spray a finish. You often have to lock in a layer of glaze or toner by spraying a coat of nitrocellulose lacquer or shellac. If your shop isn't equipped to do this, you can use aerosol cans of lacquer (made by Deft) and shellac (Wm. Zinsser & Co.), which are readily available.

Layering is the key

The human eye is a very perceptive tool. With training, it can observe at least five variables of a finish: surface defects, wood-pore and flat-grain color, finish depth, topcoat sheen and texture. Glazes and toners rely on the eye's ability to perceive depth. By visualizing what the final result will look like two or three steps ahead, I can plan glaze and toner layers that will compensate for or correct a hue that isn't quite right. (The story on p. 105 gives a brief explanation of color matching.) Each layer, whether opaque transparent or somewhere in between, affects the final color, texture and readability of the underlying wood.

Layering a finish is like building a house from the foundation up. Layers can be applied in many orders, but some are more practical than others. From the wood up, this might be a finish-layering sequence: tint and apply pore filler, dye or stain to get the right flat-grain color, correct the hue with a toner or semitransparent glaze, lock that in with a clear layer, add a thicker glaze for texture, tone where needed to add color or shade, and put on the topcoats. Toners can be added just about anytime in the layering process to change the overall color because, usually, they are nothing more than tinted finish. However, if you want to apply a heavy, textured glaze, you typically would apply it at the end of the layering. Unlike toners that can serve as their own barrier layer, glazes always need to be topcoated.

What are glazes and toners?

Glazes and toners are special stains meant to be applied over a sealed surface, rather than applied to bare wood. Glazing stains come as liquids in cans and are most often brushed or wiped on with a cloth. Toning stains come in aerosol cans (see the sources of supply box on p. 105). The pigments used as colorants in glazes make them opaque. Toners usually are a lacquer-based solution of dye and/or pigments. They're almost always thinner and more transparent than glazes, but here's where the terminology can get

Glazes make a leg look old. *The author used glazes on three legs of a table (above) to match a leg that had darkened from iron reacting with tannin. He applied a tan base color and then defined the pores and grain patterns with darker glazes.*

Wiping off a glaze changes the look. *To show how color and texture can dramatically change, the author brushes and then wipes off a burnt umber glaze on one of the oak legs (right). Mineral spirits or naphtha can be used to soften or remove an oil-based glaze layer. A sampling of brushes used for texturing is in the background.*

confusing. What some finishers call toner, others refer to as shading stain. Likewise, glazing is sometimes called antiquing. To distinguish some of the terms, I put together a glossary of common colorants (see the box below).

Great for restoration jobs and color matching

Old finishes are not uniform. They become worn in places, faded in others. They accumulate dings, dirt and wax from being used and polished over the years. To match the finish of an old piece of furniture, you have to fake the patina it has acquired, which can

Glossary of common colorants

The two most common colorants are pigments and dyes (not including substances that chemically alter wood color, such as bleaches). Pigment and dye stains can be applied to wood or as colored layers of finish.

The definitions (to simplify things, I omitted paints) at right are partially adapted from several manufacturers' literature and from Bob Flexner's book *Understanding Wood Finishing: How to Select and Apply the Right Finish*, Rodale Press, 33 E. Minor St., Emmaus, PA 18098; 1994. –D.C.

Pigments: Ground opaque particles that, when added to a binder, color wood at the surface, lodging in pores, scratches and defects. Pigment stains vary from semiopaque to semitransparent and fade slowly. Pigments are a key ingredient in glazes (see *FWW on Finishes and Finishing Techniques*, pp. 78-79).

Dyes: Tiny particles that color wood or dissolve in finish to add a transparent color layer. Dyes penetrate deeply but are known to fade. Because of their clarity, dyes offer good depth and grain readability. Dyes are often used for toning (see pp. 96-100).

Anatomy of a layered finish

A layered finish can add depth to a piece, adjust color, obscure or pronounce detail, add an aged look and permit easier repair to the finish. The order of the layers can vary. The illustration shows just one example.

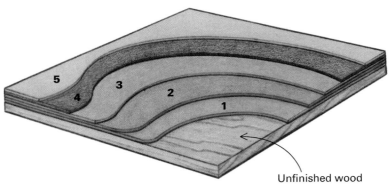

Unfinished wood

1) Tint, fill pores and dye or stain flat grain.

2) Apply sealer (may be colored).

3) Add toning layers and barrier layers (if needed).

4) Use glazing layer for final color adjustment and surface texture.

5) Apply topcoat(s) to seal, give protection and add sheen.

be complex. Mixing up trial stains (see the article on pp. 53-55) could get you the right color, but stains ordinarily are used directly on the wood. Once applied, they are difficult to remove. By contrast, glazes and toners are layered over a sealed base (see the drawing above). Glazes can add an unusual color or mimic a grain pattern. Toners can blend in a repair, hide a wood defect or create a special effect, such as shading. I use toners more than glazes, though I often use a combination of both in the same project.

Glazes and toners could be useful if you want to make new work look old or add a special look to a new piece, like a sunburst.

Glazes and toners conceivably could give more mileage to an undesirable piece of wood. For example, a glaze could be applied to a board to simulate figure. Or, to get wider stock for a panel, you could tone the sapwood so it matches the heartwood.

To lock in a layer, use a barrier

Glazes and toners can be layered one over the other or separated by a clear film (barrier) of finish. When you don't want to disturb what's underneath, you should spray on a barrier layer. I use nitrocellulose lacquer mostly and sometimes shellac. I avoid water-

Stains: A broad label applied to any mixture of pigments, dyes, resins and solvents that alters wood color. The percentage of pigment affects the clarity: Glazing and pickling stains are semiopaque, pigmented stains are semitransparent and penetrating stains are quite transparent (see pp. 92-95).

Glazes: A fairly thick oil-, varnish- or water-based stain that contains pigments. Glazes are usually brushed or wiped over a sealed surface and spread or partially removed as (or just after) the thinner evaporates. Glazes are used for antiquing, coloring pores, accenting grain patterns and adding depth to carvings and turnings.

Toners: Fast-drying solution (usually lacquer) containing dyes and/or pigments applied to a sealed surface to alter the color. Toners are sprayed on the entire surface and left to dry. Pigmented toners tend to obscure the under-color and detail; dye toners are more transparent.

Shading stains: Designed for highlighting, shading stains are specialized toners that are applied to specific areas. They can give a shaded appearance to a surface or blend regions of color. Tinting lacquers are similar products that build quickly and are used to unify tones.

Drawing: Heather Lambert

A glaze patina—The author applies dark glaze to a corner block for an old door frame to emphasize its age. After a light wash coat, he can dab on heavier coats in the recesses of the rosette and nail holes to simulate an accumulation of dirt.

Toning unifies an antique sofa table. The author often tones and glazes furniture parts separately. Here, he sprays the legs and stripped table edge with a red mahogany toner. He used pigment from a can of dark stain to glaze the edges of the stretcher. The legs were wiped with this glaze, left to dry and then shellacked.

Toner used as a shading stain—To simulate a table with a faded center, the author shades the edge of this mahogany top with a dark toner. After he rings the top with light, even coats, he can refine the look and color by spraying other toner bands.

borne lacquers because they can cause compatibility problems.

A barrier can lock in a layer of color and let you, with care, alter a subsequent layer without damaging what's under it. Lacquer barriers or lacquer-based toners can help melt one layer into the next. If a glaze layer doesn't look right, it can be removed with a rag dampened with the appropriate solvent (mineral spirits or naphtha for an oil-based glaze). Each glaze, toner and barrier layer should be thoroughly dry before you do the next. Be especially careful when spraying lacquer over oil-based glazes because wrinkling can occur if each isn't allowed to dry thoroughly. I use several thin coats of lacquer or shellac, so any solvent will evaporate completely. Certain shellacs can introduce yellowing; however, that might be what I need to give the piece a golden, aged look.

Glazes are applied and then manipulated

Glazes develop a bite on an undercoat as the solvent evaporates, but they still offer plenty of working time (5 to 10 minutes). I apply the glaze over the surface and work it until the brush starts dragging (see the photo at left on p. 102). This happens as the glaze turns flat. I can use a brush or rag to remove glaze from the high spots, leaving the recesses (see the photo on p. 103).

Sometimes I use a dry-brushing technique, which is glazing with an almost empty brush. The bristles stay soft, not tacky or stiff as they would if the glaze were drying. Dry brushing offers the most control for putting down a minimal amount of glaze. To soften an oil-based glaze, I apply mineral spirits or naphtha after the bite occurs. This gives me a bit more time to experiment and is especially useful when I'm matching wood patterns or texture.

Viscous glazes applied over a nonporous surface can be manipulated with rags or brushes to produce special effects. Marbleizing, graining, faux-finishing and antiquing are all forms of glazing. Glazing brushes come in an assortment of sizes and bristle types. Many finish-supply stores carry a good selection of them.

I prefer oil-based glazes because of better compatibility between brands and because the solvents don't rapidly affect the previous layers I've applied. To get started, it's a good idea to practice with just a couple of glazes from one product line. Then you can expand your range with confidence. As you get better, you can use glazes in more creative ways (see the top photo at left).

Toners are sprayed on and left to dry

Toners come in many pigment and dye combinations ranging from opaque to transparent. Transparent toners can be layered to adjust color without losing the distinction between the pores and the flat grain. I probably use transparent toners the most. They're ideal for shading (see the bottom photo at left) and for blending colors on components of an original piece (see the center photo). Using opaque toners can be like glazing. The color becomes muddier and the wood lacks grain definition, but this can be an advantage when, for example, I need to disguise a blemish. The thickness of the layer can be varied to get more opaqueness, too.

You can make your own toners by mixing dry pigments and/or alcohol-soluble aniline dyes in shellac or lacquer. For toning (shading) specific areas of furniture, I mix up a shading stain using lacquer and a low concentration of dye. I apply the shading stain in three or four thin layers so that I can sneak up on the color and not overdo it. I can always add another light layer, but if the color is too dark, it's nearly impossible to lighten uniformly. Every job hones your application skills and perception of color. □

David Colglazier and his wife, Laurie, own and operate Original Woodworks, an antique furniture and trunk-restoration company in Stillwater, Minn.

Color matching made easier

I often have to match colors that a client or a decorator has selected. It can be tricky finishing a piece so it goes well with a rug, the wallpaper, the couch fabric, the curtains and the other wood in the room. There are three things that make my job easier: a color wheel, stain-sample sticks and the proper lighting.

Color correction is the art of knowing which color additives are needed to make a certain hue. For instance, red can warm up brown, and green can cool it. As simple as this sounds, the permutations of hue become far more numerous by adding black and white to darken or lighten the color.

Interestingly, men have more difficulty at color matching than women because more men have color blindness in the red and green regions of the spectrum. I don't have this problem, but even so, I still need help with color decisions. I use a primary color wheel. Grumbacher wheels (called Color Computers) are available from Star Finishing Products (see the sources box at right). The wheels come with directions and a summary of color theory.

Stain sticks, a collection of stir sticks that are already stained, are also helpful. The sticks (I use Old Masters brand, but you can make your own) are

Stain sticks aid color choices—Guided by a fan of stain sticks, the author chose a glazing stain for this tabletop. The samples also helped the customer come up with a color that makes the veneer band look natural and blend with the chair fabric.

pinned at one end like a set of feeler gauges. I can fan them out (see the photo above) and ask the customer to determine the color direction. I don't have to make up a wall full of sample boards.

Back at the shop, I try to match colors under the same light that will be used to view the piece. True colors can change as a result of the light source. For example, incandescent light is rich in red; fluores-cent light is predominantly blue. A balance of cool-white and full-spectrum fluorescent bulbs is pretty close to sunlight.

Recently, I replaced the fixtures in my shop with T8 lamps made by Philips, which use triple-phospho-rous tubes. The tubes are very efficient. The light has a warm color tempera-ture and a more natural look in the shop. They've made color matching much easier. —D.C.

Sources of supply for toners and glazes

Constantine, 2050 Eastchester Road, Bronx, NY 10461; (800) 223-8087

Liberon/Star Supply, P.O. Box 86, Mendocino, CA 95460; (707) 937-0475

Mohawk Finishing Products, Inc. (H. Behlen & Bros.), Route 30 N., Amsterdam, NY 12010; (800) 545-0047

Olde Mill Cabinet Shoppe, 1660 Camp Betty Washington Road, York, PA 17402; (717) 755-8884

Star Finishing Products, Inc., 360 Shore Drive, Hinsdale, IL 60521; (708) 654-8650

The Woodworkers' Store, 4365 Willow Drive, Medina, MN 55340; (800) 279-4441

Woodworker's Supply, Inc., 1108 N. Glenn Road, Casper, WY 82601; (800) 645-9292

Creating an Antique Painted Finish

Two days and a dozen steps to a centuries-old look

by Kirt Kirkpatrick

No, it wasn't made by the conquistadors. *Though it looks like it's been in a Spanish Colonial mission for several hundred years, this hall table is really less than a year old.*

Photos: Vincent Laurence

I started experimenting with painted finishes that look old because I live in a very old region of the country. The Native American and Spanish Colonial cultures are still very much a part of the look here in New Mexico.

In collaboration with my friend Dwayne Stewart, who's a painter and professional finisher in Kansas City, Mo., I've developed a method that makes even new furniture look like it's been around for a long time.

Selecting and preparing the wood

I use old wood whenever I can, but new wood can be stained dark to make it look older.

Tool marks make a big difference, too. I eliminate machine marks with hand tools, and I gouge the wood intentionally. A 17th-century Spanish craftsman here in the desert Southwest might have had an adze, a drawknife, maybe a handplane (but likely not) and not much more. And he certainly didn't have any fancy sharpening stones. So the surfaces you see on most old furniture around here is kind of rough. I achieve a similar effect by planing against the grain in places (especially near knots), causing tearout, skewing the blade on my plane so it gouges the surface, keeping the blade intentionally dull and burnishing sharp edges. This may run counter to everything you've learned, but the results are convincing (see the photo at left).

Once I'm happy with the surface, finishing begins. Because I use latex paint and a quick-drying clear coat, I can complete the process in less than two days (see "An antique finish in 12 steps" for a thorough description of the process). Not bad for a finish that looks like it's seen some history. ☐

Kirt Kirkpatrick lives in Albuquerque, N.M. He carves and builds furniture and doors.

AN ANTIQUE FINISH IN 12 STEPS

1. Burnish the edges. Furniture doesn't age, or wear, evenly. Sharp corners, edges and other crisp details soften first. The author uses the shank of a large nail to round over the sharp edges on a tabletop.

2. For a light wood like pine, use a dark stain. Because wood changes color as it ages, the author uses a pigmented oil stain (Minwax Early American) to darken this tabletop made of ponderosa pine. But any kind of stain will do. Then he lets the stain dry according to the manufacturer's instructions.

3. Seal in the color with a clear coat. The author brushes on two coats of lacquer, but other clear finishes will work as well. Just be sure to use something with a low sheen.

4. Scuff-sand the clear coat. A quick once-over with 220-grit dulls the sheen and gives the clear coat enough tooth to hold a coat of paint.

5. Wax prevents paint from adhering, which lets the stained wood show through. Rub a bar of paraffin lightly over the edge and a bit on the top. Let the bar skip along, so the pattern will be uneven. Wax the edge more heavily, but still intermittently.

6. Apply a first coat of flat latex paint. Coverage doesn't have to be perfectly even, and it's probably better that way. Choose a color that contrasts well with the topcoat. Give it an hour or two (or whatever it says on the can) to dry.

7. Brush on a coat of hide glue. The author uses premixed liquid hide glue, but hot hide glue also works. If the premixed glue appears too thick to brush out, thin it slightly with some warm water. Mix well before applying it. A thicker coat will give you fewer, bigger cracks in the next layer of paint; a thinner coat will give you smaller cracks but more of them. Don't worry about laying down an even coat (variations in the size of the cracks look more realistic), but apply the glue in only one direction. If you're haphazard with your strokes, the crackle pattern won't look right. This is the only step you really have to be finicky about. Give the glue half an hour or so to dry.

9. & 10. Scrape and then sand the top and edges. When the second coat of paint is dry, use a paint scraper to remove paint sitting on top of the wax. The scraper also will dislodge loose chunks of paint to reveal the first layer below. Mist the surface with water, and then rub with your fingers to create an even more authentic look. Sand lightly to soften sharp edges.

8. Apply a second coat of flat latex. Make sure that the paint is flat; semigloss or gloss paint won't crackle. Keep a wet edge, move quickly and don't go over your previous strokes, or you'll fill in the cracks. This second coat starts to crackle almost immediately. Let it dry thoroughly, preferably overnight.

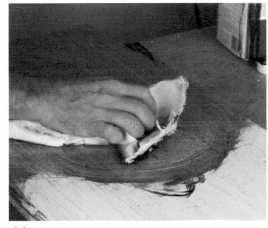

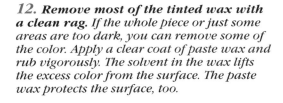

11. Apply a coat of medium- or dark-tinted liquid wax. The author uses Watco dark-satin finishing wax. This wax seeps into all the cracks and recesses and gives the whole piece a darker, almost dirty look—instant patina. Temperature affects drying time. The author usually waits about 10 to 15 minutes.

12. Remove most of the tinted wax with a clean rag. If the whole piece or just some areas are too dark, you can remove some of the color. Apply a clear coat of paste wax and rub vigorously. The solvent in the wax lifts the excess color from the surface. The paste wax protects the surface, too.

Blending several colors on a hot knife yields just the right shade for an invisible repair. After mixing the resin thoroughly with a small screwdriver, the author flows the molten resin into the damaged area. Burn-in repairs will accept virtually any topcoat.

Burning In Invisible Repairs
Hot knife and resin sticks save time and effort

by Robert Judd

Whether trying to rescue a hand-polished antique or save a chunk of exotic hardwood from the scrap pile, burn-in sticks and a hot knife can make virtually invisible repairs. A distant cousin of sealing wax, burn-in techniques have been around for centuries. Burning-in can disguise or cosmetically cover scratches, chips and other damage in a finely finished piece. The repair sticks are available in a host of colors and tints and readily intermix to match any color. Because the various resins and materials used to formulate the repair sticks

accept virtually any topcoat, the repair's finish can precisely match the original. A burn-in repair is a reversible process; you can scrape it out and start over if you don't like the color match or result. These simple repairs can save hours of rebuilding or refinishing time.

In this article, I'll look at the burn-in repair process: color matching, preparation, filling the defect, leveling the repair, adding wood-grain details and touch-up finishing. Before trying to repair your favorite piece of furniture, I suggest practicing on a scrap panel of finished wood. It's

a simple process, and the basic skills can be learned in a couple of hours. But you also can spend a lifetime perfecting those skills. If you're dealing with a valuable antique, you should consult a professional prior to attempting any repair.

Tools and materials

Burn-in repairs don't require a huge inventory of expensive tools, compressors and spray guns. A hot knife, a selection of shellac-resin sticks, a few other miscellaneous supplies and a can of spray lacquer can get you through most of the repairs

From *Fine Woodworking* (September 1993) 102:70-73

that you'll encounter (see the sources of supply box on p. 113).

The sticks are melted into place using a hot knife, either a thermostatically controlled electric knife or a manual knife with an alcohol lamp using denatured alcohol as its fuel. Don't try to use a candle as a heat source because it produces soot that mixes with and changes the color of the repair material. I've also heard of using soldering irons, but I don't advocate the practice. The iron is too hot and can burn the stick shellac, as well as the wood you are trying to repair.

I prefer the electric knife because it poses little fire hazard, and it maintains a consistent temperature. My tool of choice is a lightweight, slim and highly maneuverable knife made by Hot Tools, Inc. (see the sources box). But I also carry an alcohol lamp in my tool kit for those occasions when no electricity or lack of room makes a manual knife a logical choice.

The shellac-resin sticks are available in a wide variety of colors and tints. And different colors can be melted and mixed together on the hot knife to make the exact shade necessary for a perfect match. Some colors are available translucent or opaque, which can help make certain repairs far less noticeable. The translucent shades are perfect for repairs when just the finish is damaged and not the underlying wood. This situation is identified by no telltale color changes in the damaged area. A color change indicates broken wood fibers that will require opaque colors. But opaque and translucent colors can be intermixed to suit any repair situation.

Other than the new Concept 2000 repair system by Mohawk (see the sources of supply and the box at right), shellac resins are very brittle when cool and can chip when used on corners or other areas subject to sharp impact. The resin has no strength to hold nails or screws, so it should be used for only cosmetic repairs.

Color-matching

Probably the most important step involved in making a good repair is color matching. It is an art that takes some practice, but color-matching can be learned. Most wood has a background shade that is dominant in creating the impression of color. Quickly glance at a piece that needs repair. The color you see in that quick look is the one that you want to match. Now look closely at the piece. You will immediately notice that it is made up of many colors that are subtly blended. By carefully selecting the right shades of resin sticks, repairs also can be subtly blended.

Burning-in for beginners

As I was putting together the information on burn-in repairs, my Mohawk finishing products salesman introduced me to Concept 2000, a new repair system that was recently introduced. After working with Concept 2000, I found the system eliminates or minimizes many of the common problem areas, especially for the novice. The repair sticks are flexible, so repairs made with the new sticks won't be as fragile as the brittle traditional sticks. And the halo effect, a glossy ring left by traditional burn-in repairs, is gone because the sticks dry flat, making it easier to blend in the repairs.

Lower temperatures for better results: What really sets the Concept 2000 system apart from the traditional method is the fact that the burn-in knife is cooler than the old-style knife and need never touch the surface of the wood. Because the hot knife is kept away from the finish, there is less chance of creating more damage when making the repair. Mohawk offers a special, temperature-controlled knife for melting the burn-in sticks. However, I modified my standard burn-in knife by adding a rotary, lamp-dimmer switch for controlling the temperature. Too much heat causes the melted sticks to boil, which leaves air bubbles in the repair and darkens the color.

Repairs are made in the traditional manner of flowing melted material into the damaged area, leaving a dome-like mass. Air bubbles are removed by allowing the repair to cool for 10 to 15 seconds and then pressing on the material with a fingertip dipped in Plane Balm, Mohawk's skin and finish protector. With the easy melting, flexible repair sticks, I found this step to be rarely necessary.

Leveling the repair: To level the repair with the surrounding wood, Mohawk includes a patented device called an Ieroplane, which takes the place of a sharp chisel and allows even a novice to pare away excess material without fear of gouging the surface being repaired. The Ieroplane is a large round blade mounted in a non-marking plastic frame, as shown in the photo below. The height of the blade relative to the repaired surface can be adjusted with a top-mounted knurled wheel. The blade is adjusted to just skim the top off the mounded repair, which should be allowed to cool four to five minutes. The Ieroplane is pushed through the repair material with a slight rolling or twisting motion. Keep adjusting the blade to take off paper thin slices until the repair is almost dead even with the surface.

If necessary, further leveling can be accomplished with Mohawk's Level Aid, which is used as naphtha would be for a conventional repair. Level Aid is applied with a felt pad, a rag or 600-grit, wet-or-dry sandpaper. Limit the sanding and smoothing to just the repair area with as little overlap onto the surrounding finish as possible.

Graining can be done with appropriately colored, fine-line artists' markers in the normal manner. Spraying lightly misted coats of lacquer until the depth and gloss of the repair's finish matches the original provides a quality repair in a minimal amount of time. —R.J.

Trimming burn-in repair material flush is done without fear of damaging the surrounding finish, thanks to the Ieroplane. The Ieroplane is included in Mohawk's new Concept 2000 repair system, which makes burn-in repairs easier for the beginner.

Placing shellac-resin sticks directly on the piece to be repaired is the best way to get a sense of the color match. This technique also helps in selecting the shades that need to be blended, such as the three different colored sticks shown here.

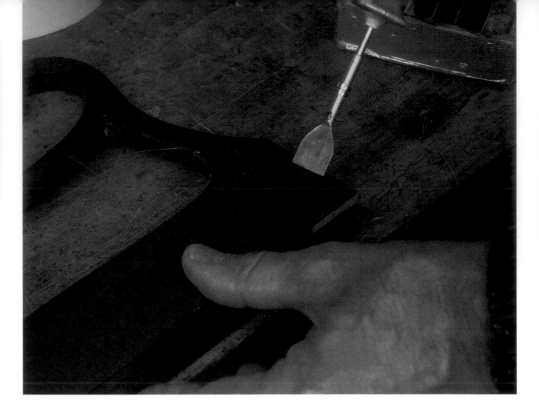

Smooth the repair with the hot knife by drawing the knife over the resin and then wiping the excess resin from the knife. Keep the knife moving because it is easy to burn the surrounding finish.

As a general rule on medium and dark finishes, if you can't get an exact match, it is better to make your repair darker than the surrounding wood. With lighter woods, it is better to err on the lighter side. This will help prevent high contrast situations, which stand out and call attention to your repairs.

A trick that helps me match colors is to place some sticks on the piece to be repaired, as shown in the photo at left above. Looking at the color *in situ* is the best way of knowing if a single stick will make a good match.

Because there are so many formulas and proprietary resins used, the manufacturers' color names can be a bit confusing. Each manufacturer has its own idea of what color "antique mahogany" or "golden oak" should be. The key is to match the wood to the repair stick color, not the name. It's all right to use a dark walnut to repair a piece of mahogany if the color match is good.

Often you will need to mix or blend colors on the knife while the resin is in a liquid state, as shown in the photo on p. 110. As a rule of thumb, if you are mixing more than three colors, you are probably in trouble; just wipe the knife clean on a rag and start again.

By purchasing a set of sticks, you will have a better chance of having the right colors on hand. I recommend buying a set of small, 2-in.-long sticks because you can get a great selection for a modest price. Even though 2 in. is the smallest size, the sticks will still go a long way because so little material is used for each repair.

Making the repair

Before starting a repair, the first step is to clean the damaged area using a rag dampened with VM&P (Varnish Makers and Painters) naphtha. This solvent will remove wax and dry in a matter of minutes, leaving a powdery residue that can be wiped off with a clean cloth. I then apply Burn-In Balm (Mohawk) or Patch Lube (Star) around the damaged areas. These thick ointments, the consistency of Vaseline petroleum jelly, act as heat sinks and help prevent burning the surrounding finish. They also act as repellents, so the resin adheres only in the damaged areas. A small bottle lasts a long, long time and makes repairs easier and neater.

Before beginning the repair, clean the knife to avoid any color contamination from residue clinging to the blade. Preheat an electric knife three to five minutes or a manual knife 30 seconds, and wipe it clean with a rag or scrape it clean with a single-edge razor blade. When you apply the knife to the stick, the resin should flow smoothly rather than bubble or boil, a clear sign the knife's too hot. After melting enough material to slightly overfill the damage, allow the molten resin to flow into the damaged area, creating a slight dome of excess material.

Wipe the knife clean, and then smooth the repair by drawing the knife over the resin, always working toward you, as shown in the photo at right above. Repeat the process of wiping the knife clean and stroking the repair at least three times or until most of the excess material has been removed. But don't try to get the fill dead

even with the knife because it's easy to damage the surrounding finish, especially if you don't keep the knife moving.

Leveling the repair

When finished with the hot knife, the repair should be slightly proud of the finish. As the resin cools, it hardens almost immediately. I shave off the remaining excess filler with a chisel I hone to a razor's edge on an 8,000-grit Japanese waterstone.

After carefully cutting back the repair, you may find bubbles or unevenness. One of the characteristics of a burn-in stick that makes it such a good repair material is its forgiving nature. Just reapply heat, and the resin will liquefy again whether it's been 30 seconds or 30 years since the repair was made. This reversibility means the repair can be pulled out if you botch the job or if a better technique is developed.

The next step in the leveling process is to wipe the resin with a felt pad and a solvent to help smooth the repair, as shown in the photo at left on the facing page. I like to use Brasiv (Mohawk) or VM&P naphtha. Often I use cigarette lighter fluid from Walgreen's. The lighter fluid is essentially naphtha, but the little flip-top can is a very handy dispenser, which keeps spills to a minimum.

Although they will rarely damage any cured finish at least 30 days old, solvents should be tested on an inconspicuous spot. Brasiv is fast acting, so it requires some care. Using a clean felt pad slightly moistened with solvent, I rapidly rub the repair. The solvent softens the resin, and the felt absorbs any excess material

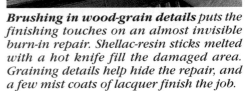

Brushing in wood-grain details *puts the finishing touches on an almost invisible burn-in repair. Shellac-resin sticks melted with a hot knife fill the damaged area. Graining details help hide the repair, and a few mist coats of lacquer finish the job.*

Buffing the repair with solvent *and a felt pad softens the resin, levels it with the surrounding wood and leaves a smooth surface. Excessive resin should first be pared away with a razor-sharp chisel.*

while polishing the surface smooth.

Many people use 400-grit wet-or-dry sandpaper to smooth repairs. This technique requires a very gentle touch and often creates more work if you damage the finish around the repair. I try not to use sandpaper and especially don't recommend it for beginners. Things can get out of control in a hurry, particularly on more modern pieces that have toner in the finish instead of being stained in the more traditional manner. Sanding, even with 400-grit paper, will cut through the toned finish in short order, and it is difficult to patch unless you are skilled with an airbrush. If you must use abrasives, keep in mind that a finish is not very thick, and you can sand through it in less time than it takes to talk about it. Try starting with less aggressive 600-grit paper, and use a very light touch.

Adding wood-grain details

At this stage, the repair should be flat and the color close to the shade of the background wood, but it still won't look quite right. The missing ingredient is the natural grain lines of the wood. The grain lines need to be duplicated to commit what the French call *trompe l'oeil*, literally, to "trick the eye." Wood-grain lines of the appropriate size and color are drawn with fine-line graining pens or painted with a brush and pigments blended with lacquer and a little retarder, as shown in the photo at right above. Artists' pens and pigments also can be used and offer an even greater selection of colors.

For best results, be sure to follow the natural grain lines. Run the pen lines past the edges of the repair, and avoid hard edges. Smooth in coloring pens and brushed colors with your finger to blur the lines. These grain lines are vital to an invisible repair, so take the time needed to get them right.

Getting the finish right

Though the repair is now smooth, grained and color-matched, it will probably still stand out. The sticks leave glossy repairs, so the sheen of the repair won't match the surrounding wood's sheen. The location of the repair and the finish of the piece determine the next step.

In most situations, the gloss of the repair can be adjusted with either Burn-In Seal (Mohawk) or Sheen (Star) aerosol lacquers. These aerosol lacquers are specifically formulated to reduce the gloss of the burn-in repair to match most wood finishes. I am not sure how they work, but they sure do the job. I lightly mist on several coats of the lacquer until the repair blends in with the rest of the finish. If necessary, you can topcoat with the original finish for a perfect match.

This technique works fine in most situations. One problem area, however, is tabletops, particularly those with a high-gloss finish. A high-gloss finish works like a mirror, reflecting light and accentuating scratches, nicks and even repairs.

Repairs to these finishes are a compromise, and no technique yields perfect results. With that idea clearly in mind, I like to use MicroMesh Abrasives, available from C.W. Crossen (see the sources of supply box), to reproduce the luster of a high-gloss finish. These super-fine abrasives, available in grits as fine as optical grade (12,000-grit) are worked with a drop or two of water from the finest grits downward toward the coarser grades, which is the reverse of the usual procedure, until a reasonable duplication of the surrounding sheen is achieved. □

Robert Judd is a professional furniture repairer and refinisher in Canton, Mass.

Paint-Grade Cabinets
Preparing wood for a demanding finish

by Lars Mikkelsen

Picking paint as a furniture finish is not just a matter of shuffling color swatches. *As Lars Mikkelsen discovered when he built these cabinets, painted work requires design decisions, materials and preparation different from clear-finished work.*

From *Fine Woodworking* (November 1993) 103:62-66

Most of us who work in wood love its color, grain and texture, and we usually build to show off these characteristics. So when a client called and asked me to make a built-in stereo and display cabinet that had to be painted high-gloss white, as shown in the photo at left, I hesitated a little. But when I saw his house and the room the cabinet was to go in, it was obvious to me that paint was what this job called for. It is a modern house, sparsely furnished, with light-filled rooms defined by strong geometric forms. It was an excellent setting for a built-in cabinet that blends architectural and furniture detailing, and a good place for paint. Once I had accepted the logic of a paint finish, and also had accepted the job, every subsequent move I made was affected by the choice of finish—from decorative and structural decisions through selection of the materials to construction and sanding.

Planning for paint

There are all grades of paint finishes, and it's important to have a clear idea of what you are aiming for before you begin. I talked with the client at length about the level to which the painting should be done. We wanted something well above the average wall-and-trim job, but taking it to the level of a grand piano would have made the cost of the prep work and the painting prohibitive. So we agreed to try for something in between: A bit of grain texture might show under careful inspection, but the overall impression should be clean and unblemished. With an understanding of what we both expected, I was ready to begin.

When designing for a clear finish, the color and grain of the wood are often the central point. A big, flat panel can be spectacular if the grain is right, and curved grain along a focal axis can pull a piece together and make an otherwise very plain design a thing of beauty. All this is lost when you paint. What you gain in return is beautiful clean shadow lines, undisturbed by grain pattern and texture. Paint emphasizes the volume of intersecting planes, and I took advantage of this in the design of the cabinet. The piece was to be built into an alcove formed by a series of sharp-edged, squared-off arches that stepped out into the room. I adapted this step pattern for the cabinet's detailing, echoing and altering the step motif, playing off it without exactly reproducing it. I would have designed differently for a clear finish because the distinctive geometric patterns and proportions I settled on would have seemed cluttered and confused had they not been painted.

I try to design built-in furniture that looks truly built-in, like the beautiful buffets so often found in Victorian houses. Thinking of trim as an important design element contributes greatly to the in-

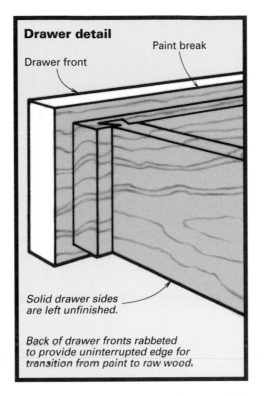

Drawer detail

Drawer front

Paint break

Solid drawer sides are left unfinished.

Back of drawer fronts rabbeted to provide uninterrupted edge for transition from paint to raw wood.

How to pick your painter

To prequalify a painter for a difficult finishing job, I would recommend asking to see what he considers his finest work. I'd also ask him to explain in detail just how the finish will be achieved. I'd have him prefinish one door panel using the materials and finish specified for the job. The client would approve that sample for color, gloss, smoothness of finish and durability, and then it would be used as a job standard. I have often volunteered to do this when the situation warranted it, or when the client was unfamiliar with my work. ☐

Dave Hughes is a professional finisher in Los Osos, Calif. For a description of how he painted Lars Mikkelsen's cabinet, see p. 116.

...see p. 116.

tegrated look that I always seek. It's easy, when designing built-in cabinets, especially painted ones, to fall into the trap of making misplaced kitchen cabinets. I try my best to avoid this by developing detailing that will give the piece a look of permanence, of belonging where it stands.

Because the piece was to be fairly big, I broke it down into four components that could be easily transported and assembled on site. I used a raised frame detail all around and between the major components. I applied these trim strips when the cabinets were set in place. This not only covered seams and edges but underscored the visual theme of the cabinet.

To take advantage of the strong shadow lines, I made all the doors and drawers inset—flush with the surrounding surface—and free of exterior hardware. With inset doors and drawers, an even gap is always important, but when a black gap line is contrasted with white paint, small discrepancies become obvious to even the untrained eye. And I was making the tolerances small, so I needed hardware with fine adjustment. I wanted concealed European hinges for the doors and chose Grass 1006 hinges on 20mm mounting plates. I picked the 1006 because it's relatively small; I was advised, though, that it won't work with inset doors that are any thicker than ¾ in. The doors are held closed and sprung open with Hafele touch latches. For the drawers, I used Accuride full-extension slides and 1041 Flexa-Touch pushers. I purchased my hardware from Capitol Hardware, 1519 Riverside Ave., Paso Robles, Calif., 93446; (805) 238-7669.

I wanted the doors painted on both sides, but for the drawers, I wanted only the fronts painted, leaving the solid-maple drawer boxes unfinished. This posed the problem of where to make the transition from painted surface to raw wood. I solved it by running a rabbet around the inside edge of the drawer front, establishing a clean, uninterrupted line for the painter to tape off, as shown in the drawing above.

Materials to fit the finish

The materials I chose for this job were determined largely by their paintability. I needed something without open pores or great differences between hard and soft grain because such differences would telegraph through paint. I ended up choosing poplar for the solid wood and shop birch plywood. Both are relatively inexpensive, mill well and require minimal preparation for painting. Other choices for solid wood could be maple, birch or alder. The main reason I chose poplar over the others was the ease with which it can be milled. For sheet goods, medium-density fiberboard is a possible choice; it paints nicely, but is extremely heavy to haul around and, therefore, easy to damage.

Stereo speakers were to be housed behind the top doors on ei-

Spraying an opaque finish on furniture

by Dave Hughes

Ask any painter familiar with high-quality finishes and he or she will tell you that furniture-grade paint finishes are far more demanding than natural wood finishes. The simple reason is that the opaque surface of the paint highlights any defects or irregularities in grain and texture. Surfaces must be sanded, caulked, puttied and re-sanded several times, and still some rubbing out and polishing may be required to achieve satisfactory results. The deeper the color and higher the gloss, the more demanding the process. With so many variables to be controlled, a patient, methodical approach is essential in applying opaque finishes.

Now, try to achieve that flawless finish inside a client's home, with kids, dogs and neighbors dropping by for a look...to be candid, I didn't have too much enthusiasm for attempting the on-site finishing of Lars Mikkelsen's cabinets until I saw them for myself. They posed a real challenge, both technically and logistically, and that is what got me involved.

On any on-site job, you have to take particular care to cover and to mask off all adjacent surfaces and any parts and hardware that won't be painted. The tape I use is 3M's Longmask, a fine-creped blue tape with high tack that leaves no residue. I rub it down with a fingernail, and it provides an excellent edge seal, allowing no paint to creep underneath. With oil-based finishes, the tape can be pulled up when the paint is dry. With latex, which has greater bridging capacity, I score a line along a straight edge with a razor blade before removing the tape.

Good lighting is also critical for a top-quality paint job. Natural light is always best, but when I do use lamps, I place them far from the work to minimize glare.

The cabinets on Lars' job were already sanded quite smooth when I began work on them, but I always count on a certain added amount of time for re-sanding, puttying and caulking because you can't really see the surface in detail until that first coat goes on. I have found it is best to fill all you can easily see; then apply a first coat of primer, and repair any small areas you have missed. The essential thing is to catch all of these before entering into the final-coats phase. This careful, methodical filling and sanding is where the patience factor really tells. For a fine finish, you must spend a certain amount of time just *looking* at every piece.

Lars had removed the doors, and I fitted each one with two small finish nails in the top and bottom edges (as shown in the drawing above) to act as stands for spraying, handling and drying. Then I set up a makeshift booth in the garage to spray the doors and drawers.

The primer I sprayed was Sherwin-Williams Hi-Build Lacquer Wood Surfacer reduced about 35% with medium-fast lacquer thinner. I used a high volume, low pressure (HVLP) spray unit, which, with its portability and reduced overspray, is particularly well-suited to on-site work. I used the HVLP unit with a Capspray fine-finishing gun.

After spraying two coats' of lacquer wood surfacer, I lightly sanded all surfaces with 400-grit wet-or-dry sandpaper that I first broke in on the backs of doors or bottoms of cabinets where dry-fall overspray accumulates. I turn the paper over and use the paper backing to abrade the knife-edges of doors, drawers and trim to avoid burning through the finish.

The third coat of primer was a final fill-coat, not really sanded, but rubbed with the back of sandpaper for smoothness. Before every operation, I used a static-free tack-rag and blew the surfaces off with the air line on the spray gun. I allowed four hours between coats of primer because that's how long it took to spray a coat on the case and all the parts. But a lacquer undercoat is generally dry and ready to sand in 45 minutes to an hour, depending on the weather.

I applied two finish coats of Benjamin Moore Ironclad fast-dry industrial enamel, which has superior leveling-out characteristics and fast set-up time. The short tack time is critical when finishing on-site to minimize dust settling onto the finish. I thinned the enamel with about 30% xylol solvent and sprayed it at orifice settings between .006 and .009, something less than half the opening you would use to paint an ordinary wall.

I alternated between vertical, horizontal and conical spray patterns as I worked to suit the intricate detailing on the cabinet doors, with the spray pressure just high enough to atomize the enamel. The Capspray gun enables me to spray in a cone pattern about the diameter of a pencil—it's practically an airbrush at that setting—which worked beautifully in the square decorative recesses of this cabinet. For the doors and frames, I switched to a 6-in. to 8-in. horizontal fan pattern.

A single coat was actually a two-step process. On the doors, for instance, I laid down a light tack-coat initially to cover the surface, rotated and tack-coated the back, and then flipped and rotated back for a full flowing coat. This method allows me to see how the material is performing and adjust viscosity, spray pattern, pressure and fluid levels before committing to a full coat. It also lets me lay down more material in one coat. I sanded lightly between coats of enamel with broken-in 600-grit paper, wiped down with a tack rag and allowed 24 hours between coats. I applied a third coat to all the doors and countertops.

When the final coat on the doors had dried hard, I removed the nail stands, puttied the holes and touched them up with two coats applied with an artist's brush. This was the only brushwork on the job.

After spraying the final coat, I took a few days away from the job before returning to do a final inspection and any necessary buffing out or touching up. The hiatus gave me some perspective and also let the finish cure hard and reach its final sheen. If you do any small repairs before the final sheen is reached, you may find they stand out later, looking either too glossy or too dull. I repair tiny blemishes by rubbing out with rottenstone or #00000 steel wool or buffing with alcohol and a tightly woven cotton cloth. A slow, hard rub with a coarser abrasive will give a matte finish while a fast, light stroke with a finer grit will yield a glossy one. By carefully adjusting the amount of pressure and the type of polishing compound, feathering out any touch-up areas and matching the sheen to the surrounding surface, you can approach a showroom finish with an on-site application.   —D.H.

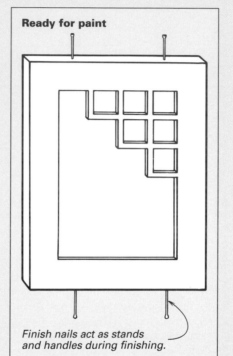

Ready for paint

Finish nails act as stands and handles during finishing.

Nail in the rail—The author shoots brads through the frame of the door to keep it from shrinking away from the panel, which could crack the paint and expose unfinished wood.

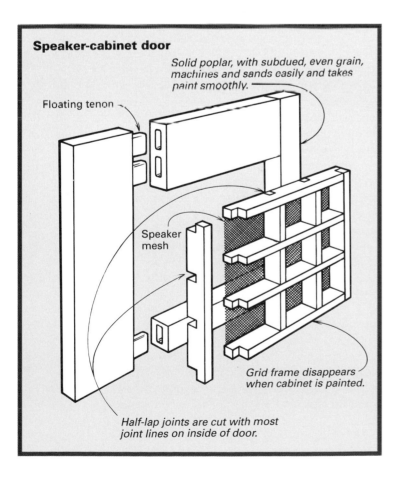

Speaker-cabinet door

Solid poplar, with subdued, even grain, machines and sands easily and takes paint smoothly.

Floating tenon

Speaker mesh

Grid frame disappears when cabinet is painted.

Half-lap joints are cut with most joint lines on inside of door.

ther side and the center door below. I made open-grid panels for those doors and covered them on the inside with sheets of metal speaker mesh (available from better stereo outlets). The mesh was painted to the same color as the cabinet and was easy to cut and install with small screws.

Joint selection

Both the finish and the siting of the cabinet were factors in my selection of biscuits for its major joinery. Using biscuits alone on a freestanding piece that could take a lot of abuse over the years might not be a good idea; but once a built-in is in place and attached to the walls, there is not much stress on the joints. So I felt this technique would be amply strong. Because the sides of the cabinet would be hidden when it was put in place, I used screws to draw the joints together while the glue set. I lipped all the plywood with ¾-in. by 1⅛-in. strips of solid poplar that I biscuited, glued and nailed on. It saves a lot of time to nail the wood on rather than clamping it, and the spackled nail holes disappear under the paint. I also find that with nailing, I can locate the lipping exactly, but with clamps, the strips are a bit more difficult to control.

Though the carcase of a built-in does not take much abuse and you can use some shortcuts in its construction, this is not true for the doors and drawers. They need to be made with the same strength and care as for any freestanding piece. I made the drawer sides of solid wood, and then I joined them to the fronts with sliding dovetails.

I joined the stiles and rails of the doors with loose tenons. The mortises for these tenons I can cut with great precision on my mortise fixture (see *FWW* #92, p. 55). The solid doors have a ¼-in. birch-plywood panel sitting in a groove. It is important that this panel never move in the groove, and thus expose unpainted wood, so I nailed it in with a few brads, as shown in the photo at left. The steps in these doors are strips of solid poplar ½ in. wide by ¼ in. thick, half lapped and glued in place. The open grids for the speaker cabinets are made with ½-in.-wide by ¾-in.-thick pieces of solid poplar, half-lapped at every joint, as shown in the drawing below. Had these doors been left clear, I probably would have mortised the end of each crosspiece of the grid into the stiles and rails. But because no grain would show, I made the grid as an independent unit with a frame of its own, with all half laps, and then glued up the stiles and rails around it.

Paint prep

It would be hard to find someone who really loves filling and sanding, but the job can be made easier and less tedious by doing as much as possible as you build. For many parts, it's much simpler and quicker to do the prep work before assembly. I carefully filled and sanded the plywood panels in the solid doors before glue-up. On all the pieces of lipped plywood for the carcase, I sanded the wood flush to the plywood with a belt sander that I slowed down with an electronic speed control. The slow speed makes this operation much easier and safer. Next I inspected all the pieces carefully and then filled and sanded any little cracks or dings that might show up later. Remember that paint really magnifies these blemishes.

When the carcases were assembled, I applied white latex caulk to all the many corners whether I could see a seam or not. I used spackle for any joint or surface that would be sanded. All this filling must be done carefully because even a hairline crack will show horribly once the paint is on. To achieve clear, crisp lines and joints, it is important to press caulk into the cracks but immediately remove all excess, leaving interior corners square rather than forming a little cove of caulk. To do this, I laid down as small

Even with end grain, it's best to scrape off most of the spackle. If necessary, apply a second time rather than build up a thick layer. Do a last round of filling when the piece has been primed. The layer of finish will highlight any imperfections.

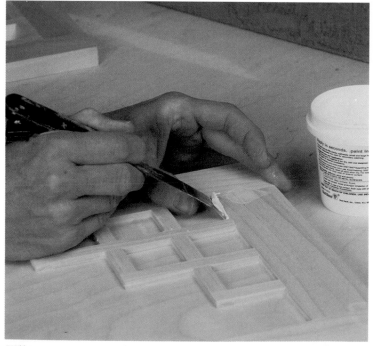

Fill every corner, whether you can see a seam or not. For long runs, caulk is best, but in tight quarters, like the door panel grids, the author uses spackle because it's less messy. With a freshly filed putty knife, he removes 95% of the filler he lays down.

a bead of caulk as possible. Then I used a putty knife that I had filed down so that it came to a knife edge and its corners were sharp and square. I probably removed 95% or more of the caulk that I applied. I don't worry about small smears of caulk or glue, but all protrusions should be removed.

After gluing up the doors, I caulked all around the groove and panel joint, cleaning it up with my putty knife. I filled the seams between the grid pieces with spackle, as shown in the bottom photo. When there's a long run to fill, it's easier to lay down a bead of caulk, but in tight spaces like the grids, caulk will make a mess. It is important to work methodically at this, so as not to miss any of the little seams. Then I took all the doors to be thickness-sanded. Some cabinet shops offer this service, and it is very worthwhile. It saves time while doing a superior job, keeping everything wonderfully flat, resulting in a beautiful, clean reflection of light when painted.

At this point, all parts had been made, filled and sanded, and all I needed to do in the shop was to fit the doors and drawers in their openings. Before fitting anything, I assembled the four individual carcases, screwing them together and shimming them as needed to get everything straight, flat and square. I glued my shims in place so that they would stay on one of the carcases. That way, when I later assembled the carcases on site, I was sure to get them exactly the way they were when I fitted the doors and drawers, saving a lot of frustration and awkward planing. I then sanded everything down to 180-grit with my random-orbit sander and broke all sharp edges by hand-sanding, creating a small roundover. A roundover always looks nice, but when painting, it is absolutely essential because paint will not adhere to sharp edges and a dark line will appear.

Installation

Now the moment of truth. No matter how many times I have done installation, it is still stressful until everything is in place. This time everything went smoothly, and the major components were quickly set and screwed together. I then shifted the unit around a bit in the wall opening to get all side margins as even as possible. I removed all doors, drawers and hardware, numbering all the hinges so that I could put them back where they came from. This makes re-installation much faster because almost no fine-tuning is needed. I left the drawer guides in place and then covered them with tape.

Though this is the point when I hand a job off to the painter, I always make certain to return when the piece has been primed. With the first coat on, previously unnoticed flaws can readily be seen, and it is the last chance to repair them without having to repaint everything. (For a detailed description of what went into the painting of this piece, see the box on p. 116.) In this case, there was nothing for me to do at the priming stage because the painter had already done any filling that was needed. I always insist on rehanging the doors and hardware myself: This is not a painter's job, and he or she cannot be expected to do it so that the doors fit properly.

The payoff

Finally, everything was done, and I could see the piece the way I had imagined it while doing the design. I was hoping my client would be as happy as I was. I got a clue when I returned for my check and found the furniture rearranged. Before, it had been facing the fireplace, and now it all faced the cabinet. □

Lars Mikkelsen is a professional cabinetmaker living in Santa Margarita, Calif.

Fill the Grain for a Glass-Smooth Finish

Simple steps are key to success with pore fillers

by Chris A. Minick

Woods like mahogany, ash, walnut and oak, which have large pores, give a natural open-grained appearance to furniture. But to get a glass-smooth surface on these woods, you have to fill the pores with a grain filler before applying the finish. Tight-grained hardwoods, like maple and most softwoods, usually don't require grain filling.

You need only a few tools to use grain fillers (see the photo at left), and grain-filling is pretty straightforward: Thin and tint the filler, prepare the surface, brush on the filler and pack the pores, remove the excess before it hardens, sand to the wood once the filler is dry, and clean off any residue. But though the process is straightforward, filling grain takes time, is messy and is generally not much fun. Even so, the results are well worth the effort, as the left side of the butternut board shows in the photo below right.

Oil-based and water-based options

Don't confuse grain fillers with the wood putty used to fill nail holes. Grain filler, also called paste-wood filler or pore filler, is a thick clay-like mixture of solvent, resin binders and finely ground minerals, often called silex. Fillers come in oil-based formulations, like Behlen's Pore O-Pac (available from Woodcraft Supply, 210 Wood County Industrial Park, P.O. Box 1686, Parkersburg, W.V. 26102; 800-225-1153) or in water-based formulations, like Hydrocote's Fast Dry (available from Highland Hardware, 1045 N. High-

Surface imperfections are magnified by pore filler, so it's critical that the wood be properly scraped and sanded beforehand. The rust colored filler used on this piece of butternut reveals even small surface blemishes (top right corner).

Grain fillers are essential for open-pored woods. Here, Minick applies water-based filler to a mahogany tabletop. Using a disposable brush, he packs the pores. He masked the edges with tape to avoid scraping filler from the routed profile.

From *Fine Woodworking* (September 1994) 108:57-59

land Ave. N.E., Atlanta, Ga. 30306; 800-241-6748). Both varieties can be purchased as a thick paste that must be thinned before use, or in a pre-thinned, ready-to-use consistency. Even though oil-based grain fillers have been around longer, I prefer water-based fillers because they work easier, dry faster and are easier to clean up. In addition, water-based fillers, once completely dry, are compatible with virtually all finishes.

Tinting the filler

Pore fillers come in a variety of wood tones, so you can match your project. They also come in off-white and in a neutral color, which can be custom-tinted in your shop. The choice of tint is a matter of taste. You may want a light, unobtrusive filler color on oak, or you may want to contrast the grain by using a dark filler. I almost always go for a darker filler because I like to bring out grain patterns. Similarly, you can pick up highlights in the wood—reds in mahogany or maroon in walnut, for example. I usually stick with earth-tone pigments, such as burnt umber (chocolate-like color), ochre (yellowish), burnt sienna (reddish) and lamp black. To my eyes, colors that are bright and bold look artificial on wood.

If you decide not to tint your off-white or neutral oil-based filler, be aware that the binders in the mixture will likely cause the filler to yellow or darken with age. This is not a problem if you use a water-based grain filler. Pigmented universal tinting colors (UTCs), available from most large paint stores, and dry fresco powders work well at coloring water-based and oil-based fillers. Japan colors (pigments ground in a varnish base), artist's oil colors and the pigment sludge found on the bottoms of oil-based stain cans are only useful for tinting oil-based fillers. For more on tinting, see the photo and story at right. In any case, make sure your coloring medium is a pigment. Transparent dye stains will not adequately color the quartz particles found in most grain fillers.

Preparing the surface

Sloppy sanding and pore fillers don't mix. That's why I usually power-sand the wood with a random-orbit sander through 180-grit sandpaper. Then I hand-sand with 220-grit to remove pesky swirl marks. Likewise, tearouts, gouges or other defects must be puttied and sanded flat before applying the filler. A poorly prepared surface will be magnified a hundred fold once the blemishes are packed with pore filler (see the photo at right on p. 119).

Pore fillers tend to seal the wood surface, which makes staining after filling difficult. If you plan to stain the wood, do it before you fill the grain. I like to use water-based dye stains under the filler because the inevitable sand-throughs are easily repaired by reapplication of the same strength dye stain. Once the stain is dry, you should seal it (I prefer shellac or vinyl sealer). There are three reasons for sealing: First, the sealer protects the stain layer from scratches during the filling process. Second, sealing before filling

eliminates an undesirable smudging effect that commonly occurs (for more on this, see p. 41). Third, because sealers smooth out surfaces, they allow easy removal of excess filler.

Applying the filler and removing the excess

Once thinned to the consistency of heavy latex paint, pore filler is ready to apply. Paint on a fairly thick coat of filler (see the photo at left on p. 119), and then pack the filler into the pores using a forceful circular motion of the brush. (This is why I like to use disposable brushes.) Stir the filler frequently because filler particles are heavy and rapidly settle to the bottom of the can.

Working oil-based fillers

by Andy Charron

Before you apply oil-based paste filler, you need to tint it to the right color for your project. The filler not only plugs up pores but also helps color the immediate surrounding areas of the wood (see *FWW* #108, p. 72). Because the silex in the filler does not accept stain, you cannot readily change filler color once it's dry. But the color can be adjusted beforehand by blending different fillers together or by adding pigments to neutral filler. You can achieve the wood tone you want through trial and error (see the photo).

Start with neutral grain filler and add pigments, such as universal tinting colors (UTCs), to get the color you like.

Besides needing tint, oil-based filler usually has to be thinned as well. If the filler is too thick, you'll need lots of elbow grease to brush it on and to rub off the excess. If it's too thin, it will be easy to apply and clean up, but it won't fill up large pores well and it will take longer to dry. Once you've thinned the filler to a creamy consistency, apply it in stages over small areas. I like to use an inexpensive stiff bristle brush to work the filler into the wood, applying it with the grain first and then going back over it perpendicularly to the grain.

Immediately after you've filled the grain (while the wood is wet), remove all the excess by scraping the surface at a 45° angle. One filler manufacturer recommends using a plastic credit card. A thin ripping of the project's scrapwood also works well. I cut one end of the filler scraper to a point, so I can get filler out of hard-to-reach places like inside corners.

Once you've scraped the surface clean, allow the residual filler to dry until it takes on a flat, crusty look (usually 5 to 10 minutes). At this point, start rubbing with a piece of burlap. When the burlap begins to weigh down with excess material, shake it out, and it will be ready to wipe some more. Finally, polish the wood with a soft cotton cloth. After the surface has been wiped off, you may need to sand it lightly. But I've found that just a firm rubbing with a clean rag usually will shine the wood to a perfectly smooth surface. □

Andy Charron is a writer and cabinetmaker living in Red Bank, N.J.

Remove excess filler from the surface with a stiff rubber squeegee (available from a glass-cleaning supply store) for water-based filler or a plastic putty knife for oil-based filler. Pulling the squeegee or pushing the putty knife diagonally across the grain minimizes the chance of removing the filler from the just-packed pores (see the top photo). If you're using oil-based filler, use coarse burlap rags to clean residual filler off the wood before it dries. The more filler you remove now, the less sanding later.

Getting a feel for the proper drying time takes practice. Generally, you can begin removing an oil-based filler when the surface starts to look dull or hazy. A light sprinkling of mineral spirits over the filler will slow down the drying and allow a bit more working time. But water-based fillers dry so rapidly that if you wait for them to haze over, it's too late. Instead, work on small patches at a time and immediately squeegee the excess filler from the surface as soon as pore packing is complete. Because the filler won't leave lap marks, you don't have to fill the entire surface at once. But sprinkling water on hardened water-based filler is no help. If you wait too long to squeegee, you'll have to sand off the excess.

While the squeegee method works quite well at removing the bulk of wet filler from large flat surfaces, turned pieces and intricate moldings are different matters. I've had some luck removing excess filler from turnings using a terry-cloth towel. I've also been marginally successful at removing dried filler from molding nooks and crannies using a shaped scraper. But I often avoid the problem by not filling turned pieces and moldings. The visibility of the pores in these regions is usually disguised because the end-grain wood will finish darker (more absorption) and because of shadows made by the profiles. To prevent filler from getting on these areas, I simply mask them off beforehand (see the photo at left).

Sand, clean and seal before you finish

Dry time (or more appropriately, cure time) of pore fillers varies significantly. While water-based fillers can usually be sanded and finished within three or four hours, oil-based fillers require two to three days to dry thoroughly. The residual solvents and oils in uncured oil-based filler can cause tiny white spots in the finish if top-coated too soon. This is particularly true when waterborne finishes and some nitrocellulose lacquers are used.

Once the filler is completely dry, sand down to the sealer, removing all the filler residue from the surface (see the center photo). Leave filler only in the grain pores. Sand carefully: It's easy to sand through the sealer coat into the base stain. Oversanding can also open up unfilled pores, which will force you to start the whole process over again. Periodically, wipe down the wood with a rag dampened with mineral spirits to inspect your progress. You should wind up with a surface that looks somewhat like the left tabletop in the bottom photo.

Because grain fillers shrink about 10% as they cure, your freshly filled and sanded wood is probably not going to be silky smooth. You can repeat the process to fill the pores completely, but I prefer to fill the small sink holes with sanding sealer (it's a lot easier). I apply a coat or two of sealer and sand it back to a flush surface. The sealer also provides a good base for the finish (see the tabletop on the right in the bottom photo). Finally, always make sure your topcoat, sealer and filler are compatible by testing your finishing sequence on scrapwood from your project. □

Chris Minick is a finishing chemist and a woodworker in Stillwater, Minn. He is a regular contributor to Fine Woodworking.

Scrape off the grain filler while it's still wet. *Wearing rubber gloves, the author drags a rubber squeegee diagonally across the grain. The scraped area to the right has already hazed over.*

Sand down to the wood (or sealer) once the filler is dry. *Minick uses 120- and then 220-grit paper to produce the fine powder shown. If the paper starts to gum up, it means the filler is not quite dry.*

Clean and seal the surface. *Wipe off filler residue, and dust with a soft cloth. Then reseal the wood before the topcoat. The mahogany top on the left has been cleaned; the right top has been shellacked.*

Finishing Brushes

*A top-quality finish starts
with the right brush*

by Jeff Jewitt

Reservoir

The divider is a
wooden cleat
that creates a
reservoir and
gives shape to
the brush.
Artist's brushes
don't have
dividers.

Applying finish with a brush seems easy enough. Dip the brush into the finish, spread the finish on the wood and then wait for it to dry. That's the theory, anyway, but many woodworkers are disappointed with the brush marks, streaks and bubbles that can mar a finish. Maybe, they may wonder, there's some secret technique. Or maybe the finish itself is to blame. Quite often, though, the problem is neither the technique nor the finish. It starts with the selection and use of the brush. Using the wrong brush or a second-rate brush makes it difficult to get first-rate results.

A brush is more than some bristles attached to a handle. Brush-making is an art. Manufacturers mix bristles of different lengths and stiffnesses for different types of brushes. In a top-quality brush, the bristles are selected and arranged by hand (for a list of my favorite types of brushes, see the story on p. 124). For a closer look at the parts of a brush, see the photos and drawings on these two pages.

Manufacturers of cheap brushes economize on the content and configuration of the bristles. They may use an oversized divider to give the brush an illusion of fullness (see the photo at right). Bristle tips on a good-quality brush have natural splits, or flags, that help hold and spread the finish. Brushes that are cut to shape after they are formed are cheaper to make, but they will be missing flags at the bristle tips. That's a good indication the brush won't perform very well.

The most important, and the most expensive, brush component is the bristle. The type of bristle determines the suitability of a brush for a particular finish as well as how it works in general. Bristles can be divided into two broad categories: natural animal-hair and synthetic-filament bristles.

The difference is inside

These two rectangular, chisel-edge brushes are made from similar parts, but the one on the right is of better quality. A thick wooden divider at the center of the brush on the left gives it an appearance of fullness, but a heavier divider means fewer bristles. The brush on the right has a smaller divider and more bristles, so it will hold and release finish more evenly.

From *Fine Woodworking* (January 1996) 116:54-57

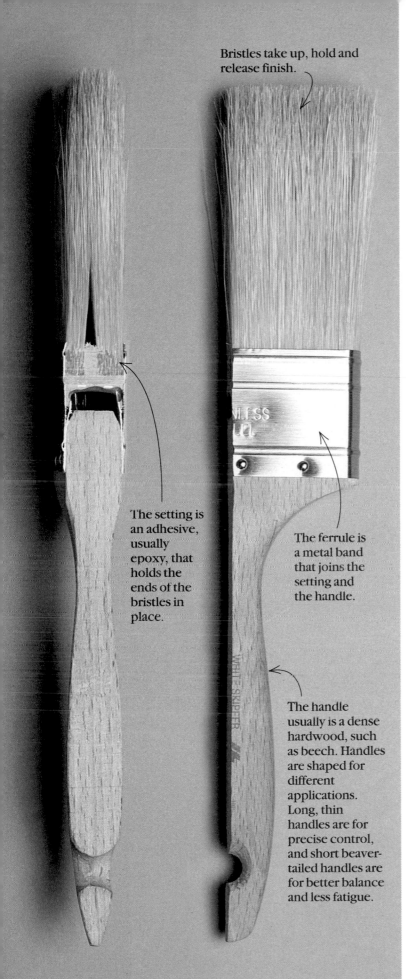

Bristles take up, hold and release finish.

The setting is an adhesive, usually epoxy, that holds the ends of the bristles in place.

The ferrule is a metal band that joins the setting and the handle.

The handle usually is a dense hardwood, such as beech. Handles are shaped for different applications. Long, thin handles are for precise control, and short beaver-tailed handles are for better balance and less fatigue.

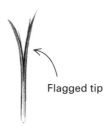

Flagged tip

Bristles are the most important part. Look for flagged tips, which help hold and spread the finish.

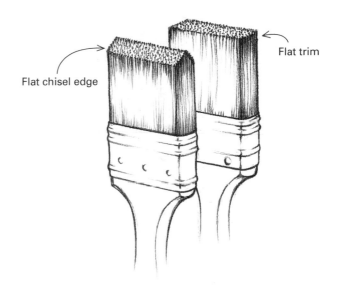

Flat chisel edge

Flat trim

Animal hair is best for solvent-based finishes

Natural-hair brushes are expensive and don't perform well with water-based finishes. But for top-quality results using oil-based varnish or paint, natural hair is unsurpassed.

Natural hair is divided into two categories: stiff bristle and soft fur. Hog bristle is used in most painting and finishing brushes. Soft fur, such as sable, camel, ox, skunk or badger, is used for varnish and artist's brushes. Two or more types of hair are often combined for specific performance characteristics.

Hog bristle is for paint and varnish. Chinese hog bristle (also called China bristle) is the best. The natural split ends on these stiff bristles allow the brush to carry a good deal more finish than bristles with smooth tips. The natural taper toward the tip gives hog bristle its strength and resiliency, or spring, which is especially important when applying paints and varnishes. The paint or varnish can be worked into the pores of the wood with the tip of the brush.

Sable is for detail work. Sable is the best natural hair for artist's brushes. Sable forms a fine, strong point when wet, making it ideal for touch-ups. Kolinsky sable is the best and most expensive; hairs from other red weasels are cheaper. All are known as red sable.

Camel is soft. A camel brush is good for lettering. The fur is not really from camels but usually from the tails of Russian and Siberian squirrels. Other kinds of squirrel hair are too coarse. Cheaper grades of camel brushes are made with ox, goat or pony hair.

Badger is best for oil-based finishes. This very soft and resilient hair is regarded as the best for flowing on oil-based finish-

The author's choice

Here's a selection of brushes that I've found to be most useful in my finishing business.

Taklon synthetic bristle brush has a tapered filament without natural splits at the ends of the bristles. This brush is made without a divider, so it has a very narrow chisel edge. I use it on small projects where exceptional control is needed. It can be used with all types of finishes. I recommend a ¾ in., 1 in. or 1½ in. brush.

Red sable is great for touch-up work. I recommend at least two sizes, a #1 and a #4.

Combination badger/skunk brush is first rate for all flowing finishes, particularly oil-based varnish and polyurethane. A 2-in. brush will cover most tasks. An expensive brush, but it's well worth it.

Chinex synthetic bristle is a good all-purpose brush. It's my favorite for water-based finishes. A 2-in. brush will cover most applications. It's an excellent tool for applying water-based dyes and stains and also can be used for solvent lacquer and oil-based varnishes.

China bristle brush is less expensive than fitch and excellent for all oil-based finishes. I use 1 in. and 1½ in. for detail work and 2½ in. and 3 in. for large surfaces. I particularly like oval-shaped brushes because they hold a lot of finish. Large oval brushes are called varnish brushes; smaller ones, 1 in. or less, are called oval sash. They also work well for effects like glazing, dry brushing and highlighting.

es. It does not have the body of hog bristle, so it's usually combined with a coarse hair, like skunk or black bristle. Pure badger-hair brushes are used for blending and highlighting in glazing and wood graining.

Ox is for lettering. Ox hair is taken from behind the ears of oxen and is silky and durable. It resembles sable but cannot form as fine a tip. It's used in lettering and sign painting.

Fitch is a combination of hair and bristle. Fitch is a confusing term because it applies to both a hair and a type of brush. American fitch is skunk hair. European fitch comes from a gray or black weasel. Fitch brushes usually are a combination of hairs—skunk on the outside for softness and bristle on the inside for stiffness. Fitch brushes are excellent for flowing finishes, such as oil-based varnish.

Synthetic bristles best for water-based finish

Synthetic bristle is a good choice for all types of finishes. It hasn't eclipsed natural bristle for the ultimate varnish brush, but synthetic bristle is constantly improving. The search for synthetic filaments to replace natural hair has been ongoing since the beginning of this century.

The first synthetic filaments were blunt tipped, similar to toothbrushes. Nowadays, manufacturers use several filaments that are tapered like natural bristle. Du Pont's Tynex and Chinex are manufactured specifically for brush-making. Taklon (a generic name) is a dyed white nylon filament with a tapered shaft and a smooth, unflagged tip. It is used extensively in artist's brushes.

Chinex is the most recent synthetic filament and is good for oil-based finishes and excellent for water-based finishes (see the photo at right). Taklon artist's brushes are exceptional for applying all finishes and usually are available in sizes up to 1½ in.

The chief advantage of synthetic filament over natural hair is that synthetic filaments absorb only 7% of their weight in water. Hog bristle and natural hair may absorb as much as 100% of their weight in water, causing the brush to become soft and floppy in water-based finishes.

Modern manufacturing can now duplicate the natural flags of bristle. These flags are made by wire wheels that create a microscopic score along the entire length of the filament so that the tip will continue to split as it wears. Synthetic filaments also are less expensive and much easier to clean because they don't have microscopic pores of natural hair that trap finish.

Brush and bristle variations

Brushes for painting and varnishing are available in flat trim, rectangular chisel, oval chisel and touch-up. Flat-trim brushes (see the drawing on p. 123) are used for exterior painting; the blunt edge works the paint into the pores and crevices of the wood. I use these brushes for applying paste wood filler. The chisel edge on rectangular and oval brushes is used where precise control is needed, such as on moldings and edges. An oval profile has more bristles so it carries more finish (see the top photo on the facing page). This is desirable for oil varnishes because the finish should flow on to minimize bubbles.

Touch-up brushes are assembled so that the tip ends in a round, fine point. These are the best brushes for detail work and painting fine grain lines in restoration work.

Buying a brush

Staining and general painting don't demand a great brush. But for applying finishes like varnish, which must be flowed on smooth-

Photos: Boyd Hagen; drawings: Michael Gellatly

Same width, more bristles. The oval chisel-edge brush (right) will hold more finish than the flat chisel-edge brush. This allows varnish to be applied in long, smooth strokes.

Synthetic bristles rival nature. Chinex bristle brushes (front) look, feel and work like the natural hog-bristle brush.

ly, a poorly made brush just can't do a good job. Be prepared to spend around $25 to $35 for a 1½-in. to 2½-in. China bristle brush of good quality.

When shopping for a brush, unwrap it. The bristles should feel soft at the tips and have spring in the overall length of the bundle. Examine the tips to make sure they have natural flags. Then pinch the whole thickness of bristles a little below the ferrule to see whether the fullness is the result of a lot of bristles (good) or a large divider (bad). Finally, fan back the brush with your hand. If the bristles come loose, don't buy the brush. And the color? The color of the bristles has no effect on performance. □

Jeff Jewitt repairs and restores furniture in North Royalton, Ohio.

Cleaning a brush

Start by wiping off the excess finish on newspaper. Then dip the brush into the appropriate cleanup solvent, and squeeze out the excess. Pour a liberal amount of dish-washing detergent on the brush (I like Dawn), and follow the steps below.

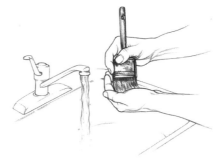

Cup your hand, and lather up the bristles with water. Swirl the bristles around vigorously.

Rinse out the soap under warm water. Bend the bristles back to force out the finish at the base of the brush, near the ferrule. Repeat this until the bristles no longer feel slimy.

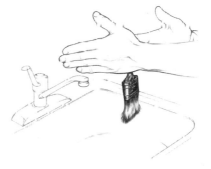

Run the bristles under cold water. Spin out excess water by holding the handle between your palms and twirling it briskly.

Straighten the bristles with a brush comb.

Wrap the bristles with paper (do not use newsprint; the ink will stain the bristles), and fold as shown. Lay the brush on a flat surface to dry. Don't store brushes in solvent for extended periods (more than four hours). The bristles will soften and lose resiliency.

Hardened finish
Soak the brush for four to six hours in a NMP (N-Methyl-Pyrrolidine) stripper such as Citristrip. Clean it as described above. Then, using a stiff wire brush, scrub the base of the bristles near the ferrule to remove the softened finish.

Index